Series Editors

W. Hansmann
W. T. Hewitt
W. Purgathofer

Bodo Urban (ed.)

Multimedia '96

Proceedings of the Eurographics Workshop
in Rostock, Federal Republic of Germany,
May 28–30, 1996

Eurographics

SpringerWienNewYork

Dr. Bodo Urban

Fraunhofer Institute for Computer Graphics,
Rostock, Federal Republic of Germany

© 1996 Springer-Verlag/Wien

Typesetting: Camera ready by editor

Graphic design: Ecke Bonk

With 71 Figures

ISSN 0946-2767

ISBN-13: 978-3-211-82876-2   e-ISBN-13: 978-3-7091-9472-0

DOI: 10.1007/978-3-7091-9472-0

Preface

In the last few years multimedia hardware and applications have become widely available on PC and workstations. Moreover, through the tremendous development and the wide usage of the World Wide Web multimedia applications have been brought over the network to many people. This book presents the results of the fourth in a well established series of international workshops on *Multimedia* organized by the EUROGRAPHICS Association, and held from May 28 to 30, 1996, in Rostock, Germany.

The workshop had the special topic *Multimedia on the Net* and was the follow up of the EUROGRAPHICS Symposium and Workshop on Multimedia held in Graz in June 1994. The workshop program consisted of an invited keynote speech and five technical sessions. The fifteen contributions selected for this volume treat topics of particular interest in current research and address actual problems of the use of multimedia in distributed applications over the network. According to the technical sessions they can be roughly structured in the parts *concepts for handling multimedia data*, *still and motion pictures on the net*, *WWW and multimedia*, *collaborative multimedia*, and *multimedia and education*.

Concepts for handling multimedia data are addressed in two contributions. The first treats a frame based presentation model for distributed information systems (Kirste), the other one presents a temporal logic formalism for specifying navigational transformation in hypermedia applications (Mere et al.).

An important data type in multimedia applications are *still and motion pictures*. For accessing images and videos via the network quality and resource controlled compression is of relevance. Two contributions address the control of image compression (Rauschenbach et al.) and video compression (Gries). Aspects of video processing and browsing including indexing, searching, and segmentation as well as knowledge based parsing are treated by a third contribution (Correia).

World Wide Web is at present the most important frame for multimedia applications on the net. Examples for *WWW and multimedia* given in this book are a three dimensional information system integrating 3D models and dynamic video data (Berka et al.), concepts for the integration of historical and cartographical data in a multimedia information system (Solka), and collaboration and joint editing on the Web using Java Applets (Park et al.)

A special aspect of multimedia applications is *collaborative multimedia*. One contribution in this book treats the integration of computer supported cooperative work and video on demand (Fukuoka et al.), the others present concepts for document handling in cooperative environments (Joseph et al.) and for media-on-demand in multimedia electronic mail systems (Tsoi et al.).

Multimedia and education treats aspects of computer based training. The contributions presented in this book discuss video-audio conferencing applications for distributed, 'just in time', and on-demand education and training (Gradinariu et al.), present concepts for content based video retrieval (Biblioni et al.), propose a concept and rules for the evaluation of multimedia and communication techniques for education (Ficarra), and describe a multimedia visualization assistance tool (Spierling et al.).

The program committee of the workshop consisted of J.Buford (USA), P.Egloff (Germany), L.M.Encarnacao (Germany), M.Gervautz (Austria), M.Gomes (Portugal), R.Guedj (France), W.Herzner (Austria), B.Herzog (USA), C.Hornung (Germany), K.Kansy (Germany), F.Kappe (Austria), B.Kehrer (Germany), L.Kjelldahl (Sweden), D.Krömker (Germany), M.Macedonia (USA), S.Owen (USA), H.Schumann (Germany), J.Teixeira (Portugal), J.Thomas (USA), B.Urban (Germany, chairman), H.Vin (USA), and P.Willis (UK), who supported the preparation of the technical program.

To conclude I would like to thank all of the authors and speakers for their effort as well as the referees for their kind support and cooperation. Special thanks go to Andreas Sandberg as well as to the many local helpers without whom the event could not have been successful. Special thanks also go to EUROGRAPHICS for their support and Springer-Verlag for publishing this proceedings, and to all those who financially supported the workshop.

Rostock, Germany   Bodo Urban
May 1996

Contents

Contents

A flexible presentation model for distributed information systems

Thomas Kirste

Darmstadt Technical University, Interactive Graphics Systems Group,
Wilhelminenstr. 7, D-64283 Darmstadt, Germany,
Email: kirste@igd.fhg.de

Abstract. One of the visions of mobile computing is to put "all information at the user's fingertips" – to allow him to operate on any data, any time, anywhere. The idea is to create an information environment providing the homogeneous access to all data and services available in the distributed, mobile computing infrastructure. A fundamental requirement for the access to such an open, distributed information system is an intelligent selection of methods for information visualization based on user requirements and available display functionality.

In this paper, a flexible concept is proposed that allows to enrich the nodes of an information structure with information about which alternative display methods can be used for what parts of the node. These *facets* are then used by a recursive view generation process for selecting suitable display methods while creating a visualization of an information structure. Influence parameters such as user characteristics, display resources, and data properties can be used to guide the selection process in order to create a presentation that optimally meets the user's goals.

1 Introduction

One of the visions of mobile computing is to put "all information at the user's fingertips" – to allow him to operate on any data, any time, anywhere. The idea is to create an information environment providing the homogeneous access to all data and services available in the distributed, mobile computing infrastructure. The term "Infoverse" will be used to denote this information environment. The Infoverse can be seen as an extension of the "Docuverse" concept defined by T. Nelson [16, 17], a distributed hypermedia structure containing and interlinking the entire human knowledge[1].

The typical infrastructure of a system for the mobile access to the Infoverse consists of a mobile end system (MES) equipped with a wireless data communication facility, and a stationary data server (SDS) that is attached to both the wireless communication link and stationary high speed networks (cf. Fig. 1). A typical MES might be a PDA (personal digital assistant) using a GSM mobile phone for wireless data communication. The SDS gives the MES access to the distributed multimedia information services available in the stationary network infrastructure. Such infrastructures are used for field service applications [6] as well as for distributed personal information management scenarios [8].

---

[1] Today, the World-Wide Web [2] provides some – but not all – of the linking functionality defined for the "Docuverse" using "tumblers" [18].

The main task of the MES is to provide a suitable user interface for these services, which means both information visualization and the support for direct interaction with these presentations.

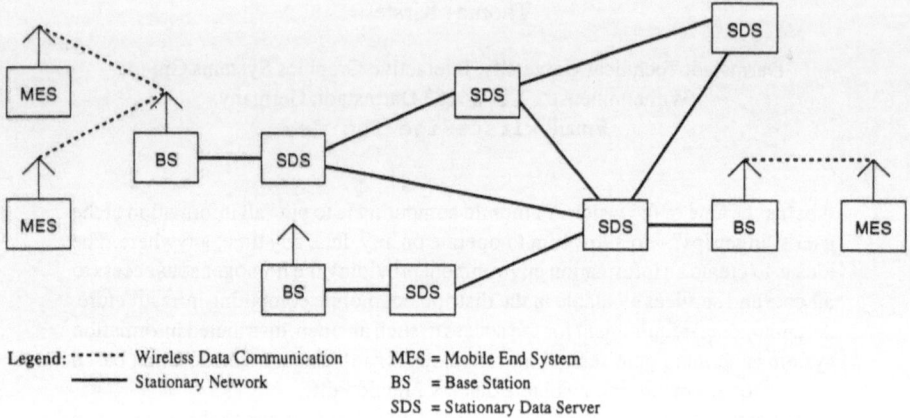

Legend: ······· Wireless Data Communication   MES = Mobile End System
——— Stationary Network   BS   = Base Station
SDS = Stationary Data Server

Fig. 1. Typical wireless information infrastructure

The wireless infrastructure shown in Fig. 1 presents some well known challenges for this task, which require special attention:

- Limited bandwidth of the wireless link (*e.g.*, 9.6 kBit/sec. in case of GSM); high bandwidth variability.
- Limited computation and storage resources of the mobile end system.
- Heterogeneous end system resources introduced by users using different end systems at different times (*e.g.*, a monochrome PDA on a business trip, a full color graphics workstation at the office.)

On the other hand, there is the challenge of the openness of the information environment – any time a new service (*i.e.*, a new data type with accompanying operations) can be added to this environment. Therefore, the MES must be prepared for situations, where the user dynamically wants to access (and operate on) data entities of a type unknown to the MES. The MES should be intelligent enough to upgrade itself with the functionality required for giving the user interactive access to this data. This requires a suitable data model for the information environment which provides a well defined way for adding new data types with their associated functionality for presentation and interaction. The MES uses this type information for determining what and how to upgrade.

With respect to the visualization functionality, it is important to support the flexible handling of alternative presentation methods. In the area of scientific visualization, it is a well known fact that different visualization methods show different aspects about the same data set [1]. Which visualization method to chose is a non-trivial process that depends on the user's informational needs, the characteristics of the data set to visualize, and the properties of the user's end system [11].

Especially for a mobile user, data access is expensive both in terms of time (due to the low bandwidth of wireless links) and money (due to the high cost of each transferred byte). Therefore, it is important to give a user the best value for his expenses – which means to let the user extract as much information as possible form a data set whose transfer he has paid for. This in turn means to support the selection of a visualization method best satisfying the user's interpretation goals. Also, the user should have the ability to switch between different alternative methods in order to extract the various informations buried in the data set.

As simple, "real-world" example, consider a "traveling manager" accessing his company's sales data for the recent months on a business trip. Depending on his interpretation goals (exact numbers, comparison between relative product volumes, trend analysis), this data should probably be presented either in tabular numeric form, as pie chart, or as line graph. Clearly, the user should be able to switch dynamically between different visualizations. Also, it should be possible to embed such data sets into larger information structures. The sales data might for example be part of the company's regular sales reports.

In closed worlds, where all data types and visualization methods are known in advance by both MES and SDS, this flexibility is more or less straightforward to obtain (e.g., "just use a Winword document with an embedded Excel spreadsheet"). But in the open environment of the Infoverse, a dynamically extensible typing for data sets as outlined above has to be available.

Another point is the flexible handling of heterogeneous end systems: on a low-resolution monochrome display, different presentation techniques have to be used than on a high-resolution color display (e.g., 2-D black & white iso-line drawings instead of a color coded 3-D height map – cf. [11]).

The point of this paper is to propose a concept for the intelligent handling of the visualization of multimedia information structures on heterogeneous end systems within the context of the Infoverse.

The central idea is to enrich the nodes of an information structure with information about which alternative display methods can be used for what parts of the node. These *facets* are then used by a recursive view generation process for selecting suitable display methods while creating a visualization of an information structure that is optimized with respect to user requirements, display characteristics and data properties.

The facet concept is embedded into a flexible, frame-based end-user data model. This model does not only support the browsing of distributed structured multimedia documents ("hypertext"), which have been deliberately created for this purpose by authors, but also the dynamic annotation, structuring, and composition of information. This is required to allow a user to embed his own working data into the global information environment.

The concepts presented in this paper have been developed within the "Data Models" working package of the MoVi project [10, 7]. MoVi (= "Mobile Visualization") is a researcher group funded by the German Research Society (Deutsche Forschungsgemeinschaft, DFG). Besides the Interactive Systems Group of the Darmstadt Technical University, members of this researcher group are the Computer Science Dept. of the Rostock University, the Fraunhofer Institute for Computer Graphics Rostock, and the

4

Computer Graphics Center Rostock.

The further structure of this paper is as follows:

Sec. 2 provides an in-depth analysis of the properties of a data model for the Infoverse, for whose instances a visualization system will have to provide suitable rendering facilities.

In Sec. 3, the concept of *facets* is developed and embedded into the data model identified in Sec. 2.

Sec. 4 covers additional issues of the facet concept relating to the detailed construction of the selection functionality.

Finally, a summary and plans for future work are given in Sec. 5.

2 Data model considerations for the Infoverse

Before developing a visualization concept for presenting the data in an information system, it makes sense to analyze the system's data model. This especially holds, if visualization information needs to be embedded into this data model.

The visualization model proposed in Sec. 3 is embedded into a data model that uses *frames* as the basic construct fore representing structured multimedia information. Frames are essentially unordered collections of *slots*, name and value pairs. (A more detailed discussion is given in Sec. 2.4.)

One reason for choosing a frame-based model as starting point is clearly pragmatic: The concepts outlined in this paper have been implemented on Apple's "MessagePad" series hand-held computing devices. These machines use a software architecture entirely relying on frames for representing data and applications [21]. Delivering data to a MES using a structuring mechanism that directly corresponds to its internal data model obviously reduces the amount of work that has to be performed by the MES for the mapping of external data into a representation that can be efficiently handled by its internal data management facilities.

However, while this pragmatic reason justifies the approach taken for a specific MES software architecture, there are also considerations of a more general kind that seem to justify the use of a frame-based data model as a *general* data model for the Infoverse. Not the least of these considerations is that a sufficiently general data model for the Infoverse has not yet been proposed.

Following, some of these considerations are outlined.

2.1 Basic features of the Infoverse

The Infoverse has to provide at least the following features:

– *Location transparency* for information services offered by the various information providers, thereby giving a user homogeneous information access, regardless of the user's (or data) location.
– A mechanism for *linking* between arbitrary data entities, regardless, whether these entities are managed by the same service or by different services (*"link-level service transparency"*).

– A mechanism for the homogeneous access of data entities, regardless of the service they are managed by ("*access-level service transparency*"). (Note that link-level service transparency can be regarded as a special case of access-level service transparency.)

Therefore, the Infoverse provides a homogeneous (*i.e.*, service transparent) and location transparent access to the information services it contains – at least with respect to basic data access and the meaning of links between data entities.

Note that the transparency aspects identified so far only simplify a *reader's* information access. The author's task is not simplified, because there are no (general) facilities for a service and location transparent *manipulation* of the data entities in the Infoverse's current manifestation (*i.e.*, the World-Wide Web).

As long as such facilities do not exist, a user is basically "left at the mercy of an information provider" with respect to the functionality available for tailoring data structures to suit the user's need.

While now a public service provider might not necessarily want a user to "play around" with the service's internal data structures, there is definitely a set of data entities a user *should* be able to modify freely: This is the user's "own" set of data files, OODB graphs, relational tables, spread sheets, etc.

2.2 The need for an expressive data model

Today, such data entities are manipulated by applications whose full functionality is not accessible through the World-Wide Web (*e.g.*, relational databases). On the other hand, these applications in general do not provide the transparency and linking features of the Infoverse. However, providing location, linking, and access transparency for a user's own data *without* losing the manipulation facilities would clearly be very important for a *mobile* user: He is able to access his own data the same way, he would access an information service in the Infoverse. He is able to cross-link between his own data structures (*e.g.*, part of a spreadsheet) and other data entities in the Infoverse (*e.g.*, a different user's spreadsheet, figures provided by a public information services containing supporting data). He could chose to allow other user's to access his data structures through the Infoverse, giving them all (or some) of the data specific functionality for operating on this data (*e.g.*, extract a column, add a column, link a set of cells into their own data base, etc.)

Today, this kind of functionality is not available – at least not without a substantial amount of CGI or Java programming, which both is quite expensive for a non-programmer user and leads to special case solutions not applicable to the problem in general (however, cf. Sec. 2.5, Point 3). For example, data to be accessed via the World-Wide Web has to be mapped to HTML-documents in order to be accessible from an arbitrary computing device (*e.g.*, another user's computer, or a visited institution's machine temporarily available to the user on a business trip). During this mapping process, important information contained in the original data entity is inevitably lost, because HTML does not provide the structural richness for defining data structures such as, say, C++. This means, only a limited subset of the operations available for the original data can be executed on this incomplete mapping (*i.e.*, operations not requiring the information

6

elided by the mapping process). Especially, manipulation of the original data set can not be performed.

This means: in order to support an integration of arbitrary data into the Infoverse *without* inherently restricting the set of operations executable on this data when accessed through the Infoverse – which is required at least for giving a mobile user access to his own data – a sufficiently flexible and expressive data model for the Infoverse is required.

2.3 Supporting incremental data definition

When looking for a suitably expressive data model, one could think for example of such object oriented models as the ODMG model [5]. These models definitely provide the required expressiveness to model any imaginable information structure.

However, within the scope of the Infoverse, there are additional considerations with respect to both the openness of the Infoverse and the ease-of-use for an end-user.

Most important, it should be easy for a user to augment existing data entities. These modifications obviously must not not affect existing functionality. But they could enable additional functionality on the enriched data entity. Such an augmentation facility is required for the annotation of foreign data entities as well as for an incremental definition of the user's own data entities (which is the same thing from a system's point of view).

Consider a user creating an address data base: He has initially thought of some interesting properties every person has, and for some time he has added entries to this database. Also, he has shared his entries with other users. It now may happen that the user wants to add a property to a person that has not been considered when setting up the data definition, because necessity of such a property has not been anticipated at that time (as a somewhat futuristic example, consider a person's home planet as part of an address). Likewise, a user sharing the address data might want to add information to a person (such as a list of points to discuss with this person) without having to manipulate the original author's data definition.

Once such an incremental data definition facility is available, it also substantially simplifies the setting up of initial data definitions. A careful analysis of all the properties that the information, which being represented by this data definition, might eventually exhibit is not necessary: Additional properties can easily be added at a later time. So, data definitions can be set up ad-hoc by the user as the need arises. They are incrementally extended, as more and more properties become known. Furthermore, data entities created by other users can be augmented with properties not anticipated by them, or not required for their specific application.

So, the *need* for an incremental data definition facility arises from the fact that the Infoverse is an open environment in the sense that neither the set of data types, nor the full set of properties of a given data type can be expected to remain stable. The incremental data definition facility then *also* supports the end-user by simplifying the setting-up of initial data definitions for the ad-hoc creation of data entities.

2.4 The frame model

One suitable data model supporting incremental data definition are *frames*. Originally, frames have been developed as a means for knowledge representation in artificial intelligence applications [14]. Powerful frame representation languages have been developed as early as 1977 (*e.g.*, FRL [19]). From this application area, frames have inherited the ability to cope with structured, fast changing information – as it also exists in the Infoverse.

Incidentally, other application areas for frame models, besides knowledge representation, have been Hypermedia-based information management systems[2] (*e.g.*, [20] and Oval [12]) and personal information management systems, such as the MessagePad [13]. (Indeed, the feature of adding "custom" properties to an address data base is exactly one of the tasks, where the MessagePad's frame system becomes directly visible to the user.)

The specific frame model described here is basically the one provided by the MessagePad's object system [21], which in some aspects is a simplified version of the object system built into the language *Self* [23].

As far as this paper is concerned, a frame is – quite similar to an object – an entity with a unique identity that contains a set of name/value pairs ("slots"). Among conventional data types, frame references may be slot values, so that frame structures can be created. Also, slot values can be *functions*, which may be invoked by message passing. Finally, frames can use other frames as *prototypes*, from which they inherit.

As an example for working with frames, consider the frames p and q, defined as follows[3]:

```
p := {a: 1, f: func() a+b};
q := {_proto: p, b: 2}
```

p is a frame with two slots, a, which contains an integer, and f, which contains a function. q is a frame with two slots, _proto, containing a frame reference (q's prototype), and b, containing an integer. So q inherits from p. As one would expect, q.b gives the value 2, q.a the value 1. The message invocation q:f() gives 3. Here, the values of f (and a, which is accessed in f) are inherited from p. The assignment q.c := 3 creates a new slot c with the value 3 in q (so, q.c now gives 3). The assignment q.a := 4 overrides the slot a inherited from p, so now q.a = 4, and q:f() = 6, but still p.a = 1.

It is also possible to define a frame

```
r := {f: func() a*b)}
```

and change q's prototype by assigning q._proto := r. So now q:f() = 8, because this time f is inherited from r.

The central differences to the conventional class/instance model of object-oriented programming are:

---

[2] The whole concept of Hypermedia is quite close to a simplified frames model. Just replace the notion "Slot" by "Link".

[3] The frame language syntax used throughout this document is based on NewtonScript [13], using the following conventions: The notation "$\{s_i : v_i, ...\}$" denotes a frame with slots s_i, which have values v_i. "$[v_i, ...]$" is a list of values v_i. "$f.s$" denotes the access of f's slot s and "$f.s := v$" is the assignment of the value v to f's slot s. "func $(x_i, ...)$ *body*" denotes function with parameters x_i. Functions are legal slot values. "$f:m(a_i, ...)$" denotes the invocation of the function stored in $f.m$ with parameters a_i (*i.e.*, a method invocation). For slots within the lexical or inheritance scope of the current expression, the "$f.$" prefix can be omitted.

- The dynamic addition/removal of slots to/from frames, which enables incremental data definition and also data reuse/data sharing.
- The prototype-based dynamic inheritance mechanism that allows a frame to inherit slots from arbitrary other frames. This supports conventional class-like inheritance as well as powerful data sharing. The last point is specifically important in the case of PDA class machines, where storage is a scarce resource.
  This and the previous point also clearly separate frames from static object based models such as *Obliq* [4].
- The availability of type information at runtime enables the handling of unknown frame structures (*i.e.*, structures that have been created by other users). This information can be used, for example, to create structure-specific visualizations, as is done in Oval.

Frames therefore provide a dynamic environment that allows the user to flexibly create, augment, and modify information structures to suit his personal needs. So, frames seem to be suitable as end-user data model for an integrated information environment.

As a side observation, it is very interesting that frame structures can be used for the definition of interactive applications. The most prominent example for this is probably the MessagePad's programming language "NewtonScript" [13]. This means, frames integrate a powerful end-user data model *and* a means for defining non-trivial interactive applications. Consequences are:

- The user himself may create applications ad-hoc. This provides the required functional extensibility and tailorability of data and service access.
- The *same* system services (*e.g.*, frame migration and replication, frame caching) can be used for managing the access of data and applications.

2.5 Concluding remarks

With respect to the discussion presented in this section, there are some important points to keep in mind:

1. The superficial analysis for the properties of an object model for the Infoverse given so far is not deep enough to serve as a well-founded argument in support of the frame model. A much stronger argument in favor of this model is the fact that software architectures sharing many similarities with the Infoverse successfully employ frames for modeling data structures (and applications).
   More research is required in order to determine if a frame model is indeed the best choice for a distributed data management environment such as the Infoverse. Nevertheless, the intuitive match between the facilities of a frame model and the features required for the Infoverse seems to justify at least a closer look.
2. Note that the frame model is nothing "new". It is not the claim or goal of this section to introduce a new data model. The interesting point made here is rather that in order to integrate personal data management into the Infoverse, one needs a data model that is substantially stronger than what is currently anticipated in, *e.g.*, the World-Wide Web. The frame model has been picked from a range of existing data models merely as an especially promising candidate.

3. There have been some claims in this section about what can not be done in the World-Wide Web, which deserve further explanation. Of course, Java is powerful enough to implement a more flexible data model such as frames. It is also quite straightforward to think of some SGML mark-ups (or some other suitable syntax) for embedding frames into HTML pages. So, a frame model can be implemented *on top* of the existing WWW technology. The claims about the deficiencies of the WWW should therefore rather be read as "there exists yet no concept of a data model providing the capabilities as outlined above". Once such a model has been chosen, it could then be implemented on top of the WWW.

4. Finally, some words about legacy and proprietary data. It is probably not realistic to expect ever information provider to upgrade his data representation to conform to a however flexible data model. Also, some information providers might want to trade functionality for efficiency by using a proprietary data model. This means, any future data model for the Infoverse must anticipate the problem of proprietary and legacy data.

   A basic solution is of course simple: as long as the data model provides byte strings as one of its basic data types, together with sufficient functions for operating on byte strings, such "foreign" data formats can be embedded into the general data model (which here serves as a "container" for this data). Even special functionality on this data can be represented by using the data model's byte string operations. Of course, the applicability of general purpose Infoverse functions that rely on knowledge about the internal structure of a data entity is limited in this case.

In the next section, the central proposal of this paper, a model for supporting the flexible visualization of frame structures, will be introduced.

3 Frame Visualization

3.1 Basic frame visualization

Because frames inherently provide runtime information about their slots and the value types contained therein, it is in principle possible to create a mechanism for the automatic display of arbitrary frame structures – very similar to the "Pretty-Printing" facilities of LISP [22], such as described in [24]. The availability of such a mechanism is very important in an environment, where anytime the user may encounter unknown frame structures.

However, this basic concept assumes the visualization methods for each value type to be fixed. Within the Infoverse, this is unacceptable. As outlined in the introduction, alternative display methods have to be supported at least for the following two reasons:

– Depending on the available presentation resources, different display methods have to be selected for the same data.
– User preferences for different visualization methods should be observed. Also, the user should be allowed to switch between visualization methods in order to see different aspects of the same data.

A possible solution is, for example, provided by systems such as Oval and HyperPicture [9]. Here, the runtime system ("Session Manager") knows a *number* of alternative visualization methods for each data object. Upon object display, an appropriate method is selected based on user preferences and resources. The user may afterwards switch between different methods.

Unfortunately, this solution is not sufficient within the scope of a global information system: The display methods known to the creator of a frame structure may not necessarily be known to a later user of this structure. In addition, it is usually not known which slots contain "interesting" information and which ones are merely used for internal purposes.

Therefore, each frame should be able to provide information about the display methods useful for visualizing frame information. This approach is used in principle by NewtonScript: The display method to be used for a frame can be defined by the frame's _proto-slot.

The solution concept proposed in this section is essentially a unification of these two techniques, based on the concept of *facets*.

3.2 Facets and views

The extended visualization model consists of the following elements:

Facets. Facets have two tasks:
- They define groups of slots that can be presented together in a meaningful way.
- They can map these slot groups to display methods that are appropriate for visualizing the slot values.

The idea is to use a frame's facets for determining *which* information of the frame to display and *how* to do the rendering.

Display methods. A display method is the definition of a function which is able to visualize a set of values with a given structure (*e.g.*, a string and a list of integers). A display method is *applicable* to a frame, if the frame matches the *structural constraints* of the display method. These constraints are defined by the set of slots the frame must contain and the types of the values contained in these slots.

Facet views. Facet views display a facet of a frame using a specific display method. Also, they allow the user to switch between the different display methods applicable to the presented facet.

Frame views. Frame views are responsible for orchestrating the display of the various facets of a frame. In addition, specialized frame views can be provided for presenting *sets* of frames. For this case, they may support layout techniques such as tables or graphical overviews ("structure maps") and the consistent selection of facets across the whole frame set.

3.3 Facet declarations

Every frame may include facet declarations which the visualization system expects to find in a slot named facets. The value of a frame's facet slot is a *facet declaration frame*. Each slot in the facet declaration frame contains a *facet declaration*, the slot name of a facet declaration is the *facet name*. A facet declaration is itself a frame consisting of an (optional) *template definition* (a slot named `template`) and an (optional) *display method definition* (a slot named `display`).

The content of a template definition is a frame whose slots contain *value expressions*. These value expressions may be:

- Constants.
- Functions with a single parameter.
- Path expressions.

When the view system creates the visualization of a frame's facet, it does not apply the facet's display method directly to the frame. Rather, it instantiates the facet's template from the frame and applies the display method to the instantiated template frame. This allows to define (quite arbitrarily) derived frame structures, whose contents is better suited for a facet's visualization problem than the original data itself (see Sec. 3.5 for a detailed example).

Template instantiation proceeds as follows: constant values remain unchanged. Functions are called with the original frame as parameter, they may then perform arbitrary evaluations whose result is used as slot value for the instantiated template frame. Finally, path expressions (such as `'a.b.c`) can be used to "pull" a value buried deeper in the frame structure upwards into the template frame. (A path expression `'path` is really a shorthand for the template function `func(f) f.path`.)

The `display` slot of a facet declaration defines the set of display methods that are – from the frame creator's point-of-view – applicable for presenting the instantiated template frame. The value of this slot can be:

- The name of a single display method.
- A frame whose slots contain alternative display methods (the slot names are the alternative's names). The value of an alternative method slot may be a display method or again a frame that contains a `method` slot, whose value is the desired method, and other slots that will be passed as parameters to this method (see Fig. 3 for an example).

Consider the following frame:

```
f := {
  facets: {facet1: {template: {string: 'stringSlot},
                    display: {simple: 'simpleFrameDisplay,
                              fancy: 'fancyFrameDisplay}}
           facet2: {template: {number: 'numberSlot}
                    display: 'numberFrameDisplay}},
  stringSlot: "Some Text",
  numberSlot: 1234}
```

This frame defines two facets, `facet1` and `facet2`. The `template`-slot of `facet1` defines a single-slot template frame that will contain the value of `f.stringSlot` upon instantiation, and which should be displayed using either the display method `simpleFrameDisplay` or `fancyFrameDisplay`. `facet2` will display the value of `f.numberSlot`, using the display method `numberFrameDisplay`.

3.4 The view generation process

The view generation process is defined by the three core functions buildView, buildFrameView, buildFacetView, and the respective display method, which call each other recursively. A rudimentary definition of the core functions and a sample display method is given in Fig. 2, using NewtonScript inspired pseudo-code. Based on these functions, the visualization system proceeds as follows when called through buildView with a value (*e.g.*, a frame structure) to visualize:

- buildView determines if the value to visualize is structured (*i.e.*, a frame) or simple and calls the respective specific view creation function. (The parentView parameter contains the view into which to embed the view created for value.)
- For frames, the function buildFrameView is called. It first creates a child view that will contain the frame's different facet views. Then it selects the first facet to visualize, instantiates its template, and calls the function buildFacetView with the instantiated template frame.
- buildFacetView selects an appropriate display method using the facet declaration's display slot and possibly information about additional local display methods that may be applicable. It then calls the selected display method with the instantiated template frame. (Facet and display method selection are further discussed in Sec. 4.)
- The display method is responsible for displaying the instantiated template frame in a suitable way. The sample method simpleFrameDisplayMethod simply iterates over all slots in the template, creating a label and a value view for each one. The value view is created by recursively calling buildView, thereby closing the circle.

3.5 An example

This section gives a small example illustrating the use of the facet model. In Fig. 3, a sample frame structure including facet declarations is given. The different renderings of this frame structure generated by choosing different facets and display methods are shown in Fig. 4 to 6.

This frame structure illustrates the following features of the facet model:

- The declaration of multiple facets for a frame (*e.g.*, the sales and oview facets for the top level frame).
- The declaration of multiple display methods for a facet (*e.g.*, the fancy and simple display methods in the sales facet of the frames fstruct.tbl and fstruct.y.c).
- The use of deep-structure value access in the definition of a facet's template (*e.g.*, the m slot of the top-level frame's sales facet template). Note how this is used to create a display that presents the message fstruct.y.c and the table fstruct.tbl at the same level in Fig. 4. Compare this with the direct rendering of the frame structure in Fig. 6.

```
buildView: func(parentView,value)
  if IsFrame(value)
    then buildFrameView(parentView,value)
    else buildImmediateView(parentView,value)

buildFrameView: func(parentView,frame) begin
  childView := buildFrameContainer(parentView);
  facet := selectFacet(frame);
  template := facet.template;
  instTplFrame := instantiateTemplate(template,frame);
  buildFacetView(childView,instTplFrame,facet);
end

buildFacetView: func (parentView,instTplFrame,facet) begin
  displayMethod := selectDisplayMethod(facet);
  call displayMethod with (parentView,instTplFrame)
end

simpleFrameDisplayMethod: func(parentView,instTplFrame)
  foreach slot,value in instTplFrame do begin
    buildSlotLabelView(parentView,slot);
    buildView(parentView,value)
  end
```

Fig. 2. Core functions of the visualization system

– The use of on-the-fly computations in the definition of a facet's template (*e.g.*, the v slot of fstruct.y's facets.oview template, which sums up the individual unit numbers in the frame's a slot, displaying a grand total to the user).

Once displayed, a facet view allows a user to dynamically switch between different display methods for the same facet, as shown in Fig. 4. Note that the visualization layout may change in response to switching a display method.

Fig. 6 shows a rendering generated by choosing *no* facets and display methods. In this case, the original frames are directly used as instantiated templates, whose slots and values are displayed using standard methods. Note that this is also done with frames lacking facet or display-method definitions, such as fstruct.z. This defaulting mechanism allows to handle the display of arbitrary frame structures without requiring the author to spend extensive thoughts on useful facet definitions. These can easily be added at a later time.

4 Method and facet selection

When visualizing the frame structure, the visualization system has to determine two aspects for each frame:

```
fstruct :=
{facets: {sales: {template: {m: 'y.c, t: 'tbl}},
          oview: {template: {a: 'y, b: 'z}}},
  x: 1, /* some internal value of no interest to the user */
  y: {facets: {oview: {template: {m: "Company total ... ",
                                   v: func(f) begin local s:=0;
                                              foreach v in f.a do
                                                 s:=s+v;
                                              return s
                                   end}}},
      a: [400,280,460,380],
      c: {facets: {sales: {template: {text: 'bla},
             display: {fancy:  {method: 'directTemplateView,
                              .../*fancy text style params*/},
                       simple: {method: 'directTemplateView,
                              .../*simple text style params*/}}}},
            bla: "Sales Report:\nHere is the recent ... "}},
   tbl: {facets: {sales: {template: {value: 'dta},
                  display: {fancy: 'graphTableView,
                            simple: 'textTableView}}},
          dta: [["Sales", "1993", "1994", "1995", "1996"],
                ["Prod. A:", 100,110, ...], ...]},
     z: {m: "Company sales area", p: ... /* Image Reference */}}
```

Fig. 3. Sample frame structure

- Which of the frame's facets to visualize (`selectFacet`).
- Which display method to use for the selected facet(s) (`selectDisplayMethod`).

Both selection processes are guided by user requirements, available resources, and data characteristics. As outlined in Sec. 1, this is a non-trivial task in general.

The basic idea here is to use a weighting mechanism for introducing an an order on display methods, as suggested in [11]. Each method is provided with a *fitness function* $f : D \times R \times U \rightarrow V$, where D is the set of *data characteristics* (*e.g.*, "multivariate data"), R the set of *resource characteristics* (*e.g.*, display resolution), U the set of *user requirements characteristics*, and V a linear ordered set of *fitness values*. A concrete characteristics tuple $c \in D \times R \times U$ defines a partial order on a set of display methods M based on the fitness values assigned to the methods by their fitness functions when applied to c. (In other words: $\forall m, m' \in M : m \geq_c m' \Leftrightarrow m.f(c) > m'.f(c) \vee m = m'$.) The best method $m \in M$ (*i.e.*, the largest with respect to $\geq_c$, as one would expect) is then chosen as initial display method. (If more than one method qualifies as best, the order of declaration is used.)

While this basic mechanism is straightforward, finding a concrete definitions of D, R, and U, as well as the values of f for individual display methods, is difficult (what, for example, is the complete set of user requirements characteristics?) This analysis is

◆**Facet** Sales (Fancy)　　　　　　　　　◆**Facet** Sales (Simple)

m:	**Sales Report:** Here is the recent year's sales data for A, B, and C. Note that while A and B have become more or less stable since the drop in 1994, C still needs attention.
t:	Prod. C: ... (graph)

m:	Sales Report: Here is the recent year's sales data for A, B, and C. Note that while A and B have become more or less stable since the drop in 1994, C still needs attention.			
t:	**Sales** 1993 1994 1995 1996			
	Prod. A: 100 110 150 160			
	Prod. B: 120 100 150 140			
	Prod. C: 180 70 160 80			

Fig. 4. Display of facet sales using display method fancy (left) and simple (right)

◆**Facet** Overview　　　　　　　　　　◆**Facet** None

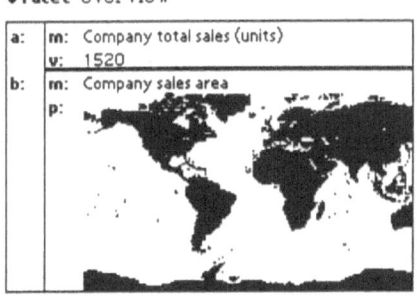

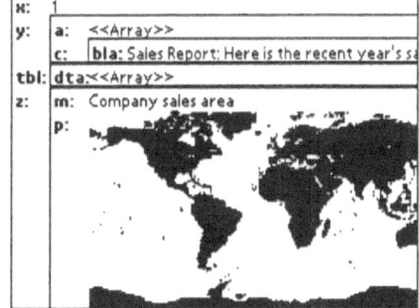

Fig. 5. The oview facet　　　　　　　**Fig. 6.** Using standard visualization

part of ongoing research in MoVi. See [11] for more information.

It is important to notice that these functions may not rely solely on the information stored in a frame's facet declarations. Because of the Infoverse's openness, a user's end system may contain display methods that are not contained in the frame's facets (and vice versa). Therefore, the set of facets applicable to a frame and the set of display methods applicable to a frame's facet have to be computed dynamically. With respect to computing the *effective set* of display methods for a facet, the simplest choice is to intersect the facet's method set with the set of applicable methods that are available locally. (A display method is applicable to a facet, if its structural constraints are matched by the facet's instantiated template frame.)

If the intersection is empty, the system may decide to dynamically down-load one or more of the unknown display methods named in the frame's facets. This down-loading is supported by the mobile frame model outlined in [10].

The visualization system may also choose to offer local applicable methods that are not contained in the facet declaration's method set as additional alternatives.

Furthermore, it may be useful to dynamically create additional facets for a frame. The computation of these facets is based on using the frame as its own instantiated template frame, against which the structural constraints of those local methods are matched, which are not yet used in a facet of the frame. These methods can then be grouped based on the equality of their structural constraints, each group forming a dynamic facet.

5   Conclusion

5.1   Summary

The purpose of this paper has been to introduce a flexible presentation model for open, distributed information systems. This model should allow to embed presentation information into distributed data structures, while at the same time supporting the flexible and dynamic choice between alternative presentation methods, based, *e.g.*, on user preferences and display characteristics.

In the first part of the paper, the essential aspects of an open, distributed information system, especially from the viewpoint of a mobile user, have been analyzed. These considerations have been based on the integrative concept of the Infoverse. An important observation has been that in order to support manipulation functionality in the Infoverse – which is required at least for embedding personal information management – a suitably expressive data model is required. It has then been argued that "frames" could be a possible candidate.

The second part of the paper has concentrated on the definition of a suitable visualization model and its embedding into the basic frame model. The central idea of the visualization model has been to enrich frames by the concept of *facets*. A facet maps parts of a frame to alternative presentation methods, providing the information required for choosing which parts of a frame can be displayed meaningful and how to do the rendering. This choice may be influenced by user requirements, data characteristics, and display capabilities.

5.2   Future work

The visualization process of the facet model introduced in Sec. 3 has been implemented on a MessagePad. The screen-shots in this paper have been generated by applying this implementation to the frame structure shown in Fig. 3.

However, while the fundamental viability of the concepts introduced in this paper is proven by this implementation, there still remain numerous open questions. Some of them are outlined below.

- Obviously, the concrete definitions of the selection functions and their parameters, as outlined in Sec. 4 is an important part that is yet missing. (Currently, preferences for facets and display methods are selected by hand.) Ongoing work in MoVI is expected to provide a solution here.
- Another important aspect is geometry management and the parameterization of display methods: it depends on the user's entry point into a frame structure, at what level in the display hierarchy a frame will be displayed. This influences the amount

of space available for displaying facets of this frame. So there must be a mechanism for describing and handling the dynamic layout of display methods over a broad range of available "screen real estate". Because switching facets may change the space required for a view, this geometry computation must also be carried out for views while they are displayed.

- A related aspect is the definition of layout constraints between different component frames in a composite frame. Such a constraint may read, for example, "component frames a and b must always be displayed side by side using the same facets". The definition of such constraints is especially required for the description of the coherent rendering of frame structures representing compound multimedia documents. In the terminology of MHEG, a suitable constraint mechanism effectively allows to overlay (and merge) multiple final form presentations over the same data structure.
- Finally, besides the plain selection of a visualization method, another important aspect is to decide at what time to present which components of a structured data set. This decision depends on the user's shifting focus of interest and directly influences the scheduling of requests for the data set's components.

It is possible to exploit the specific processing sequence of frame visualization and the frame structure for a high level optimization of networked frame access. Specifically, the following techniques are easy to support in a network scheduler:

Prefetch: Because the frame structure can be analyzed automatically, it is possible to support prefetch based on such a structural analysis: While a frame is being displayed and the system is otherwise idle, pointers to other frames may be extracted from the frame's slots and followed, prefetching the destination frames to the user's terminal system.

Structural detail-on-demand: For component frames containing less important information, the access and visualization of these frames can be delayed until the user actually requests the display (*e.g.*, by clicking on a place-holder, similar to the "Delay Image Loading" option of the "Mosaic" WWW Browser [15]). The visualization is then dynamically extended by adding the component frames.

The development of such a network scheduler is part of ongoing research in MoVi. See [3] for more information.

As concluding remark, it should be noted that through a slight extension of the basic frame model, *application partitioning*, the dynamic distribution of application functionality across the available network nodes, can be supported. See [10] for a brief outline of this *mobile frame model*.

Acknowledgments

I would like to thank all my colleagues in the MoVi project – Jörge Bönigk, Andreas Heuer, Bernd Kehrer, Susanne Lange, Astrid Lubinski, Uwe Rauschenbach, Anke Rieck, Andreas Sandberg, Jürgen Schirmer, Heidrun Schumann, Bodo Urban – for encouragement, motivation, and critical questions regarding the concepts outlined in this paper.

The work presented in this paper has been funded by the German Research Society (Deutsche Forschungsgemeinschaft, DFG) as part of the MOVI researcher group.

References

1. Arndt, S., Lukoschek, K., Schumann, H. Design of a visualization support tool for the representation of multi-dimensional data sets. In *Proc. 5th Eurographics Workshop on Visualization in Scientific Computing*, Rostock, Germany, 1994.

2. Berners-Lee, T., Cailliau, R., Groff, J., Pollerman, B. WorldWideWeb: The Information Universe. *Electronic Networking: Research, Applications and Policy*, 1(2):52–58, Spring 1992.

3. Bönigk, J. System Architecture and Exchange Strategies for Mobile Visualization. In IMC'96 [7].

4. Cardelli, L. Obliq – A language with distributed scope. White Paper, Digital, Systems Research Center, March 1994.

5. Cattell, R.G.G. *The Object Database Standard – ODMG'93*. Morgan & Kaufmann, 1994.

6. Davies, N., Blair, G., Cheverst, K., Friday, A. Supporting adaptive services in a heterogeneous mobile environment. In *Proc. Workshop on Mobile Computing Systems and Applications (MCSA'94)*, Santa Cruz, CA, December 8–9 1994. IEEE Computer Society.

7. *Proc. Workshop on Information Visualization and Mobile Computing (IMC'96)*, Rostock, Germany, February 26–27 1996.

8. Kirste, T. An infrastructure for mobile information systems based on a fragmented object model. *Distributed Systems Engineering Journal*, 2(3):161–170, 1995.

9. Kirste, T. INCH – *Ein Konzept für* Interactive Computational Hypermedia *auf der Basis einer funktionalen Objektinterpretation*. Shaker Verlag, Aachen, Germany, 1995. ISBN 3-8265-0748-7.

10. Kirste, T. The MOVI Project – Introduction and Modeling Concepts. In IMC'96 [7].

11. Lange, S., Rauschenbach, U., Schumann, H. Alternatives for the presentation of information in a mobile environment. In IMC'96 [7].

12. Malone, T.W., Lai, K.-Y., Frey, Ch. Experiments with Oval: A radically tailorable tool for cooperative work. *ACM TOIS*, 13(2):177–205, April 1995.

13. McKeehan, J., Rhodes, N. *Programming for the Newton*. AP Professional, 1994.

14. Minsky, M. A Framework for Representing Knowledge. In Winston, P.H., editor, *The Psychology of Computer Vision*. McGraw-Hill, New-York, 1975.

15. NCSA. Mosaic.
    http://www.ncsa.uiuc.edu/SDG/Software/Mosaic/NCSAMosaicHome.html.

16. Nelson, T.H. Replacing the printed word: A complete literary system. In Lavington, S.H., editor, *Proc. IFIP Congress 1980*, pages 1013–1023. North-Holland, 1980.

17. Nelson, T.H. All for One and One for All. In *Proc. Hypertext '87 (November 13–15 1987, Chappel Hill, North Carolina)*, pages v–vii. The Association for Computing Machinery, 1987.

18. Nelson, T.H. Immense storage management. *Byte*, 1988.

19. Roberts, R.B., Goldstein, I.P. The FRL Primer. AI Memo No. 408, Artificial Intelligence Laboratory, MIT, Cambridge, Mass., 1977.

20. Shibata, Y., Katsumoto, M. Dynamic Hypertext and Knowledga Agent Systems for Multimedia Information Networks. In *Proc. Hypertext'93 (November 14–18 1993, Seattle, Washington)*, pages 83–93. The Association for Computing Machinery, 1993.

21. Smith, W.R. The Newton Application Architecture. In *Proc. IEEE Computer Conference*, San Francisco, 1994.

22. Steele Jr., G.L. *Common Lisp: The Language*. Digital Press, second edition, 1990.

23. Ungar, D., Randall, B. Self: the power of simplicity. In *Proc. OOPSLA'87 Conference*, pages 227–241, Orlando, Florida, 1987. Published as *SIGPLAN Notices 22*, Dec. 1987.

24. Waters, R.C. GPRINT: A LISP Pretty Printer Providing Extensive User Format-Control Mechanisms. AI Memo No. 611, Artificial Intelligence Laboratory, MIT, Cambridge, Mass., 1981.

This article was processed using the LaTeX macro package with LLNCS style

Specifying navigational transformations in hypermedia. A temporal logic framework

M. C. Meré* and G. Rossi+

* System Engineering Department-UERJ and CNPq,
e-mail: cmere@omega.lncc.br

+ D.I. PUC-Rio, LIFIA-UNLP and CONICET,
e-mail: grossi@info.unlp.edu.ar

Abstract. In this paper we present a temporal logic formalism for specifying navigational transformations in hypermedia applications. Using temporal logic it is possible to specify both the static and dynamic aspects of the navigational structure of such applications. We present our framework in the context of the Object-Oriented Hypermedia Design Methodology (OOHDM) though it can be applied to other methods involving graphs as the specification structure for navigation. We show that the power of the temporal logic formalism is enough to deal with concepts, like aggregation, interruptions, backtracking, etc., and compare our formalism with others in the hypermedia field.

1 Introduction

In the last four years there has been growing interest in hypermedia design models and methodologies. The "Web explosion" has made evident certain problems suffered by the final user like getting lost in the hiperspace, cognitive overhead, etc. As new Web browsers begin to include new navigation and interface functionality, designers are faced with the need to clearly organize contents, navigation strategies and interfaces in their applications. We strongly believe that most usability problems can be solved during the specification and design step of the development cycle. In this paper we focus on a narrow though critical problem of hypermedia applications: the specification of the navigation structure, in particular the specification of navigational transformations and its impact on the final application in the context of the Object-Oriented Hypermedia Design Methodology.

The structure of this paper is as follows. In section 2 we present the Object-Oriented Hypermedia Design Methodology (OOHDM) and introduce the problems related with navigational transformations, in section 3 we discuss the temporal logic framework with some examples, emphasizing the treatment of aggregations. Finally, in section 4 we compare our formalism with other related approaches and discuss some further work.

2 OOHDM

The OOHDM is a model-based approach, considering the hypermedia application development process as a four activities process, namely conceptual modeling, navigational design, abstract interface design and implementation. They are performed in a mix of iterative, incremental and prototype-based styles of development.

During Conceptual Modeling, a model of the application domain is built using well known object-oriented modeling principles [9] augmented with some primitives such as attribute perspectives and sub-systems. Conceptual classes may be built using aggregation and generalization/specialization hierarchies. There is no concern for the types of users and tasks, only for the application domain semantics. The product of this step is a class and instance schema built out of Sub-Systems, Classes and Relationships.

In OOHDM, an application is seen as a navigational view over the domain model. This view is built during Navigational Design taking into account the types of intended users, and the set of tasks they are to perform using the application. Different navigational models may be built for the same conceptual schema thus expressing different views (applications) on the same domain. We describe the navigational structure of a hypermedia application by defining navigational classes such as nodes, links and access structures that reflect the chosen view over the application domain and a Navigational Schema showing the static relationships among navigational classes.

The navigational structure is defined in terms of navigational contexts, which are induced (in different ways depending on the type of class) from navigation classes such as Nodes, Links, Indices, and Guided Tours. Navigational Contexts are useful for organizing the navigation patterns that may be followed by a user.

During Navigational Design we also define the way in which navigation will proceed by specifying transformations in the navigational space, i.e. the set of accessible navigational objects at a given time.

During Abstract Interface Design, an interface model is built. The interface model specifies which interface objects the user will perceive and, in particular, the way in which different navigational objects will look like, which interface objects will activate navigation, the way in which multimedia interface objects will be synchronized and which interface transformations will take place.

Finally, by mapping the navigational and abstract interface models into concrete objects, i.e., those available in the chosen implementation environment, the author produces the actual hypermedia system to be run. In particular the abstract interface model can be implemented in a straightforward way on top of available hypermedia platforms such as Hypercard, Toolbook, Scriptx, etc.

A deeper discussion about OOHDM may be found in [7,8,10,11,12,13,14].

2.1 Navigational Transformations. Why?

While the navigational schema shows the static navigational structure of a hypermedia application as a graph with nodes and links, many of them exhibit complex dynamic patterns while navigation proceeds.

For example we may want that a set of nodes remain open and accessible until certain link is followed (see for example [3]). Although we must not confuse these dynamic patterns with pure interface effects (a menu pop-up, some attribute that remains hidden until you push a button, etc) it is clear that during navigational design we must precisely specify what happens each time a link is followed in terms of the set of accessible navigational objects. Suppose we have the simple navigational schema in Figure 1 showing class city as an aggregation of city places and a link to their history. The example is adapted from the Touring Amsterdam system [3] in which similar problems are presented. We will not address interface problems but purely navigational ones: which nodes are shown and when. We do not care about how they will be shown (this is done during Abstract Interface Design).

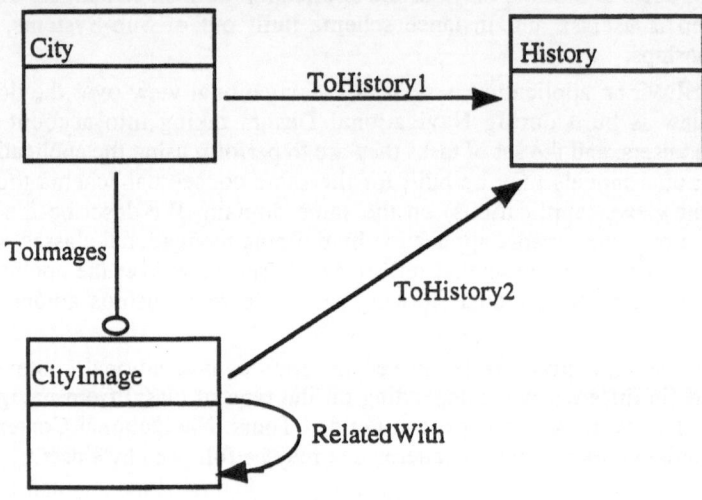

Fig. 1. A simple navigational schema

It is possible to navigate from a city to one of its images and from both the city or an image to the node describing the history. The pre-defined navigational behavior in OOHDM prescribes that when a node is left, it is removed from the navigational space until it is further activated. However, in this simple example we could specify a slightly different behavior: city and city images may co-exist in the navigational space but when a link to the history is selected only this latter node remains available. In a multi-windows environments this may be implemented by allowing to have two different windows opened one for a city and the other for a city image that are mutually exclusive with the window for the history.

Also, let's suppose that when we active a link from an image to another image (of the same city) the node of the previous image is closed but the city remains available.

Note that the previous example of navigational transformations is particularly useful when City has some media attribute, for example, an audio recording that we want to continue when we explore images, but instances of History have their own recording (or video) and thus we do not want both media to be played at the same time. Also, we may specify the abstract interface in a way that images do not appear in a separate window but in a frame inside city nodes.

While the specification of how navigation will proceed is important in typical hypermedia applications they are critical in distributed environments or in Web applications.

Specifying the behavior of navigational objects when a link is traversed may be done
in different ways. Moreover, although it is true that when we implement a hypermedia
application, navigational behavior must be usually written using a scripting language
(like Toolbook's OpenScript, Hypercard's Hypertalk, Scriptx or Java) it is important
to precisely specify at a design, implementation-independent level which the desired
transformations will be.

In the next section we explain our temporal logic framework and show the
specification of navigational transformations for the previous example.

3 The Logical Approach to Formal Specifications

3.1 The Temporal Logic Framework

In this work we explore how to specify the navigational behavior of hypermedia
applications using a linear discrete temporal logic. Using this approach we also have a
deductive system that permits querying and verifying properties satisfied by the
application.

Moreover, our specifications are as weak as possible, stating only those properties of
the application necessary to meet the designer specification. Such specifications leave
the implementer free to choose the best possible implementation.

Informally, we consider that there are different time points which may yield different
truth values of propositions. We assume that the set of time points is infinite, discrete
and linearly ordered with a smallest element (like the natural numbers set ordered by
the $\leq$ relation). In order to describe the possible variety of the truth values of a
proposition A at different times, the logical language supplies us with operators (or
connectives) which enables us to formulate new propositions related to some
reference point. Besides that, we have the connectives and quantifiers of a many-
sorted first-order logic language (with equality predicate symbols for each sort).

In this work we use the following temporal connectives:

ξ A, meaning that property A holds at all time points after the reference point and at
the reference point too ("always").

ζ A, meaning that there is a time point after or equal to the reference point at which
A holds ("sometimes").

$O A$, meaning that A holds at the time point immediately after the reference point
("next").

$\Omega(A, B)$, meaning that if there is a following point at which B holds then A holds up
to that point, else A holds permanently ("weak until", also called ``unless'').

A formula A, without temporal connectives, is true if and only if it is true in the
current or reference moment ("now").

A comprehensive discussion about temporal logic issues can be found in [6,2].

Clearly, the design of the navigational structure of hypermedia application is a
critical step in the construction of these applications. The use of formal methods may
be a good alternative to help the author in the process of specifying the navigational

behavior of a hypermedia application. Also, this behavior will have an immediate impact in the application's usability as they can help readers navigate through complex documents.

Using our temporal-logic based formalism we are able to specify both the static navigation structure and the navigational behavior of the application. Actually, we have an adequate conceptual tool for both designing the application and for querying the design against desired properties.

The navigation process in a hyperdocument can be thought as a sequence of states transitions, i.e., a certain action a takes the program from state s to state s'. This transition would represent the traversal of a simple link in some hypermedia application, in which case s is the state before the traversal and s' is the state immediately after it, and a denotes the link being active.

To specify such situation we must specify the set S of all possible sequences. Therefore, a navigation process satisfies the specification if the set S of its execution sequences is equal to the set of execution sequences that the temporal logic specification satisfies.

All execution sequences are infinite; terminating programs are represented by having an 0-ary action that closes all the nodes forever, and therefore it closes the navigation. This semantics also justifies the adoption of an infinite temporal domain.

Following the logical approach [16], we shall formulate the specifications within the formalism of first-order logic. Thus, a specification is an axiomatic presentation of a theory in many-sorted first-order logic and the properties described by such specification are the consequences of the presentation.

More precisely, a logical specification consists of two parts: declarations and axioms. A declaration part or *signature* contains a description of all the symbols involved, including *sort, function and predicate symbols* (with their arity, domain and codomain). They are the elements of the specification. The sorts and functions will be assigned a rigid interpretation (time-independent interpretation), whereas the predicates will be non-rigid.

The *axioms* or property part is a set of formulas (a presentation of a theory) that define the properties that the symbols have. The properties are *static* or *dynamic*. A property is static if it is independent of the time, i.e., the formula have no temporal connectives. An example of this kind of property is the structural properties of the navigational schema, i.e., the formulae that specify which nodes are related by which links. Dynamic properties establish how the state of the elements is modified during its lifetime. Syntactically, these formulas have temporal connectives. Examples of this kind of property are the formulae that specify which nodes are closed and which are opened when a link is traversed.

Given a temporal specification we may ask queries like: will node a be eventually opened?, is there a session in which both a and b are opened before c ?, etc. We can then use the underlying deductive system to verify if our specification meets these properties.

3.2 Logical Specification of Hypermedia Applications

We will next show how we specify the static structure of the simple hypermedia application discussed in section 2. In Figure 2 we present a temporal logic specification for the static properties (the underlying graph). The treatment of dynamic properties will be presented in Figure 3.

The logic specification S corresponding to the graph of the application in Figure 1 has the following set of symbols: sorts N and L meaning the set of (types of) nodes and the set of (types of) links between them and sorts *SetOf(N)* and *SetOf(L)* meaning sets of (types of) nodes and set of (types of) links, respectively. The predicate symbol *Enab* indicates what links are enabled in each node at each moment. For each (type of) node we have a constant (or function) symbol of type N that represents it, for each (type of) link we have a constant (or function) symbol of type L. Also, we have a constant that represents a set of nodes and two constants that represent sets of links. We also have a predicate symbol *Open* indicating which node is opened in each moment and two predicates (in_N and in_L) that point which elements are in each set.

The (static) properties of this specification establish in which node a link can be active (the domain of the link) and define a node by all the links beginning in it. We should also establish the node where each link arrives (its codomain), but this property can be expressed together with the dynamic characteristics.

The specification of finite sets using first-order logic is well-known (see [5]) and we assume to have these axioms in our theory though we don't write explicitly them. In the figures below we consider that the axioms holds in each instant of time, i.e. there is a connective ``always" in from of each axiom.

$$
\begin{aligned}
&\textit{Sorts:} \quad\quad N, L, SetOf(N), SetOf(L)\\
&\textit{Pr edicate Symbols:}\\
&\quad\quad Enab \subseteq L\\
&\quad\quad Open \subseteq N\\
&\quad\quad in_N \subseteq N \times SetOf(N)\\
&\quad\quad in_L \subseteq L \times SetOf(L)\\
&\textit{Function Symbols:}\\
&\quad\quad City: \to N\\
&\quad City\,\mathrm{Im}\,age: \to SetOf(N)\\
&\quad\quad History: \to N\\
&\quad ToHistory_1: \to L\\
&\quad ToHistory_2: \to SetOf(L)\\
&\quad To\,\mathrm{Im}\,ages: \to L\\
&\quad \mathrm{Re}\,latedWith: \to SetOf(L)\\
&\textit{Axioms:}\\
&\textit{Structural Pr operties:}\\
&Open(City) \leftrightarrow Enab(ToHistory_1) \wedge Enab(To\,\mathrm{Im}\,ages)\\
&\forall x: N(in_N(x, City\,\mathrm{Im}\,ages) \to (Open(x) \leftrightarrow \exists y, y': L(in_L(y, ToHistory_2) \wedge\\
&\quad in_L(y', \mathrm{Re}\,latedWith) \wedge Enab(y') \wedge Enab(y) \wedge (\forall z, z': L\, in_L(z, ToHistory_2) \wedge\\
&\quad in_L(z', \mathrm{Re}\,latedWith) \wedge Enab(z') \wedge Enab(z) \to y = z \wedge y' = z'))))
\end{aligned}
$$

Fig. 2. Logical specification of a graph

The dynamic properties express the changes in the status of nodes and links that navigation through a hypermedia application produces. The dynamic properties can be classified in *navigation graph*, *initial, final* and *transformational properties*.

The navigation graph properties establish general properties common at all hypermedia applications. Such properties must express consistency conditions of the navigation operation. To express them, we need a new predicate symbol, *Act*, meaning that a link is active, or in other words, that a link is being traversed. Another interesting property is that we can make active a link only if it is enabled and that we can make active (travel through) only one link at a time. We also consider that it is always possible to follow an enabled link, thus navigation proceeds.

The transformational properties are the particular dynamic characteristics of the hypermedia application that we are specifying. They establish the codomain of the links and what nodes are closed or remain opened when we travel through a link.

The initial condition establishes the initial status of the hypermedia application. We need a predicate constant *BEG* that initializes the process. In the same way, the final condition allows to close a section, we use a predicate constant $STOP$ for this purpose.

Consider as an example the following specification of the dynamic behavior of the application discussed in section 2.

Pr*edicate Symbols*:

$Act \subseteq L$

BEG

$STOP$

Navigation Graph Pr*operties*:

$\forall i, j: L \ (Act(i) \wedge Act(j) \rightarrow i = j)$

$\forall l: L \ (Act(l) \rightarrow Enab(l))$

$\forall x: N \ \forall l: L((Open(x) \rightarrow Enab(l) \wedge Act(l)) \rightarrow O(\exists x' : N \ Open(x') \wedge x \neq x'))$

$\forall x: N \ (Open(x) \rightarrow (\exists l: L(Enab(l) \rightarrow Act(l)) \vee STOP))$

Transformational Pr*operties*:

$Act(To \text{Im} ages) \rightarrow O(\exists y: N \ in_N(y, City \text{Im} ages) \wedge Open(y)) \wedge OOpen(City)$

$Act(ToHistory_1) \rightarrow O \ Open(History) \wedge O \neg Open(City)$

$\forall l: L \ in_L(l, ToHistory_2) \rightarrow (Act(l) \rightarrow O \ Open(History) \wedge O \neg Open(City))$

$\forall l: L \ in_L(l, Re latedWith) \rightarrow (Act(l) \rightarrow O(\exists y: N(in_N(y, City \text{Im} ages) \wedge Open(y) \wedge$

$\quad (\forall x: N \ in_N(x, City \text{Im} ages) \wedge Open(x) \rightarrow x = y))) \wedge OOpen(City))$

$\neg Open(City) \rightarrow \forall y: N(in_N(y, City \text{Im} ages) \rightarrow \neg Open(y))$

Initial Condition:

$BEG \rightarrow Open(City) \wedge (\forall x: N \ x \neq City \rightarrow \neg Open(x))$

Final Condition:

$STOP \rightarrow O(\forall x: N \neg Open(x))$

Fig. 3. Logical specification of behavior

The transformational properties show the effects of the action *Act* over the attributes *Open* and *Enab*. *Act* is an action that changes the status of nodes and links from one moment of time to the next. Because the node *History* doesn't have any enable link, when *History* is reached the navigation must end.

The predicate constant symbol *STOP* can be a button that allows to exit the system in each or only in some desired windows, i.e. it allows to quit the application. Formally, *STOP* changes the status of nodes and links and in the formal semantics the action *STOP* closes all the nodes forever.

Notice that in the specification above, all the links of all the open nodes are enabled. For example, if in the instant s_0 we initialize the navigational process, we have that the node *City* is open and the links *ToHistory 1* and *ToImages* are enabled (and the nodes *CityImages* and *History* are closed). If the link *ToImages* is active, then in the instant s_1 we will have that the nodes *City* and *CityImages* are open (and the node

History is closed) and the links *ToHistory₁*, *ToImages*, *ToHistory₂* and *RelatedWith* are enabled and therefore, any of them can be active.

In the example of section 2, each city can be related to several images, this is the reason because we have chosen to consider *CityImages* as a set. Moreover, from each image it is possible to go to another image or to the history of the city. Therefore, we consider that *ToHistory₂* and *RelatedWith* are sets of links, one link of each kind for each image. This approach can be more general to cope with a community of several cities (each one with its own history and its set of images) interacting between them. It is enough to add a new sort whose elements are the patterns with the desired behavior (in this example, each pattern is formed by the nodes City, History and the set CityImages and the links between them).

In some applications the links can be traveled backward or forward. To specify this case, it is more convenient to have in our logic connectives for expressing strict past time[1] : ΔA means that A was always true in the past (``always in the past") and $\nabla A$ means that $A$ was sometimes true in the past (``eventually in the past"). The time semantics we have in mind is the same as before, the set of naturals with their order relation $(N, \leq)$. We also add to the logical language a new predicate symbol *Back* meaning the result of going backward in the time sequence. In our formalism it is not difficult to express what to travel back is: to go back in an open node X results in a new state where the open nodes are those that were open at the past time immediately before X was open. Specifying backtracking, we can leave for a later implementation step decisions such as: what the backtracking of the first node is; if the nodes that were open after the node where we are applying backtracking remain open or not and, because a node can be open and closed several times, what exactly past point of time must be considered to go back.

Another problem that we want to discuss is the case when a link is active but after that it can be interrupted. In this case, we may use a logic with continuous frame time (like $(R, \leq)$ or $(Q, \leq)$, the set of rational or real numbers with their order relation) but we will not have the next operator, as it doesn't exists a successor element in the line time. Another possibility could be a logic with intervals of time, but a discrete one. We prefer to use the semantics frame of naturals because is the more intuitive framework for our application problem.

We need to add some more predicate symbols to specify this case. We consider that a link can be enabled, initialized or interrupted. The navigational properties must establish that: it is possible to initialize only a link at a time, enabled links are the only ones that can be initialized, a link can be interrupted only if it is initialized. It is important to note that in this case, not to interrupt a link is the action that changes the states in the time sequence. The other actions don't change the current states in the time sequence.

4 Related work and concluding remarks

---

[1] Strict past time is the notion of time that doesn't include the present moment as part of the past. Moreover, the past of a formula A in the initial moment has always true value.

We have briefly discussed the use of temporal logic to specify navigational transformations in hypermedia applications. We have shown that we can generate a modular, understandable specification that can be later used by the implementer to generate a running application. Unambiguously specifying the behavior of navigational objects is a key aspect to success in these applications. We have used our formalism to specify complex applications that have been later implemented in different application environments (like Toolbook, HTML, etc)

Other authors have used formal techniques to specify the navigation and interface structure of hypermedia applications.

For example in [15] branching temporal logic is used to expressing some dynamic properties a document should exhibit during browsing and a model checking approach is used to verify that these properties are met by the system (expressed as an automaton). In this case temporal logic is not used as an specification tool but only as a verification tool. Our approach is different because we want to specify and later verify using the same formalism.

In [17] the authors use statecharts to specify the behavior of a hypermedia application. Their approach is interesting because they also take into account interface aspects.

Finally, in [4] it is shown how to use an interval temporal logic to express temporal constraints. In this case we are focusing a different problem, the specification of navigational transformations but obviously both approaches can be merged.

We are now working in some research issues related with our formalism; first we are extending our framework to incorporate the dynamics of the interface in a logic specification by being able to "explode" some predicates into others containing information about the structure and behavior of the interface.

We are also studying the use of the Metatem tool [1] to obtain an executable algorithm from the specifications discussed in this work, since both our framework and Metatem are based on the same kind of temporal logic.

Finally we are planning to adapt the Metatem tool to a visual definition environment in which navigational transformations are graphically specified, the corresponding temporal formulas are derived from that specification and can be later executed by Metatem.

References

1 Barringer, H., Fisher, M., Gabbay, D., Gough, G., Owens, R.: MetateM, a framework for programming in temporal logic. University of Manchester, T.R. 1995 (e-mail: barringer@uk.ac.man.cs).

2 Gabbay, D., Hodkinson, I., Reynolds, M.: Temporal logic, mathematical foundations and computational aspects.,Vol 1. Oxford Science Publications, 1994.

3 Hardman, L., Bulterman, D., Van Rossum, G.: Links in hypermedia, the requirements for context. In Proc. Hypertext'93, ACM, pp 183-191.

30

4 King, P: Towards an ITL based formalism for expressing temporal constraints in Multimedia Document. In Proc. of Workshop on Executable Temporal Logics, 1995. (e-mail: prking@cs.UManitoba.ca).

5 Manna, Z., Waldinger, R.: The logical basis for computer programming, deductive reasoning, Vol. 1. Addison-Wesley, 1985.

6 Pnueli, A.: Applications of temporal logic to the specification and verification of reactive systems, a survey of current trends. In De Bakker, J.W., De Roever, W.P., Rozenberg, G. (eds): Current Trends in Concurrency, overviews and tutorials. Springer Verlag 1986 (Lecture Notes in Computer Science, vol. 224, pp: 510-584).

7 Rossi, G., Schwabe, D., Lucena, C., Cowan, D.: An Object-Oriented model for designing the Human-Computer interface of hypermedia applications. In Proc. of IWHD'95. Springer Verlag, forthcoming.

8 Rossi, G., Schwabe, D., Garrido, A.: Design issues while building computational hypermedia applications. In Proc. of the Second International Workshops on Adding hypertext functionality to computer applications, Washington, March'96.

9 Rumbaugh, J., Blaha, M., Premerlani, W., Eddy, F., Lorensen, W.: Object Oriented Modeling and Design. Prentice Hall Inc., 1991.

10 Schwabe, D., Rossi, G.: From domain models to hypermedia applications, an Object-Oriented approach. In Proc. of the International Workshop on Methodologies for Designing and Developing Hypermedia Applications, Edinburgh, September 1994.

11 Schwabe, D., Rossi, G.: Building hypermedia applications as navigational views of information models. In Proc. of the Hawaii International Conference on System Sciences, Hawaii, January 1995.

12 Schwabe, D., Rossi, G.: The Object-Oriented Hypermedia Design Model. Communications of the ACM, August 1995.

13 Schwabe, D., Rossi, G., Barbosa, S.: Systematic hypermedia design with OOHDM. In Proc. of the ACM International Conference on Hypertext (Hypertext'96), Washington, March 1996.

14 Schwabe, D., Rossi, G., Barbosa, S.: Structured WWW site design. Presented at the Workshop on Hypermedia Research and the WWW. ACM Hypertext'96, Washington, March 1996.

15 Stotts, P.D., Furuta, R., Ruiz, J.C.: Hyperdocuments as automata, trace-based browsing property verification. ACM ECHT Conference, Milano, 1992.

16 Turski, W.M., Maibaum, T.S.E.: The specification of computer programs. Addison-Wesley Publishing Company, 1987.

17 Zheng, Y., Pong, M.C.: Using Statecharts to model hypertext. In Proc. of the ACM European Conference on Hypertext, Milano, December 1992.

Quality and Resource Controlled Transmission of Images

Uwe Rauschenbach
Randolf Schultz
Heidrun Schumann

University of Rostock
Computer Science Department
D-18051 Rostock
Germany
Email: {urausche, rschultz, schumann}@informatik.uni-rostock.de

Abstract. This paper presents an image transmission protocol which allows to transmit images controlled by resources and quality demands. Depending on these parameters, the reduction of image data, the selection and the configuration of a compression algorithm are done automatically. The automatic selection mechanism is based on the results of an investigation of image compression agorithms we conducted in order to find out the strengths, weaknesses and configurability of JPEG, fractal and wavelet-based compression.

Keywords: Image transmission, Image compression, Image quality, Protocol

1 Introduction

Mobile computers, wireless data transmission and globally distributed information spaces (e.g., the WWW) are widely available now and create new technological challenges. Especially the transmission of image data is very bandwidth-demanding, and techniques of image data reduction and compression have to be used. This paper deals with the transmission of images from a server to a mobile client computer, where one has to cope with lots of constraints limiting resources, like bandwidth and processing power. The paper addresses two aspects of the problem:

First, we discuss the results of an investigation of image compression agorithms we conducted in order to find out the strengths and weaknesses of several lossy compressors and their configurability.

Second, we propose an image transmission protocol which allows to transmit images controlled by resources and quality demands. Depending on these parameters, the reduction of image data, the selection and the configuration of a compression algorithm are done automatically.

2 Investigation of Image Compression Algorithms

2.1 Motivation

Our goal was to develop a control mechanism that accepts quality and resource parameters and calculates a set of configuration parameters for a certain compression algorithm so that the resulting image quality and the use of resources matches the given values. This mechanism is intended to be the core of a protocol for the quality and resource controlled transmission of images.

There are a lot of different compression algorithms for images. Some are standardized, accepted and widely used like JPEG. Other new approaches, namely fractal compression and compression using wavelets, are relatively unknown regarding their strengths and weaknesses. To select a major compression algorithm to use for the transmission of images over a low-bandwidth network, we investigated and compared JPEG, wavelet and fractal based compression.

Lossy algorithms achieve the best compression ratio. Certain parameters control the compression ratio and thereby the loss of quality caused by the compression/decompression process. However, they do not directly correspond to the image quality or to the amount of resources saved by the compression. Thus, our experiments had to clarify this correlation.

2.2 Evaluation Criteria and Procedure

Regarding image transmission over low bandwidth links, we used the following criteria to evaluate a compression algorithm's quality:

- maximum achievable compression ratio
- compression and decompression costs (CPU time)
- subjective image quality at a certain compression ratio
- dependence on image content
- configurability
- support of progressive or hierarchical encoding
- symmetry of costs for compression and decompression

It is difficult to judge the quality of images observed by humans. Often, "technical" measures like the signal-to-noise ratio or comparisons of the statistical distribution of colors are used. The drawback of these signal characteristics is that they don't take the special capabilities of the human perceptual system into consideration. PQS [1], a quality judgement system which does consider these, is unfortunately limited to monochrome images. Thus, we used our own

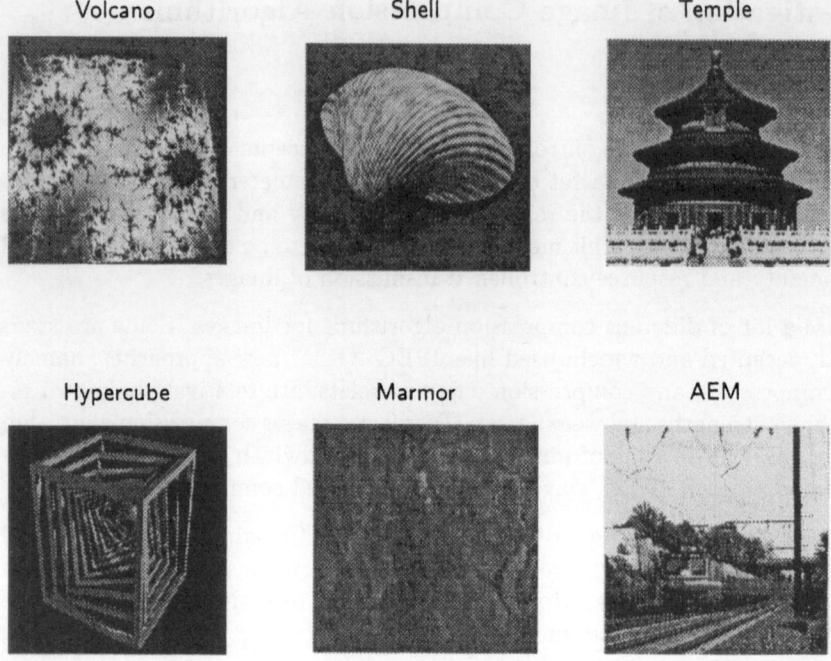

Figure 1: The test images

subjective criteria to judge image quality:

- good (no visible alterations)

- medium (visible artifatcs)

- poor (heavy distortions)

We selected a set of six images (see figure 1) with different characteristics as the test data set. Attention has been paid to cover a wide range of features, e.g. scanned photographs (AEM, Temple), computer generated images (Hypercube, Shell), images with fine lines (AEM), Fractals (Volcano) and textures (Marmor).

We used the JPEG implementation of the Independent JPEG Group, the wavelet implementation EPIC, which is based on Daubechie's wavelet, and the example implementation of a fractal compressor by Yval Fisher. Each compressor can be configured by one or more parameters, which influence quality and compression ratio. In the case of more than one parameter, the parameter which had the greatest influence on the compression ratio has been selected in preliminary tests. A test suite has been implemented which iterates the selected parameter for each compressor and each image within a predefined range and and with a predefined step size. CPU time and compression ratio for each compressor/decompressor run has been recorded, and inverted difference images between the original image and the particular compressed/decompressed images have been computed for quality judgement by a human observer.

2.3 Evaluation results

criteria	JPEG	Wavelet	Fractal
maximum compression ratio	1:160	1:350	1:375
compression ratio, quality: good	up to 1:30	up to 1:30	up to 1:25
compression ratio, quality: medium	up to 1:70	up to 1:90	up to 1:50
compression ratio, quality: bad	up to 1:160	up to 1:350	up to 1:375
compression time (factor)	1	*5	*20 (average)
decompression time (factor)	1	*3	*5
dependence on image	medium	big	big
configurable	yes	yes	yes
detail on demand, progressive	yes	yes	no
symmetric	yes	no	no

Table 1: Results of the evaluation

Table 1 shows the results of the evaluation:

- JPEG is the fastest and most stable compression method (i.e. independent from image data to a high degree, see figure 2a).

- JPEG is the only symmetric method.

- Wavelets and fractal compression are several times slower than JPEG during compression as well as during decompression.

- Wavelets and fractal compression are much more image-dependent than JPEG

    - compression ratio breaks down on fine structures (c.f. performance measures for the "volcano" test image, figures 2b and 2c).

    - better compression than JPEG on textures (c.f. performance measures for the "marmor" test image, figures 2b and 2c).

- The compression time of a fractal encoder depends to a high degree on the compression ratio (see figure 2d).

- Wavelets deliver better image quality at high compression ratios than JPEG and fractal compression - however, at the cost of a long computing time.

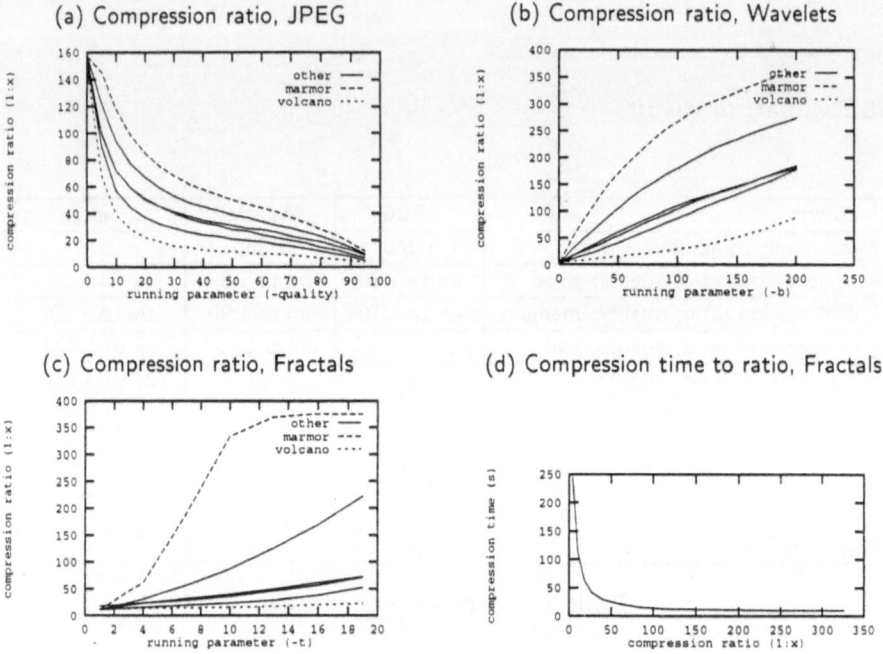

Figure 2: Experiment results as diagrams

Tests done subsequently using other implementations than the three mentioned above confirm the trends we found. Since JPEG is the fastest algorithm and allows better prediction of the compression ratio given the image quality (and vice versa) than wavelet and fractal based compression, we selected this compression method for use in our image transmission protocol, which we will describe in the rest of this paper.

3 Image transmission protocol

3.1 Motivation

In a mobile environment, transmission bandwidth, client display resources and client processing power are limited. Transmission bandwidth can be saved by using image compression methods, and the images must be adapted to the client's

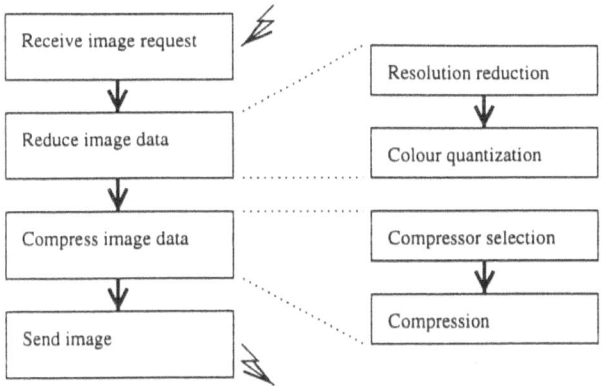

Figure 3: Tasks of the image server

display resources. Our quality and resource controlled image transmission protocol has been designed to consider these aspects.

The basic idea is to do all necessary reduction at the server side in order to save transmission bandwidth and client processing power. In a first step, all those parts of the image can be removed which can't be displayed at the client. This includes the reduction of the resolution as well as the reduction of the number of colors. In a second step, lossy or lossless data compression can be applied in order to decrease transmission bandwidth demands furter. When applying lossy data compression, quality requirements of the user should be accepted and mapped to the parameter values of the compression algorithms. Our protocol is designed to adapt the image to the client's display before compressing it, and to automatically select and configure an appropriate compression algorithm.

3.2 Features

For an effective image transmission, the protocol must have the following basic features:

- To reduce communication costs, the protocol must use compression techniques which can be either selected automatically depending on the image type (e.g., JPEG for photographs or JBIG for scanned documents) or explicitly by a client request.

- Images must be cropped, scaled, resampled and quantized at the server side according to the client's display resources in order to save communication bandwidth and to reduce the workload on the client system when displaying the image, as stated above.

- It must be easy to extend the knowledge base of the protocol by new compression techniques.

- The protocol should support the separate transmission of several resolution or quality levels as they are offered by some compressors (e.g., Progressive JPEG). This allows the use of detail-on-demand and progressive refinement techniques, which lead to shorter response times and enable a high degree of user control over the transmission process.

3.3 Description of the Protocol

Request processing and structure. The basic tasks of the image server are illustrated in figure 3. As the protocol works with knowledge about the display parameters of the client in order to provide a default mechanism, we must distinguish two types of requests: contact request and image request. When the client contacts the server for the first time, it sends the *contact* request which contains the following information:

- Client address

- List of available decompressors

- Screen size and resolution

- Colour depth

- Palette

To fetch an image, the client sends an *image request* which is structured as follows:

- Image identifier

- Client address

- Requested quality or compression ratio

- Flag: successive refinement requested

- Requested compressor (optional)

- Requested image resolution (optional)

- Requested image size (optional)

- Requested cropping coordinates (optional)

- Requested color depth (optional)

• Requested palette (optional)

Where the first four fields of the request are mandatory, the optional fields can be used by the client to override default values and the automatic selection process. This facility offers the client a flexible way to control the image handling on the server.

Data reduction. The adaptation of images to the client's display resources can lead to a significant decrease of the data volume. Figure 4 illustrates the process. Take, for instance, a 1280x1024 pixel true color image, which has a size of 3.75 Mbyte. Adapting it to a monochrome 320x200 pixel PDA screen leads to a data volume of 7.8 KByte, the adaptation of the same image to a 640x480, 256 color laptop display reduces the image data size to 300 KByte - without compression!

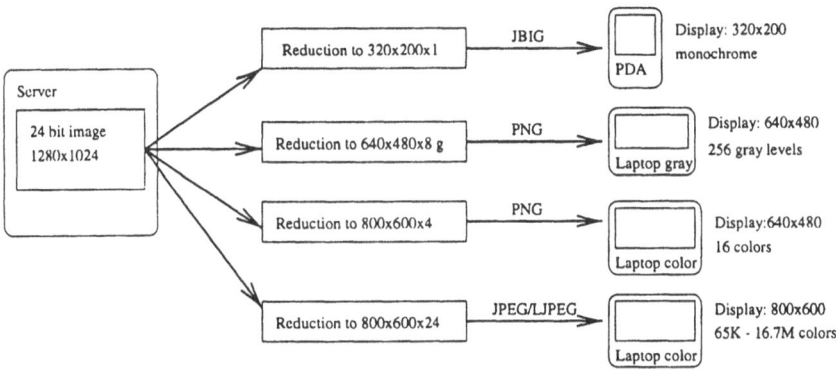

Figure 4: Image handling for different display types

Two steps are necessary to adapt the image to the client's display resources. First, the image size is reduced according to the requested or the client's default values. This can be done either by scaling (default) or by cropping if the client specifies a cropping rectangle. In a second step, the colors of the image are adjusted to fit the client's resources. This is currently done by octree [4] quantization and Floyd-Steinberg dithering [3]. Optionally, the image is adapted to the palette of the client.

Compressor selection and configuration. After the data reduction of the image, a compression algorithm is selected based on the color depth of the image, the achievable compression ratio or quality and the client request. Figure 4 illustrates the selection process for clients with different display capabilities. One interesting result of our tests has been, that JPEG is not always superiour over the lossless(!) PNG image format [5], when compressing color images with a number of bit planes between 3 and 7 and a -quality parameter between 60 and 95. The dependency is shown in figure 5.

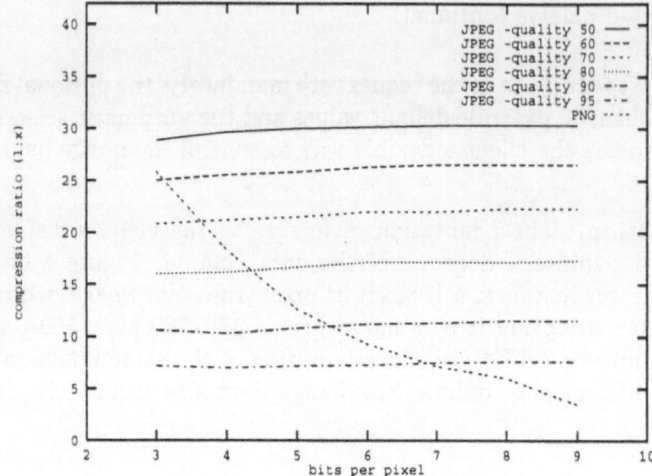

Figure 5: PNG versus JPEG

As this example shows, for the selection process knowledge about the properties of each compressor is necessary, which is stored in an extensible knowledge base. It contains the following facts for each compressor:

- suitability for images of color depth N

- lossy or lossless compression

- support of progressive refinement

- maximum achievable compression ratio

- configurability

- list for control parameter lookup, consisting of tuples of control parameter values, color depth values, compression ratios and image quality measures

- command line with placeholders for input file, output file and parameter value

Currently, the selection process consists of two steps:

1. From the list of available compressors, all algorithms are selected which are suitable for the color depth of the reduced image.

2. From the resulting reduced list, the algorithm is selected which meets all the criteria specified in the request. If no such algorithm exists, the one with the highest achievable ratio or quality is chosen.

If the selected compression algorithm is configurable, a configuration stage is necessary after the selection.

Parameter (-quality)	Compression ratio	Subjective image quality
30	1:40	20
40	1:35	30
50	1:30	40
60	1:27	50
70	1:22	60
80	1:17	70
90	1:11	80
95	1:7	95

Table 2: Configuration of the JPEG compressor

Either the desired compression ratio or the desired quality of the image can be requested by the client. Given the results from our compression algorithm investigation, we can now parameterize the compressor in such a way that the requested ratio or quality is achieved with a certain accuracy. This is done by looking up the nearest corresponding parameter value from the table or computing it by interpolation. Lookup supports the parameterization using more than one parameter, too. Table 2 shows the mapping between the parameter -quality of the JPEG compressor, the average compression ratio and the subjective image quality for 8 bit images.

The used JPEG implementation can be controlled by the parameter -quality, which, however, does not influence the image quality directly. Instead, it serves as a scaling factor for the quantization matrix. We found in our experiments that the -quality parameter does not exactly correspond to the subjectively perceived image quality. As many metrics for the term "quality" exist which may be highly dependent on the application domain, we chose to supply generic quality values in a range between 0 and 100 percent. The user of the protocol is free to define a mapping from his quality metric to the generic values.

Having decided which compression algorithm and which parameters to use, the parameters are passed to the compressor by replacing the placeholders in the command line by the current values. The compressors are considered to be external command line tools, which are called using operating system functions. Temporary files are used as a means for data exchange. This mechanism offers great flexibility.

4 Conclusions and Future Work

We presented the results of an investigation of the image compression algorithms

JPEG, wavelet and fractal compression as the basis for a quality and resource controlled image transmission protocol. Since JPEG was found to be the fastest and most stable algorithm, we selected it for use in the image transmission protocol, which we proposed in the second section of this paper. This protocol considers quality demands and client resources. In a two-step process, the requested image is reduced to fit the client's display resources and compressed using an image compression algorithm that has been selected and configured according to the clients quality or data volume requirements. An extensible knowledge base supports the incorporation of new image compressors.

Some problems remain to be solved and need further work:

- The quality judgement of the compressed images should be repeated with a greater number of subjects.

- If not all criteria are met, the current selection algorithm returns the compressor with the highest achievable compression ratio. This has to be changed to return the compressor which meets most of the criteria. Assigning weights to the criteria can help resolving in conflicts.

- Support for connection breakdown handling should be added.

- An image compressor which creates thumbnail catalogues to support visual search operations (as described in [2]) should be integrated. This includes the extension of the request structure to support lists of image IDs in one request.

- A generalized handling of data reduction and data compression modules is needed to support, e.g., alternative dithering or scaling methods.

Acknowledgement

This work is part of the MoVi Project supported by the German Science Foundation (DFG) under contract no. Schu 887/3-1.

References

1. Lu, J.; Algazi, V.R. and Estes, R.R.: Comparison of Wavelet Coders Using the Picture Quality Scale (PQS), invited paper, in: Szu, H.H. (ed.): Wavelet Applications II, Proc. SPIE, Vol. 2491, pp. 1119-1130, April 1995.

2. Burton, C.A.; Johnston, L.J.; and Sonenberg, E.A.: An Empirical Investigation of Thumbnail Image Recognition, in: Proceedings Information Visualization 95, October 30-31, 1995, Atlanta, GA, pp. 115-121

3. Floyd, R. and Steinberg, L.: An Adaptive Algorithm for Spatial Gray Scale, in: Society for Information Display 1975 Symposium Technical Papers, 1975, 36

4. Gervautz, M. and Purgathofer, W.: A Simple Method for Color Quantization: Octree Quantization, in: Magnenat-Thalmann, N. and Thalmann, D. (eds.): New Trends in Computer Graphics, Springer, Berlin, 1988, pp.219-231

5. Crocker, L.D.: PNG: The Portable Network Graphic Format, in: Dr. Dobb's Journal, Vol. 20, July 1995

6. Jaquin A.: Image Coding Based on a Fractal Theory of Iterated Contractive Function Systems, SPIE Vol. 1360, Visual Communications and Image Processing 1990

7. Hilton Michael L., Jawerth Bj"orn D., Scngupta Ayan, Compressing Still and Moving Images with Wavelets, Multimedia Systems, Vol. 2, No. 3, 1994

8. CCITT Draft Recommendation T.82, ISO/IEC Draft International Standard 11544 Coded Representation of Picture and Audio Information - Progressive Bi-Level Image Compression, 1992

9. Fischer, Y. (ed): Fractal Image Compression: Theory and Application, Springer, New York, 1995

10. Pennebaker, W.B. and Mitchell, J.L.: JPEG Still Image Data Compression Standard, Van Nostrand Reinhold, New York, 1993.

Components for video processing applications

Nuno Correia, Nuno Guimarães

INESC, R.Alves Redol, 9, 6o., 1000 Lisboa

email: {nmc,nmg}@inesc.pt, http://amadeus.inesc.pt

Abstract. This paper presents a set of software components for video processing and browsing. The current framework comprises a toolkit, with objects for video segmentation, processing, and support for interactive applications. An approach to video modeling and model reuse for knowledge based parsing of multimedia information is outlined. Some applications of the toolkit and auxiliary tools are described with emphasis on WWW related aspects (generation of HTML and Java based documents).

1   Introduction

The widespread use of video, for entertainment and information purposes, make it an appealing medium for computer processing, storage and dissemination. Advances in storage capabilities and computational power anticipate a future where video can be treated like any other data type, e.g. text. Text has received great attention over the years and applications for indexing, searching, and storing, text based information are common in all computer platforms.

Video introduces new problems given its temporal nature and the amounts of storage needed for even a few seconds of broadcast quality video. Work in this area attempts to integrate video in application development frameworks and support most of the functionality presented by text based systems. Some of these capabilities include indexing: the ability to find significant events in a video stream avoiding sequential search; searching: the ability to find occurrences of a given object or pattern; segmentation: separation of a video stream in its structural components.

In this paper, we present a software architecture and several software components to support video at the application construction level and to provide some of the processing functionality described above.

The present work has its roots in the MADE (Multimedia Application Development Environment) project [8]. This project had the goal of defining an object oriented framework for construction of multimedia applications. The generic object model in MADE supports active objects and other features such as delegation. On top of this model several object sets for user interaction, constraint management and time based media were also developed. Time based media classes, such as audio and video, derive from a superclass where all temporal management and synchronization mechanisms were introduced [2, 7]. The development of this toolkit, influenced the construction of the components and software presented on this paper in section 2.1.

In section 2.2 our approach to video modeling is also presented. The following section outlines the main characteristics of some video processing applications and its capabilities as content providers for WWW information services. The paper closes with some conclusions drawn from the experience gained so far. The remainder of this section discusses some related work and foundational technologies.

1.1 Related work

Three major classes of systems should be considered as related work: systems for video segmentation; systems for visualization and browsing; systems for generation of new documents from video sources.

Video segmentation is the ability to split a video stream in its components. The structure of a video is, in general, derived from the original process of video capture using a video camera or other device. A shot is a sequence of frames (each image in the video) between the time in which the recording device is turned on and turned off [5]. Shots can be grouped in sequences. Work on this area attempts to recognize the cuts between camera shots [10, 4]. Additional cuts can be introduced during the editing process of the video, so these should also be identified. In the present work, our usage of the word shot includes shots where cuts are a "user-defined" condition, and not only an artifact in the original stream. A "user-defined" condition can be the difference in image content in successive frames exceeding a given threshold.

Differences between images can be computed at pixel level, but the more robust technique of color histogram differences is commonly used. Differences of size in compressed M-JPEG (motion-JPEG compressed movies) sequences are used in the Motion Picture Parser [6].

The process of video segmentation can be highly improved if a model of the information exists beforehand. This is the case in the TV news parsing system described in [15] and in our WeatherDigest application described below. Both of these applications are built specifically for a given model. In our approach to video modeling (sec. 2.2) we tried to overcome this limitation by defining generic video models that can be reused.

Other area of interest is structure visualization and browsing. Several tools fall in this category: the hierarchical browser [9], the VideoSpaceIcon [14], Media Streams [5], and Rframes [1]. These tools allow fast browsing using advanced user interface concepts to represent the video information and structure.

The last set of systems considered uses video material and generates documents or applications in other forms. Examples of this work include the Salient Video Stills [13] and some recent work in hypermedia document generation [11] and access to long video segments [12].

2   Software architecture and tools

This section describes the software architecture in terms of classes and their functionality. These tools can be used either for interactive applications or for off-line processing of video information. The approach to video modeling is presented next. Video modeling is used to improve the parsing process.

2.1   Object model

The object model for video processing, depicted in fig. 1, contains data modeling classes and tools for image processing and visualization. The data modeling classes are instantiations of some of the fundamental concepts in video structure and segmentation units. These include the Image class as a model for a frame, the Shot class, a group of images with temporal and spatial continuity and the ShotSequence which groups several shots using semantic criteria such as news shots, sport shots, etc..

The Image class implements functionality for image manipulation at pixel level. The Shot classes inherits the temporal attributes such as duration and frame rate from the TimeSync class. Composite objects (ShotSequence), also derive from TimeSync in order to include the attributes related with temporal management.

An important difference from the present work is that relations between objects in MADE (as it happens in general with authoring systems) are purely synthetic and for presentation purposes only. In the toolkit for video processing, objects represent structural components in the original video stream. Therefore, the object network is an abstraction of the original video, with the advantage of being a computer model suitable for further processing.

The toolkit includes a set of classes for video signal processing named generically tools. These tools include filters for image enhancement, contour detection, histogram computation, etc.. An important class of these algorithms are the cut detection tools. They are based on the notion that frames belonging to a single camera shot have similar properties and thus, boundaries or cuts can be detected if the difference between two sequential images exceeds a given threshold. In our current framework, we have implemented the following: pixel intensity differences between frames, histogram differences between frames and frame sizes differences in MJPEG (motion-JPEG compressed movies) files.

Additional classes for visualization and browsing are called Views. There are several views that can be applied to a given shot. These include the movie view (a player with VCR like controls) , the X-ray view (for detection and visualization of camera movements), the Cube view (originally developed by Eddie Elliott, MIT Media Lab) for quick browsing of video sequences and cut visualization. A Shot class can be associated with one or more Views, depending on the application.

Data modeling classes can be associated with different IO handlers, both input and output of video information. Each IO handler manages a given file format.

The set of classes above can be used to implement both the data acquisition and processing functionality and the manipulation and display mechanisms required by interactive applications.

This toolkit was first implemented in g++ in Sun workstations running Sun OS 4.1.3 and later ported to Borland C++. Some of the IO handler mechanisms were also rewritten to allow for the smooth integration of new video file formats.

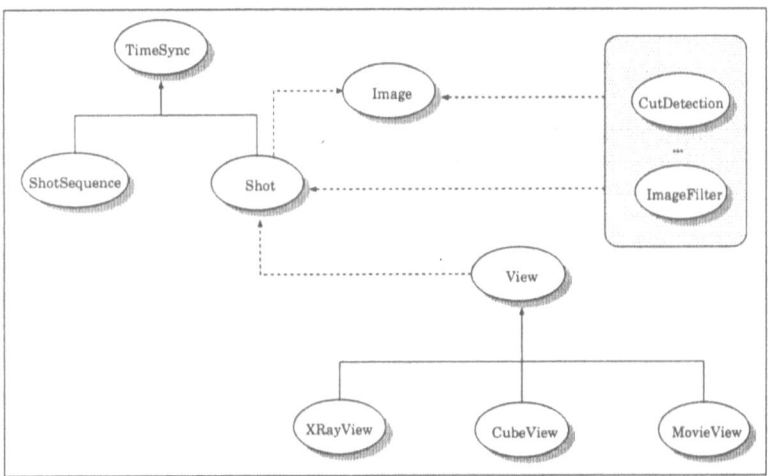

Figure 1: Object Model

2.2 Video modeling

Video parsing is a very complex task given the amount of information and the way that information is combined and presented. This task can be made considerably easier if the applications have a-priori knowledge about the information domain. In this approach the problem can be simplified to the process of matching the incoming video stream with the pre-defined model.

Accordingly to this idea, we defined a language for video modeling, to be used in video processing applications. This language has constructs for the definitions of video segments roughly with the same meaning as shots. The segments are defined based on its start and stop conditions. As an example, we can identify a segment that starts with a given frame and stops when the difference between the histograms of successive frames exceeds a given threshold (fig. 2.1). Additional conditions can also be used, such as to consider only the video segments where the camera movement was a zoom.

Several of these conditions can be combined in macros with a higher level meaning: commercial shot, news item shot, weather forecast shot.

```
layout "prog";
group
    label ("Group 1");
    while (ABSFRAME < 1000) do
        start (HISTDIFF(ABSFRAME, "start.jpg") < 10)
          label(ZOOMIN(ABSFRAME, ABSFRAME + 10, TRUE), "Close-up" );
        stop  (HISTDIFF(ABSFRAME, ABSFRAME+1) > 50) ;
    od ;
end ;
```

Table 2.1: An example of the video modeling language.

The result of applying the model in table 2.1 is a set of objects describing the video information, some of them with labels indicating that a zoom-in camera movement was detected.

We are now developing a graphical editor for this language. This editor will represent the video (and audio) stream in several timelines allowing for the definition of conditions in each of these timelines. Possible timelines are: the differences between histograms, the audio signal amplitude and the camera movements representation. The input for the editor are representative samples of a given information domain. The edited models will be stored in a database and used whenever an application processes a previously modeled information type.

3   Applications

In this section we outline the main characteristics of some applications built with the components and techniques described in the previous section.

3.1   Video browser

The significant units for the video browser are the shots, understood as a set of frames with temporal and spatial continuity. The browser can load a video stream and split this stream in its shot components using cut detection algorithms. Additionally, it can load a textual description of the shot sequence from a previously generated file.

Each shot is represented in the browser main window by an icon which is the first frame in the shot. The shots can be selected by point and click and then be played using several of the views described in section 2.1.

The browser has a built-in mechanism for HTML generation from the shot sequences. For each sequence, a page can be generated and each shot is represented by the first frame as in the browser main window.

Figure 2 depicts the user interface with the Cube view and a motion removal filter.

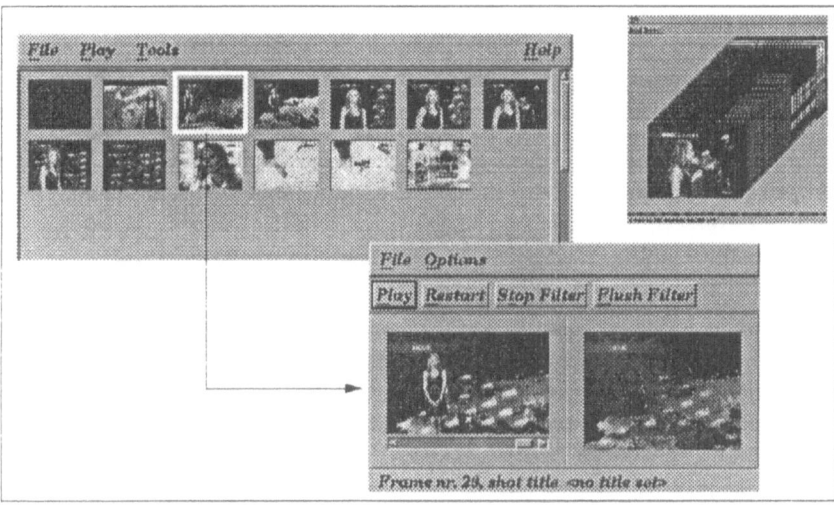

Figure 2: Video browser

3.2 WeatherDigest

WeatherDigest [3] is a simple application that illustrates the importance of information models. We identified the model for TV weather forecasts as a sequence of changing maps while the anchorperson is speaking. Each of this map transition can be identified with one of the cut detection algorithms that we developed. For each of these transitions a image is saved. All of the images are then combined in an HTML page mapping the sequential temporal structure of the TV weather forecast in the spatial structure of the page. In some shots, motion removal algorithms were applied to remove the anchorperson from the map, thus generating a synthetic image that was not in the original video stream.

3.3 News analysis

This set of applications for content analysis resulted from the cooperation between our computer science group and a group of social scientists with background in content analysis of TV programs. Previous experiences occurred in 1990 and 1995 with the goal of comparing political and social orientations of several television channels. In these experiences no computer support was used: the method was based on VCR tapes and manual classification.

This analysis was centered on filling forms including the news items subjects, durations of anchorperson shots and new shots, icons, etc.. Our system attempts to automate the analysis process so that all the repetitive tasks, such as duration measurement can be carried out much faster. The approach taken was to consider the meaningful semantic events in the video stream and capture them, while preserving their understandability and the temporal relations between them. To do this, models for TV newscasts were taken into account [15]: the structure of a generic program is a sequence of shots that include either the anchorperson commenting a particular item or live video related to that item. Additional characteristics such as that the initial seconds of the anchorperson's introduction provide enough data to characterize the news item were also used.

These observations resulted in a system where all significant transitions are detected, the frames corresponding to those transitions are grabbed together with some seconds of audio information. The result is a sequence of timestamped images and associated audio segments.

The images are then grouped by time and by news item in HTML pages for quick browsing and annotation (Internet Assistant was used allowing for annotation while browsing). Additionally the system generates CSV (Comma Separated Values) files that can be imported in commonly used spreadsheets such as Excel. These tables include all the timing information that can be derived automatically and place holders for the remaining information needed in the analysis process.

This application was implemented with some of the components in the object model including the Image class and some image processing tools (cut detection algorithms). As described, browsing and visualization is done with standard HTML browsers so our specific view objects were not used.

3.4   Video dissemination using WWW

Some of the described applications generate HTML files as output. This proved to be a very efficient way to provide content based browsing of the video information given the availability of HTML browsers in many different platforms and mainly for the possibility of remote access to this information. Although the news analysis applications were designed mainly for content analysis, its output can also be used for anyone interested in a quick browsing of the video programs. Samples of the output results of the application can be accessed at URL http://amadeus.inesc.pt.

We are also developing Java based tools for accessing this information. The first application developed is a simple Animator applet (reusing the Animator applet that comes with the distribution) with controls to play, stop, pause and resume the animation (fig. 3). This applet can be used to view the captured video frames corresponding to transitions and audio files in a synchronized way.

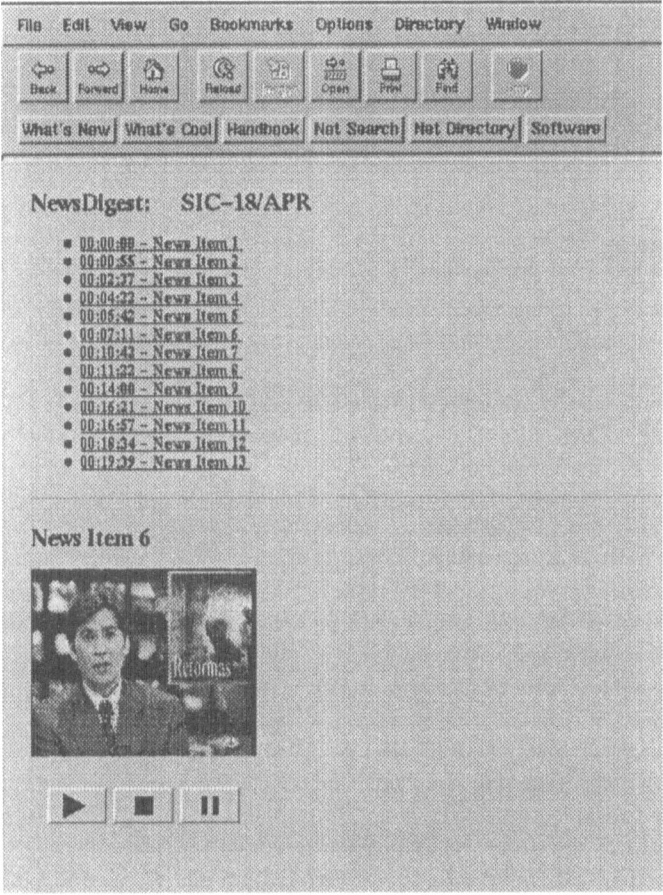

Figure 3: Java applet for news browsing

4 Conclusions

In this paper we presented several tools and techniques for video processing. The tools and models were evaluated and validated in several applications for video browsing, analysis and repurposing.

A major conclusion obtained from the results of the work done so far is the ability to understand and reuse video information in commonly used platforms using semantic knowledge of the domain. The developed applications show the importance of using these models. Our approach for model edition and storage is an attempt to generalize this concept.

The developed tools are very promising for repurposing existing video information given the characteristics of WWW access tools such as Java based systems. These systems can be used to provide both the content and the appropriate viewers modeled as objects for a given content model.

52

Acknowledgments

This work was partially financed by JNICT (National Board for Scientific and Technological Research). We would like to thank Inês Oliveira, João Martins (aka Jota), António Grilo and Artur Caetano for their contributions.

References

[1] F. Arman, R. Depommier, A. Hsu, and M. Chiu. Content based browsing of video sequences. In *Proceedings of ACM Multimedia'94 Conference, San Francisco, CA, USA*, pages 97–104, 1994.

[2] N. Correia and N. Guimaraes. Time and Synchronization Objects for Multimedia Application Construction. In *Proceedings of the Fourth Eurographics Workshop on Object-Oriented Graphics, Sintra, Portugal*, 1994.

[3] N. Correia, I. Oliveira, J. Martins, and N. Guimaraes. WeatherDigest: an experiment on media conversion. In *Integration Issues in Large Commercial Media Delivery Systems*, volume SPIE 2615, pages 50–61, 1995.

[4] A. Dailianas, R. Allen, and P. England. Comparison of automatic video segmentation algorithms. In *Integration Issues in Large Commercial Media Delivery Systems*, volume SPIE 2615, pages 2–16, 1995.

[5] M. Davis. Media streams: An iconic language for video annotation. In *Proceedings of the Symposium on Visual Languages, Bergen, Norway*, 1993.

[6] E. Deardoff, T. Little, J. Marshall, and D. Venkatesh. Video Scene Decomposition with the Motion Picture Parser. In *Proceedings of the IS&TSPIE Symposium on Electronic Imaging Science and Technology, San Jose, CA, USA*, volume SPIE 2187, pages 44–55, 1994.

[7] A. Lie and N. Correia. Cineloop Synchronization in the MADE Environment. In *Proceedings of SPIE/IS&T/IEEE Multimedia Computing and Networking'95, San Jose, CA, USA*, volume SPIE 2417, pages 225–232, 1995.

[8] MADE. MADE 1 (EP 6307): Technical Annex, March 1992.

[9] M. Mills, J. Cohen, and Y. Wong. A Magnifier Tool for Video Data. In *Proceedings of CHI'92, Monterey, CA, USA*, pages 93–98, 1992.

[10] K. Otsuji and Y. Tonomura. Projection Detecting Filter for Video Cut Detection. In *Proceedings of ACM Multimedia'93 Conference, Anaheim, CA, USA*, pages 251–257, 1993.

[11] B. Shahraray and D. Gibbon. Automated authoring of hypermedia documents. In *Proceedings of the ACM Multimedia'95, San francisco, CA, USA*, pages 401–410, 1995.

[12] Y. Taniguchi, A. Akutsu, Y. Tonomura, and H.Hamada. An intuitive and efficient access interface to real-time incoming video based on automatic indexing. In *Proceedings of the ACM Multimedia'95, San francisco, CA, USA*, pages 25–34, 1995.

[13] L. Teodosio and W. Bender. Salient Video Stills: Content and Context Preserved. In *Proceedings of ACM Multimedia'93 Conference, Anaheim, CA, USA*, pages 39–46, 1993.

[14] Y. Tonomura, A. Akutsu, K. Otsuji, and T. Sadakata. VideoMAP and VideoSpaceIcon: Tools for Anatomizing Video Content. In *Proceedings of INTERCHI'93, Amsterdam, The Nederlands*, pages 131–136, 1993.

[15] H. Zhang, G. Yihong, S. Smoliar, and T. Yong. Automatic Parsing of News Video. In *Proceedings of the IEEE ICMCS'94 Conference, Boston, MA, USA*, 1995.

Analysing the Quantization Parameters for Quality Assessment of Digital Video

Volker Gries
Email: vgries@informatik.uni-rostock.de
ANOVA Multimedia Studios Rostock GmbH
Joachim-Jungius-Str. 9
D-18059 Rostock, Germany

Abstract. In this paper we deal with the quality of digital video. After the standardization of the video format it is the responsibility of the user to choose any parameters for encoding. This choice is important for the produced video quality. After a general discussion of the term quality in relation to digital video we analyse processes and parameters for encoding with regard to its influences on the video quality. In fixed bitrate encoding the bitrate control of the encoder has the main influence on the produced video quality. We introduce a tool for analysing the output of an encoder by decoding the bitstream and visualizing the quantization parameter stepsize in relation to the complexity of a video frame. Our investigations are embedded in the development of a dynamic scalable MPEG encoder / decoder, that enables the dynamic variation of encoding parameters to achieve better video quality.

Keywords: Image Quality, Digital Video, Video Compression, MPEG

1 Introduction and motivation

In the context of transmission of digital video, mobile computing and multimedia on the net the quality of digital video gains rising importance. A design of multimedia applications with complete control of the quality of digital video sequences is necessary.

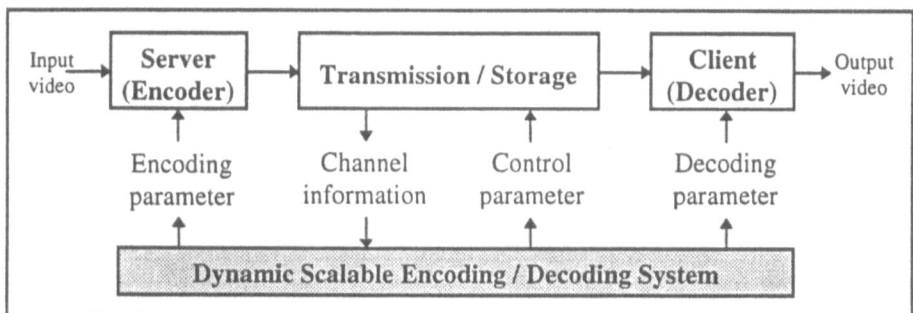

Fig. 1. DYSCO project overview

Figure 1 shows a block diagram of video transmission in a typical client server model used in our investigations in the project Dynamic Scalable MPEG Encoder / Decoder (DYSCO[1]). A server provides digital video information in MPEG1 format for transmission to any client. In the desired configuration this server carries out an online sampling and encoding in realtime. The transmission is carried through a network with

---

[1]The project DYSCO has been funded in the cource of a programme „Produkterneuerung in den neuen Bundesländern (PEP)".

changing bandwidth. The client decodes the video information, that is immediately presented then. The overall process operates with a loss in quality of the output in relation to the input video. The emerging losses should be as low as possible. We can describe each part of the process with its main parameters influencing the quality of the presentation. To realize a dynamic control of quality we at first have to clarify the question what influence the separate parameters have on the video quality. In addition there are dependencies between the parameters. Dynamic scaling of parameters for encoding and decoding means that we have to find the appropriate parameters for a dynamic quality control. In the project DYSCO our investigations are used in applications capable for varying parameters during an online video transmission to influence video quality or to react to the needs of the transmission.

Just mobile computing and mobile visualization can suffer from our work. Mobile computing is characterized by dynamically changing bandwidth of networks and limited resources that often force high compression of data. Compression algorithms that achieve the best compression ratios are lossy and decrease the quality of images. In the context of mobile computing there is a need of a control mechanism that accepts quality and resource parameters and calculates a set of parameters for a certain compression algorithm so that the resulting video quality and the use of resources matches the given values [3].

This paper is organized as follows. In section 2 we give a definition for the term video quality and we discuss the fundamental problem of quality assessment for digital video. We consider some typical coding artifacts using a classification to resolution degradation, edge busyness and image persistance. We ask for the reasons and give some examples.

In the third section we deal with the generation and processing of digital video regarding its quality. For practical studies we use digital video in MPEG1 format. We examine each part of the process for its losses and show some of the dependencies to other parts of the processing. Some practical experiences for the handling of MPEG coded video are presented then.

Section 4 describes the practical analysis of encoding step quantization. In fixed bitrate coding the parameters of quantization are used to control the amount of bits for encoding a picture. Therefore quantization plays a keyrole for data reduction and achieving a distinct quality of video. We give a short introduction to common models for bitrate control. The output of a bitrate control mechanism can be analysed with a tool we have developed. The analysing tool makes it possible to check general parameters and especially quantization parameters.

2 Quality of digital video

In this paper the term video quality refers to the quality of decoded video presented at the client's side. From this the following questions arise: How to assess or measure quality? When is a quality better than another? Which criteria should we use to evaluate quality? The difficulty to answer these questions is a result of difficulty in generalizing the subjective evaluations like: „it looks fine", „I like it", „it doesn't look fine but the essential is to recognize", „there is hardly nothing to recognize". In this field there are some investigations connected with the research in laws of human perception. In [2] the quality of a presentation intended for human perception is defined by the degree in which the communicative goal of the presentation is reached. The goal is to find an optimal ratio between the information provided for the human observer, and the amount of information which is perceived by the human observer. Therefore the human observer, the kind of coded information, the communicative goal, the application area and the presentation environment influence the quality of a presentation.

Digital video is different from analogous in some characteristics. During its processing the frames of a video sequence run through an indistinct mass of procedures that decrease the quality. We can assign the output video to an input video and if we assume that the quality of the output video can not be better than the quality of the input video, we can lead back the question of quality assessment to the question for the differences between input and output. These differences are perceptable as artifacts in the ouput video. In literature general video coding artifacts and its reasons are discussed at no length. Often it is difficult to separate a type of artifact from another and reasons for it can be very complex. Very often more than one reason is responsible for an artifact and some artifacts are typical for a concrete application. The development of new applications leads to new types of artifacts. The American National Standards Institute (ANSI), Accredited Standards Committee T1, Working Group T1Q1.5 is drafting interface performance specifications for digital video teleconferencing / video telephony (VTC/VT) and digital television. From the produced catalogue of video motion artifacts associated with video compression we give an extract of some coding artifacts that are very perceptable to the observer. A more detailed description can be found in [6], [8], [11].

2.1 Resolution degradation

The characteristic of artifacts in this class is a reduction in resolution where we can distinguish between temporal resolution degradation (less frames per second) and spatial resolution degradation (less information to describe an area of a frame).

Blocking, Checkerboards. There are rectangular or checkerboard patterns over the coded and afterwards decoded video frames not present in the original. These artifact is caused for instance in block-based encoders by coarse quantization.

Blurring, Smearing. The coded and afterwards decoded video frames have lost edges and details present in the original. There are several causes for that artifact. For instance, in predictive encoders the so-called Slope Overload appears, if the predicted value, the value to be coded, exceeds a limit given by the encoder's quantization characteristics. That leads to a blurring of sharp edges then. The effect depends on the used prediction algorithm too.

Jerkiness. The original smooth and continuous motion appears as a series of distinct snapshots in the coded and afterwards decoded video sequence. One reason for that artifact is the omitting of frames in order to reduce the amount of data and repeat other frames for compensation.

2.2 Edge busyness

The characteristics of artifacts in this class is that outlines of moving objects are displayed with randomly varying activity.

Mosquito Noise. There are some small „objects" around moving objects in the coded and afterwards decoded video frames not present in the original. The effect looks like mosquitos flying for instance around a person's head and shoulders, therefore the name. A reason for that artifact is block-based processing of video frames. A block of a frame contains the information of the moving object in the foreground as well as background information. The quantization noise caused by the moving information in the foreground leads to the described effect in the background.

Dirty Window. Observing the coded and afterwards decoded video gives the impression of looking through a dirty window because of disturbing specks and some parts of the video are not updated as expected. The artifact appears if the video codec reaches data compression by updating and transmitting only the changing parts of video frame. If the threshold for the decision to transmit a part of frame or not was chosen too coarse, the dirty window effect appears.

2.3 Image persistance

In the coded and afterwards decoded video frames moving or changing objects appear that were faded some frames earlier in the original. The reason for that artifact is the inertia of the encoder to react to the changes of video information.

3 Losses in coding and decoding

3.1 Analysing of processes to its losses

Corresponding to the given objectives we do analyse the processing steps encoding and decoding regarding to its importance for video quality, using the MPEG1 standard as a basic application. We have classified the processes to its losses and the results of our investigations are presented in table 1. Processes are classified as lossless, if the input data to the process and the output data from the process can be transformed in one another 1:1. Of course, in the reality we always have a limited precision that leads to losses but these losses are not caused by the process itself, so we neglect them. In the case of lossy processes we only can discuss the amount of quality degradation and its reduction. In decoding and realtime encoding we have to follow a strict timing. Some processes are realized with losses therefore, although they are really lossless. In practice sufficiently fast algorithms are often used accepting the losses. In the following we discuss the assignment of processes to these classes, presupposing that the basics of video coding in MPEG are well-known. For a more detailed discussion about MPEG encoding we refer to [1], [7].

Preprocessing. Prior to the encoding the video frames are treated with a preprocessing, which is very important for the video quality. During preprocessing the sampling together with a format conversion is done. this process is lossy however with a proper choice of parameters sampling frequency and precision it can be achieved, so that losses are not perceptible in the video output. For MPEG encoding video frames are often converted to the Source Input Format (SIF). That conversion is not necessary but makes possible a quality comparable with the Video Home System (VHS) using a bitrate of up to 1,5 Mbit/s. The format conversion leads to a high data reduction. The resulting losses are to compensate using appropriate conversion filters, that its perceptable effects are low. MPEG1 does not support video in interlaced mode. The demanded conversion leads to a decrease of quality. MPEG encoding is based on blocks, where luminance and chrominance are processed separately using the YC_bC_r colour system. Human perception is more sensitive to differences in luminance than in chrominance. Therefore a subsampling of chrominance values is used, which is a lossy process. Because of the block-based processing of video frames the blocking artifact is possible. It is possible to avoid or reduce the blocking by using proper filters during the subsampling and the appropriate parameters during the following encoding.

Encoding.   The encoding starts with a Discrete Cosine Transformation (DCT). Each block of a video frame is transformed from the spatial domain to the frequency domain that works without any losses and is not to be influenced by any parameters. The idea of DCT is to separate frequency areas and to process them in a different manner. Low frequencies correspond to the global structures in the frame whereas high frequencies describe sharpe edges and fine details. The following step of encoding, the quantization, is processed dependent on the frequency. Quantization is lossy and can be influenced by the stepsize and weighting of the frequencies. Weighting is processed with a matrix, where a recommendation is proposed in the standard. The degree of quantization is controlled using the parameter stepsize. A high value for the stepsize leads to a coarse quantization, a better data reduction but in addition to a decrease in video quality. Quantization is a key feature in achieving a good data reduction efficiency with attention to the video quality. The following entropy coding has no influence on the video quality.

The frames of a video sequence can be encoded using different procedures, that differ in the presence or absence of motion compensation (MC). The MC is a predictive coding method and in MPEG encoding it is processed on tha basis of macroblocks. The principle is to find out if a macroblock of the frame can be described as a shift of a macroblock in a reference frame that has already been coded. If it is possible the macroblock is described with its difference to the reference macroblock, that is indicated with a coded shifting vector. MC is possible with preceding and/or following reference frames and leads to a more compact representation of a video sequence. The drawback of MC is a restricted possibility of random access to single frames because predictive coded frames can not be decoded separately. To compensate this drawback the video sequences are devided into Group of Pictures (GoP). In the beginning of each group a frame is coded without MC. These frames are intra coded (I-frame) and serve as access points in the video stream. Intra coded pictures are reference frames for the predictive coded pictures (P-frame) or bidirectional predictive coded pictures (B-frame). Coding efficiency is the greatest in the case of B-frames but the quality of B-frames is low in relation to I-frames or P-frames. It is the responsibility of the user to choose the size of groups. The coding of frames in one of the different motion compensation modes is only resticted by a few limits in the standard. The MC can be influenced through the parameters size of search area in the reference frame, the accuracy of motion vectors, the matching criterion   and   through the   search algorithm. The matching criterion fixes the

Table 1. Overview of characteristics of MPEG encoding and decoding relating to losses

Process	Step	Lossless	Lossy	Often lossy caused by implementation
Preprocessing	Sampling and format conversion		×	
	Subsampling of chrominance, generation of macroblocks		×	
Encoding	DCT	×		
	Quantization		×	
	Entropy coding	×		
	Motion compensation (MC)	×		×
Transmission / Storage		×		
Decoding	Inverse entropy coding	×		
	Inverse quantization	×		
	Inverse DCT	×		×
	Inverse MC, buffering of reference frames	×		
Postprocessing / Presentation	Format conversion	×		×
	Expansion of chrominance to the resolution of luminance and colour conversion	×		
	Presentation	×		

conditions if a block in the reference frame match with the block to be coded. The ideal case is an exact match but in practical implementations a threshold for permitted deviations is used. This handling leads to losses which are rizing with the magnitude of deviations. In addition the MC depends in the time available for searching the reference macroblocks. If for a distinct macroblock there is no reference block found during the available time, this macroblock is intra coded without any MC. If this happens very often for a frame, the bitrate is temporally rising. In fixed bitrate coding this rising of bitrate has to be compensated through a more coarse quantization. This leads to a lower quality because of quantization noise. Because of the deviations while matching the blocks and the relation to the quantization in fixed bitrate encoding, the motion compensation is classified in table 1 as lossless from the algorithm's viewpoint, but the implementation often operates with losses.

Storage, Transmission. In our discussion we suppose that storage and transmission of the bitstream happens in a lossless environment, although it is an idealistic point of view refering to the practice.

Decoding, Postprocessing and Presentation. All steps of decoding, postprocessing and presentation can be processed without losses and therefore we have classified them as lossless in table 1. However the demand for realtime decoding and presentation of the video sequence leads to simplified algorithms and additional losses in video quality. The same evidence is valid for postprocessing. If a format conversion of video frames is necessary the used filters and methods are decisive for the video quality. In order to present the video on a computer screen a colour conversion from YC_bC_r to the RGB system with the well-known formulas is necessary.

3.2 Parameters and parameter dependencies

After analysing the processes we pay attention to the parameters of processes and the parameter dependencies now. In table 2 we examine main parameters for encoding a video sequence. The alteration of a parameter can influence another parameter which we name parameter dependency. There are some essential demand to the coded bitstream from the applications side. Beside the video quality the random access to any frames, error robustness, the costs for coding and decoding (delay, resources), processability with editors and the possibility for playing in trick modes belongs to these application dependencies. Whether the coded bitstream satisfies these demands depends on the parameters used. Each parameter has an effect on the characteristics of the generated video bitstream.

Table 2. Parameters and parameter dependencies

Parameter	Application dependencies	Parameter dependencies
Bitrate	Video quality	Quantization parameters
Quantization parameters (step-size, weights for frequencies)	Video quality	Bitrate
Parameters of MC (search area, precision of vectors, time, matching criterion)	Video quality Costs for coding	Bitrate Quantization parameters
Horizontal and vertical frame resolution	Video quality Costs for coding and decoding	Bitrate Input buffer size
Framerate	Video quality Costs for coding and decoding	Bitrate Size of group of pictures, type of coding
Input buffer size	Costs for decoding	
Size of group of pictures, type of coding, ratio between intra and predictive coded frames	Random access Error robustness Trick modes Editability Video quality Costs for coding	Parameters of MC Quantization parameters Bitrate
Periodical repetition of header information	Error robustness Editability Random access Costs for decoding	Bitrate
Size of slices	Error robustness	Bitrate

Table 2 shows that the bitrate is an essential parameter for coding and transmission. The maximum value for the bitrate is often constrained by external demands, for instance the bandwidth of a network for transmission or a norm for a compact disc

(CD-i, Video-CD). The higher the available number of bits per time for encoding a sequence is, the better is the video quality. We assume fixed bitrate encoding for our applications to satify the decodeability of the bitstream with a great variety of decoder architectures.

The frames of a video sequence have a variable complexity and therefore need a different number of bits to encode with a constant quality. In fixed bitrate coding a mechanism is necessary that controls the bitrate, in most cases with the help of quantization. It is the aim of the bitrate control to distribute the quantization over the frames so that artifacts caused by quantization would not be perceptible.

Because of permitted deviations with the matching criterion and the influence on the quantization in the case of success or failure with the block search the motion compensation has an influence on the video quality. The size of search area and the used search algorithm have an essential effect on the success of the motion compensation, but on the delay for block search, too.

The greater the horizontal or vertical resolution of frames is, the higher is the amount of bits needed for encoding or the video quality would decrease. Frames with a higher resolution lead to a higher delay of encoding or decoding. In addition more memory resources are needed for buffering of reference frames with a higher resolution. The same connection between the costs for encoding and decoding and the same relation to the bitrate is valid in the case of the parameter framerate. The number of frames per time has an influence on the size of groups of pictures if we assume, that because of random access, an intra coded frame is necessary each half of a second.

The demanded size for the input buffer is critical if a decoder is able to decode a sequence or not. If this parameter is chosen to small it is perhaps not possible to use bidirectional prediction for encoding the frames. This is the relation of input buffer size to the motion compensation.

The number of frames per group and the ratio between intra and predictive coded frames are important for the random access characteristics of the encoded bitstream. Using motion compensation decreases the possibilities for editing the video sequence and leads to a delay for encoding. If an error occurs, in the worst case the decoding can restart with the next intra coded frame. The choice of coding type is important for the bitrate and video quality. MPEG encoding supports different weights for the frequencies for different frame types. Therefore we have marked the quantization as dependent from the coding type in table 2.

Within a bitstream it is possible to periodically repeat the header information for instance for the sequence layer. This enables an earlier restart of decoding after an error occured. Additional repetition of information needs additional bits for coding. Therefore these bits can not be used for encoding the frames themselves then.

The MPEG standardization group has offered a set of recommendations for the choice of some parameters. The adherance of this constrained parameter set is not necessary but guarantees that encoded bitstream is decodeable with most architectures that are available.

3.3 Experiences with the handling of MPEG video with a high quality demand

Beside the already discussed influences of parameters on the quality of the video, in our practical tests it has become obvious, that some additional influences have to be observed. We want to present our experiences now. The quality of input video material, additional filtering methods during the preprocessing, the characteristics of the video scenes and the used encoding architecture are important facts for the final quality of output video.

Video material. The quality of video material is the foundation of the quality of final video output. The following principle is valid: the higher the quality of input video material is, the higher is the quality of MPEG video. The quality of analogous video sources depends on the used method for recording the video tape.

Filtering. In order to achieve a high video quality without perceptable artifacts caused by format conversion it is necessary to do the preprocessing of video frames very carefully. This implies the question whether there is a generalized method for preprocessing. Are there any special filtering methods that guarantee a high quality for any video sequences? In the reality there are smoothing filters and colour correction filters used to support the following encoding. If the analogous video material was copied several times a noise is perceptible on the tape. This noise would be interpreted as fine structures and details by the encoder and would lead to a lower coding efficiency. Therefore often noise reduction methods, well-known from the analogous video technology, are used. It is not possible to recommend one method of preprocessing of all possible video scenes because of the great variety of quality levels for the input video and the character of sequences.

Video scenes. Observing different MPEG encoded video scenes in quick succession it is obvious that video quality depends on the characteristics of the video scene and is not constant for instance over the length of a video film. Whereas some video sequences were processed by the encoder very well, there are some other video scenes for which the encoder produced a lower quality. It is system-dependent that there are some limits which make the MPEG encoding of video scenes with distinct characteristics very difficult. These characteristics are for instance filigree structures, lots of details, texts and regular fine pattern, fast zooming and fast panning over a fine structured area, and therefore video sequences with such a characteristic are named „MPEG killer“. No film producer can be limited in his creativeness with the reason in mind of a used technology but the knowledge in this connection and the conscious application of such design funds would help to achieve a better quality of MPEG video.

Architecture. Another practical problem is the choice of coding architecture. The first class of architectures are realtime encoders, which do the encoding together with the sampling in realtime. Such devices operate very economical because of saving time. However the quality of video produced by offline encoders is much better. Offline encoding requires the sampled frames on a storage medium. High storage capacities are often needed. Another solution is a hybrid architecture. It consists of a realtime encoder which encodes the video in a first pass. In dialog with the user some critical parts of the video scene can be marked then and offline encoded in the second pass. Both produced bitstreams can be put together then replacing the old critical parts.

Additional information and experiences in the practical handling of MPEG video are given in [4].

4 Bitrate control and the analysing of quantization parameters

Bitrate control is a central problem in designing video sequence compression systems. To investigate the behaviour of a bitrate control system in relation to the produced quality of video sequences we have developed an analysing tool. It works on the basis of decoding the video bitstream and visualizing important parameters, especially quantization parameters. Before we give an overview, which investigations are possible with that analysing tool, we introduce the bitrate control problem first.

4.1 Bitrate control problem

The bitrate control is a mechanism in the encoder which regulates the balance between fixed bitrate and quality of video frames. In the case of MPEG encoding it is done through the control of the quantization parameter stepsize. The bitrate control has got two objectives: (1) the quality of pictures should be as uniform as possible and (2) the use of available amount of bits as close as possible. These objectives lead to contradictory settings for the encoding parameters what is called the bitrate control problem.

The quantization should be configured in dependence to the content of the video frames. The content of a video frame is described over its complexity. A video frame with a high complexity usually needs more bits for encoding than another frame with a low complexity. Figure 2 shows the block diagram for two basic solutions to the bitrate control.

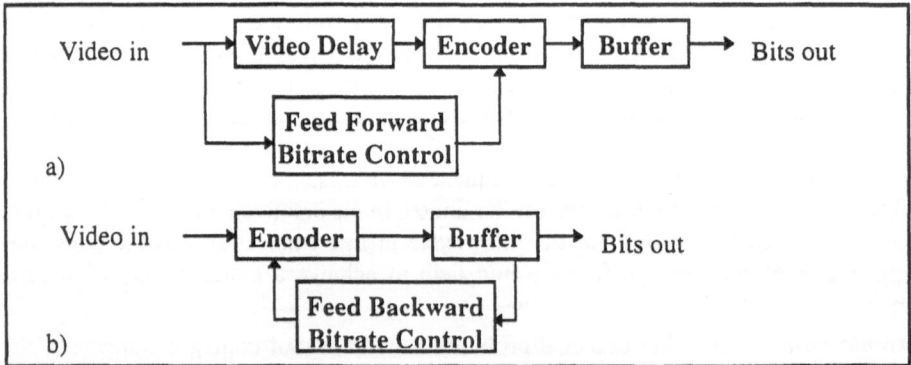

Fig. 2. Bitrate control solutions; (a) Feed Forward Bitrate Control, (b) Feed Backward Bitrate Control

In the case of Feed Forward Bitrate Control the relations between encoding parameters, the produced video quality and the bitrate are well-known prior to the encoding so that the evaluation of settings to the encoder is possible. For instance, it is possible to predict the quality produced, when choosing a distinct bitrate for a video frame with a distinct complexity. Hence, a major problem with Feed Forward Bitrate

Control is, that for most systems the needed relations between bitrate, encoder settings and quality has to be computed, which implies a serious computational burden.

In the case of Feed Backward Bitrate Control the relations between encoder settings, quality and bitrate are unknown. Consequently the bitrate can temporally overflow the fixed limits while encoding a frame with a distinct complexity and distinct encoder settings. This overflow has to lead to a change of encoder settings. Therefore the amount of produced bits is checked periodically through the bitrate control using a buffer. Since the buffer is accessed frame by frame from the decoder this temporal overflow or underflow of bitrate is permitted. Strictly speaking, the bitrate is constant means, that the bitrate is constant frame by frame or each GoP in the bitstream uses the same amount of bits. With Feed Backward Bitrate Control the computational complexity remains acceptable, so it is used in nearly all of today's MPEG encoder implementations, despite the fact that bitrate is controlled with lower precision.

In [5], [9] and [10] some practical implementations for bitrate control algorithms are explained in detail.

4.2 Analysing of quantization parameters

We have developed a tool enabling the analysis of an encoded video bitstream and the visuatization of relations between quantization parameters and complexity of video frames. This analysis is necessary and helpful when studying the output of a bitrate control system. At first we give some information about the functions of the analysing tool. After that we will explain what investigations are possible with the help of the tool.

Figure 3 shows a typical analysing session with that tool. The user can step through the stream frame by frame with a parsing control dialog. The decoded image and the information about sequence, group of pictures and the picture layer are presented. With a colour coding the quantization parameter stepsize and the complexity of the decoded frame can be visualized. The complexity of each macroblock is computed similar to [10]. We use the Mean Absolute Difference (MAD) between the luminance values of each luminance block and an average for intra coded macroblocks and the Mean Absolute Difference between the macroblock and its reference block if the macroblock was predictive coded.

For intra coded macroblocks the average value dc_k (k=0...3) for each luminance value y_k of each 8×8 luminance block k of a macroblock is calculated at first using:

$$dc_k = \frac{1}{64}\sum_0^{64} y_k(i, j), \quad i = 0...7; j = 0...7.$$

Also possible is to set

$$dc_k = y_k(0,0),$$

because the coefficient $y_k(0,0)$ is an approximated average of all values in the block k. Then we calculate the mean absolute difference of luminance values y_k from the average value dc_k with

$$\Delta_k = \frac{1}{64}\sum_{i=0}^{7}\sum_{j=0}^{7}|y_k(i, j) - dc_k|.$$

The complexity Δ of a macroblock is given by summation of single values Δ_k of each luminance block

$$\Delta = \frac{1}{4}\sum_{k=0}^{3}\Delta_k .$$

This Δ is directly used for the colour coding of complexity in the analysing tool.

For predictive coded macroblocks we calculate an average of vector lengths of forward and backward motion vector first. If both vectors exist we use an average value of both for colour coding, otherwise the according available vector is used directly.

Additionally, it is possible to view the used quantization weights for a video sequence with the analysing tool.

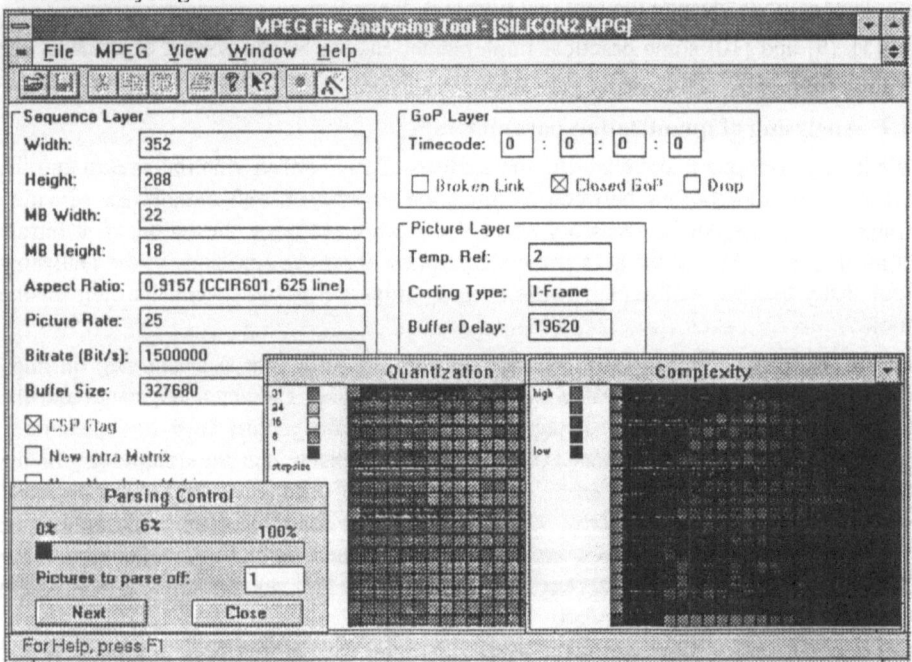

Fig. 3. Typical session with the analysing tool

The analysing tool is used to investigate the following problems:

- Checking of general parameters of an unknown video bitstream, if problems with its use occur
- Studying the behaviour of a bitrate control of a MPEG encoder with the help of the visualization of quantization parameters
  - Is the quantization parameter set in dependence to the complexity of video frames?
  - Are there sudden changes in the quantization unless the complexity of the frame would motivate this?

In figure 4 two typical visualizations of the parameter quantization stepsize and the corresponding complexity of the video frame are shown. It is obviously perceptable in figure 4a that quantization is set in dependence to the complexity. Macroblocks with a higher complexity are quantized more coarsely than macroblocks with a lower ones. Consequently the necessary quantization is distributed well over the frame and quantization noise is quite invisible.

Figure 4b shows a distribution of the quantization stepsize over the frame with a sudden rise of values, although the complexity of the frame is quite uniform. In this case a buffer overflow was detected by the bitrate control algorithm. The control mechanism tried to compensate the rising amount of data with a more coarse quantization. This leads to a local decrease of picture quality perceptable in the decoded frame.

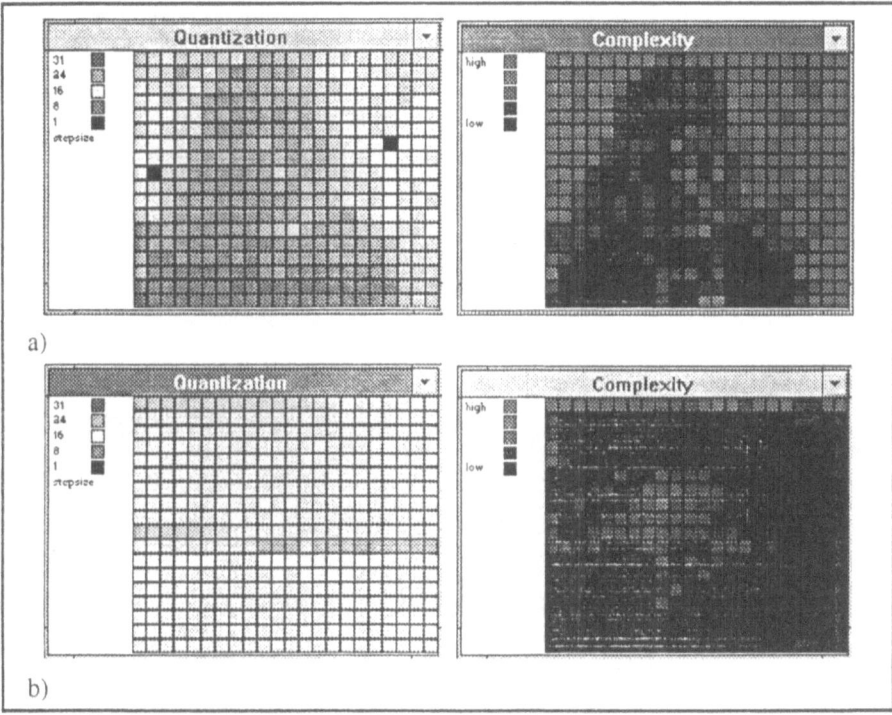

Fig. 4. Two corresponding visualizations of quantization stepsize and complexity; (a) Quantization stepsize follows the demands of the complexity, (b) Sudden rise in quantization although the complexity is uniform

5 Conclusions

In this paper we have investigated the processes and parameters while encoding and decoding of video sources regarding to its influence on the quality of presented video frames, using the MPEG standard as a reference video format. It was shown, that predominant the preprocessing and quantization in the encoding process are lossy. Additional decrease of quality is caused by the implementation of time-critical processes during the motion compensation, during decoding and during postprocessing. The parameters bitrate and quantization, the parameters of motion compensation, the horizontal and vertical resolution of video frames, the framerate and the ratio between intra and predictive coded frames have an influence on the video quality. The parameters bitrate and quantization are influenced by changing most of the other parameters. It is shown that bitrate and quantization are connected to another when coding with fixed bitrate. We introduced an analysing tool for video bitstreams that visualizes the parameter quantization stepsize in relation to the content of video frames. With the help of that tool we can study the behaviour of a bitrate control of an MPEG encoder. When bitstreams are generated using the fixed bitrate mode, this analysing is important for the quality of video frames. In our practical investigations we analysed different video bitstreams generated by different encoders. We found out some differences but additional investigations are necessary. Investigations up to now helped us to assess different encoders to its capabilities. Additional investigations are to execute in order to find the appropriate parameters usable as a dynamic quality control.

How this additional investigations could look like? With the help of an encoder architecture we could generate a series of MPEG bitstreams from a video source, each bitstream with a varying parameter candidate. A measure of Mean Square Error (MSE) or any other objective measurements could give a first evidence whether the parameter changing influences the video quality. A subjective quality test could establish then, whether these changes are perceptable through a decrease of quality, and whether subjective quality tests correlate with the objective measurement.

References

1. Le Gall: „A Video Compression Standard for Multimedia Applications", Communications of the ACM, Vol. 34, April 1991

2. Gerfelder, Müller: „Quality Aspects of Computer Based Video Services", Proceedings 1994 European SMPTE Conference Convergence of Imaging Media, SMPTE, Cologne, September 1994, pp. 44-67

3. Gries, Schultz, Schumann: „Quality and Resource Controlled Transmission of Images and Video in a Mobile Environment", Workshop IMC '96, Information Visualization and Mobile Computing, Poster Presentation, Rostock, February 1996

4. Gries, Meißner: „Qualität von MPEG-Videos", Radio Fernsehen Elektronik, Berlin, (to appear 1996)

5. Keesmann, Shah, Klein-Gunnewiek: „Bitrate Control for MPEG Encoders", Signal Processing: Image Communication, Vol. 6, 1995, pp. 545-560

6. Murakami, Hashimoto, Hatori: „Quality of Band-Compressed TV Services", IEEE Communications Magazine, October 1988, pp. 61-69

7. Musmann, Werner, Fuchs : „Kompressionsalgorithmen für interaktive Multimedia-Systeme“, Informationstechnik und Technische Informatik 35, Febrary 1993

8. Netravali, Haskell: „Digital Pictures“, Representation, Compression and Standards, Plenum Press, 2nd Edition 1995

9. Puri, Aravid: „Motion-Compensated Video Coding with Adaptive Perceptual Quantization“, IEEE Transactions on Circuits and Systems for Video Technology, Vol.1 No. 4, December 1991

10. Viscito, Gonzales: „A Video Compression Algorithm with Adaptive Bit Allocation and Quantization“, Visual Communications and Image Processing '91, Proceedings of SPIE, Vol. 1605/205, November 1991

11. Wolf: „Features for Automated Quality Assessment of Digitally Transmitted Video“, U.S. Department of Commerce, National Telecommunications and Information Administration, Report 90-264, June 1990

Three–Dimensional Information System on the World Wide Web

Roman Berka, Martin Brachtl, Aleš Holeček, Martin Novotný Jan Přikryl,
Pavel Slavík, Jiří Žára

Czech Institute of Technology,
Department of Computer Science and Engineering,
Computer Graphics Laboratory

Abstract. With the advent of new technologies it is possible to create information systems that provide the required information in a user-friendly and natural way. New software tools allow us to generate realistic three-dimensional scenes which the user can walk through while searching for desired data. The nature of the information can be of two kinds. Static data, including for example the names of the professors, the location of labs etc. Dynamic data is the second kind and it can be illustrated by the presence of persons in seminar rooms or labs, processes that take place in the labs like measurements, long lasting experiments and so on. In this paper we present a solution that allows us to integrate both kinds of information into one information system. For the description of the synthetic scenes the Virtual Reality Modeling Language is used. Capturing of the dynamic process in the real environment is mediated by video camera. To get maximum information from the surrounding world, we provide an interface to control the viewing direction of the camera from an arbitrary distant location. This allows for retrieving specific information from an arbitrary place in the real environment. The actual and synthetic three-dimensional information is integrated into one system. In the network environment it is possible to distribute both kinds of information and to create a basis for discussions.

Keywords: Multimedia, WWW, VRML, three-dimensional, geometric modeling, Java, Perl, hyperlinks.

1 Introduction

Many information systems exist in the university environment that provide the students and the visitors with comprehensive information about the departmental profile, facts about the staff and with other useful information. The first systems of this kind appeared already several years ago, and were text based. Usually they were designed in the form of pure database with a traditional user interface.

The advent of multimedia and other new technologies significantly influenced the structure and the principles of the new information systems. Incorporating multimedia into the information systems changed not only the user interface, but also impacted the contents of the databases themselves. There exist several authoring tools for multimedia applications that allow creating presentations where besides text other media like pictures, sound and video can also be included. A database that offers a user-friendly interface and presents the data in an interesting way appears to be much more attractive to common users than the traditional one.

Generally multimedia can be divided into two classes:

- local to one machine (CD ROM oriented)
- distributed (network oriented)

In this paper we will deal with the second case only. For the distribution of multimedia applications, the framework of the *World Wide Web* (WWW) is going to be considered. The information in the environment of WWW is usually annotated in the form of *HyperText Markup Language* (HTML) programs. These programs are usually capable of satisfying all the requirements of complex multimedia application [2]. The main feature of such a system built on a multimedia platform is the graphical user interface that allows very easy specification of the user's requirements.

University information systems created in the WWW environment became a sort of standard at all major universities around the world. The speed at which this new information technology was adopted is really striking; the first systems of this kind appeared in 1994 [1] and nowadays they can be found very frequently. Although these systems have many advantages to offer, there is still plenty of space for improvement. This concerns for example the fact that there is usually information missing about the spatial layout of the university, faculty and/or department. Such information can be crucial for visitors and also for students who take their first courses in the department. A typical task is to find a certain laboratory or an office of a particular professor. Another task could be discussion about safety in a certain parts of the department (e.g. for the evacuation measures that should be taken in the case of fire).

To provide support for solving these problems within the frame of the information system, it is necessary to find a representation of the departmental layout that will contain as much information as possible. In the most simple case the layout is represented in the form of a ground plan of the department. As this information is of 2D nature, quite a lot of important data that could be crucial for the decision making is missing. The correct solution is to extend the system to a 3D model of the department. To support the interaction among users (or to allow a distant access), it is advisable to create this model in the environment of the WWW.

2   Tools for description of 3D models

There exist many systems (geometric modelers) for authoring 3D models of geometric objects and creating of 3D scenes. Some of them already support a creation of 3D scenes with hypermedia features typical for the WWW environment. For the annotation of such scenes the *Virtual Reality Modeling Language* (VRML) is usually used. VRML has become the de facto standard for description of 3D scenes on WWW. The VRML language was designed to describe models in a wide range of complexity. It could be used to annotate a simple scenes consisting of several primitives as well as hierarchical description of complex and textured architectural models.

To specify a scene (world) in VRML a subset of the Open Inventor^{TM} file format is used. To this subset some new features were appended to allow creation of links to subscenes and to provide the hypermediality of the model [3]. Important feature accelerating the rendering of large worlds is implementation of various *Level of details* (LOD). This concept allows for defining several geometrical representations for one 3D object. A browser (renderer) can switch among multiple representations according to the distance from the observer, required image quality and/or performance capability of the client computer.

Typically, all objects placed far from a viewer are displayed using only a few flat shaded polygons, whereas objects in the center of the user's interest are displayed in full detail and are textured. This approach is particularly useful for visualization of the worlds on various computing platforms starting from simple PC's up to high performance SGI machines.

Since the VRML language was designed with respect to full utilization of graphics accelerators, only polygonal objects are supported. A small set of primitives (cone, cube, cylinder, sphere) and polygonal meshes are the basic geometric objects. Color, light, texture and transformation properties can be defined for each geometric element.

3 Overview of the designed system

As a part of the research conducted in the area of multimedia by the department of Computer Science and Engineering at the Czech Technical University we have decided to exploit all the multimedia features of the WWW environment and design a user friendly information system. The main goal of this project is to offer extensive information for visitors and students, but also to mediate the life at our department to the wide Internet community.

The VRML language has been found suitable for the representation of the Department building and offices. The correspondence between certain objects like doors or information boards in the 3D world and the information about people, places or activities has been easily ensured by exploiting the hypermedia features provided by VRML and HTML. Proper configuration of browsers (Netscape for HTML documents and WebSpace for VRML files) makes the system fully interactive and user friendly. The realized system can be logically divided into two parts:

- the building where the department is located and its surroundings
- the description of the internal layout of the department and related information

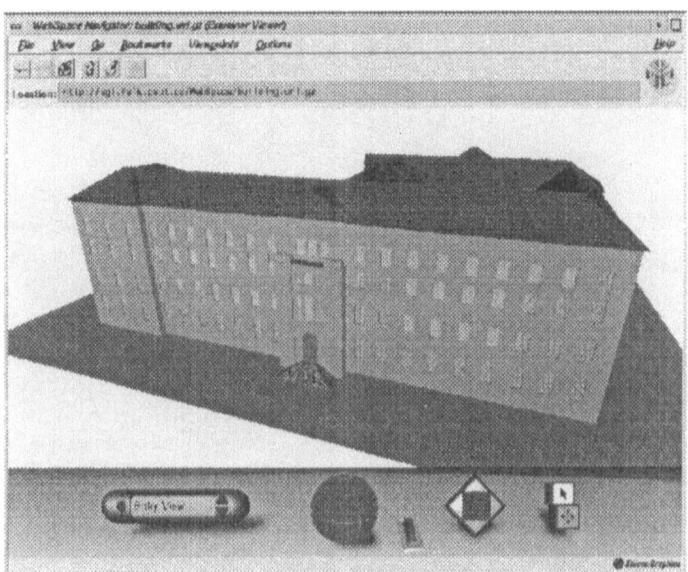

Fig. 1. Model of the university building

Both parts have been modeled using VRML and HTML languages. In the first part, we have intended to emphasize the historical background of the university location and the building itself. This led to the idea to allow the user to interactively walk through both the historical and the nowadays environment. It is possible to see the changes that appeared in the last 80 years and to make a proper comparison with the current state (Fig. 1).

The department itself is located in two stories of one of the university buildings. Both stories have been completely modeled including the staircase between them (Fig. 2). This way the user can also walk through the department. It is possible to click on any door in the department and to get information whose office it is. Using the features of the VRML it is possible to link this information with the home page of the person that resides in the office. The user can obtain both the idea where the office is located in the building as well as detailed information about the person residing in the office.

Another feature of the presented system is that it offers information about the size of each room and in such a way it is possible to plan allocation of equipment in the labs, etc. As the information system is on the WWW anybody equipped with a proper set of browsers can walk through the department and get on-line information.

In order to fully cover the department, precise models of laboratories and offices will be created. The first step was the creation of a 3D model of the Computer Graphics Laboratory (Fig. 3). Although this model depicts almost every little detail in the laboratory layout, it does not provide any information about the actual life and people working there. This kind of data can be perceived

Fig. 2. Model of the department interior

as a function frequently changing with a place and time. The next step was to link this fine granularity data to the information system.

First we have provided a web page with snapshots of the laboratory, which were taken every 5 minutes. For obtaining the pictures we have used cameras connected to three of the Silicon Graphics workstations placed in the lab. Since the cameras were fixed on the top of the computers, observation has been mode of the people in the laboratory, in the way the cameras will point. Also the time interval between the picture taking limited the observer in finding out the desired information. To improve the quality of this service a special gadget has been developed that allows for controlling one of the cameras from an arbitrary distant location with an access to the WWW.

4 Interactively controlled camera with the WWW interface

WWW is not a moderated information source, and a significant majority of the accessible data is provided as is. There is no warranty on the contents or the currency of the information and it is up to the user to decide, if it is out of date or valid. Different proposals have been made for the publishing etiquette on the WWW (e.g. Webiquette). But again it is up to the maintainer of the actual web home page to choose the contents and form of the page.

According to our beliefs, every information system should hold only the most recent and valid data. Of course we have realized that some information can have a long lasting character (e.g. names and faces of the professors at the university information desk). Our research with the camera is oriented toward capturing data frequently changing in time. We attempt to fully exploit the multimedia character of the World Wide Web environment, to distribute the most recent

Fig. 3. Model of the Computer Graphics Laboratory

data in understandable form. The tools being built into the framework of this project should allow the user of the WWW to interactively check for validity or even request the most recent data.

We have identified the main issues of the project as follows:

- using **other input** for obtaining the information, not a human
- **preventing collisions** of the users requests, while accessing the input device

4.1 Experiment

To observe and simulate behavior of such a system which is exposed to the above described conditions, we have decided to conduct an experiment within our computer laboratory. The main idea is to extend the information provided about the laboratory by a *user controlled snapshot* of the room. The visual information from the room can be perceived as the data frequently changing in time. As mentioned above, to capture the information, we use a small video camera installed in the laboratory. Unfortunately the viewing angle of the camera can not cover the entire area of the room. That is why a gadget was created which would allow the user to obtain a picture from any desired small area of the lab. The device rotates the camera in a nearly 360 degree range and can be controlled from any remote location on earth which has WWW access.

4.2 Hardware

The main component of the device is micro-controller 89C2051 which provides us with the RS 232 serial interface and controls a servo which rotates a platform holding the camera. The micro-controller has been programmed to read a set of commands from the serial line and produce the required number of impulses for the servo. The set of commands is very simple. Table 1. contains a brief overview of the syntax and the semantics of the commands. The communication protocol is bi-directional and synchronous. Before a new command is issued to the gadget, the controlling computer is waiting for the previous command to be finished. The rest of the hardware used for the construction of the device was more or less standard.

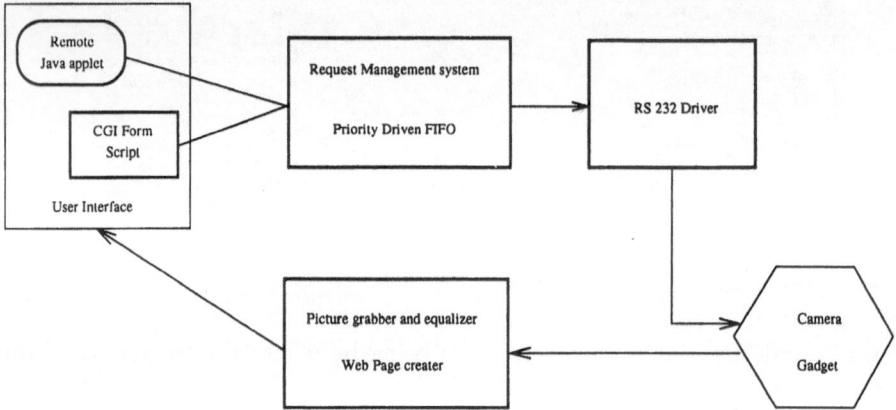

Fig. 4. Hierarchy of the software package controlling the gadget

4.3 Software

The above described hardware is only one part of the experiment. The other part, and maybe an even more important part is the software which works as an interface between the WWW and the serial port of the controlling computer. This software package consists of four independent parts (see Fig 4):

User interface; In this part we fully exploit the possibilities given by the HTML and Java programming languages. The user interface is based on a sophisticated form operating above a CGI scripts written in Perl and using a click sensitive map (Fig. 5). Currently an Java applet is being implemented to allow for orientation in a 3D model of the laboratory. This applet should provide the user with the possibility to specify a trajectory on which the camera will capture a movie. This will then be transferred to the user as a compressed MPEG format.

Fig. 5. Examples of the front end of the user interfaces for the remote control of the camera. Picture on the left shows a simple interface based on HTML v2.0 form. The right snap depicts the Java applet for camera control.

Request management system; This part of the software is designed to avoid collisions when accessing the device. This appears to be a standard database problem which could be solved by applying the *First In First Out* (FIFO) strategy [5]. Because we wanted to increase the overall performance of the system we have implemented *Priority driven* FIFO. It offers the possibility for a request to be satisfied before another request which has arrived earlier. The main reason for this is that the rotation of the camera requires a certain amount of time. If the requests for capturing pictures would be located on the opposite side of the range (see Fig. 6), a lot of time would be lost with the camera rotating to the new positions. Sorting the incoming requests by the means of polar coordinates makes it possible to satisfy more requests within the same period of time as using only FIFO. The reason for this effect is obvious.

On the other hand using the priority driven FIFO may result in the situation, where a request is waiting too long to be satisfied. It has to be ensured that each request will be fulfilled in a reasonable time. This is done by modification of the priority driven FIFO concept. We change the position of the camera to satisfy the request which has the next closest polar angle coordinate without changing the direction of the camera rotation. After the last request in the current direction is fulfilled, the direction of rotation is changed, the request queue is resorted and the process starts over again with the camera rotating in the opposite direction.

Serial Port Driver; It was written to control the data flow on the serial port of the UNIX machine. This C program intermediates the actual communication

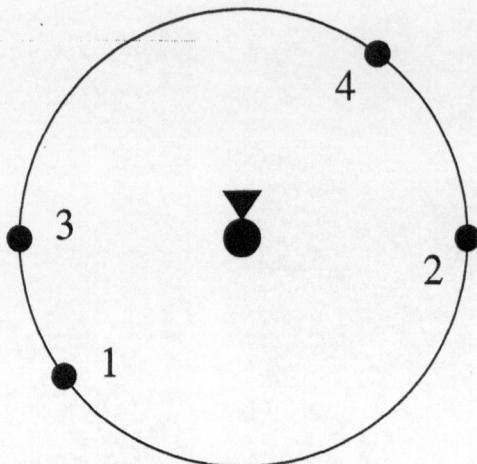

Fig. 6. Possible sequence of incoming request, where the priority driven FIFO can decrease the time needed for dispatching the required data. The numbers depict angles in which the camera is required to snap a picture.

of the computer with the gadget. It accepts the commands in the form shown in Table 1. extended by the commands for the camera (e.g. capture an image). It does not include any higher level of intelligence for the queue management.

Page Maker; The software is responsible for presenting the data to the user who requested it. In case there was a static picture required, we create a WWW page containing the image with some more interesting facts about the camera added. In case an animation was requested we create a page with a reference to the MPEG movie and some of the frames from the movie. This way the user has one more chance to decide if the movie should be transferred over the network, since this procedure may be quite time consuming. Captured data are removed from the disk after a while.

5   Conclusion

The departmental information system that integrates three-dimensional information both real and synthetic was presented. The system described works in the WWW environment allowing thus the access to information from any location around the world with WWW access. Three-dimensional information provided via models described in the VRML is linked with information of a non-geometric nature (information about professors) annotated in HTML. The information from the real world was acquired by means of the distant driven camera.

The experiment with the camera is a good example of how to incorporate a machine driven input device into an information system. In our case the infor-

Table 1. The definition of the simple language, which was defined to control a gadget for camera rotation from a workstation.

Command	Description	Response	Semantic
I	check the range find and set the middle position	"i" "g"	command acknowledgment the operation is finished
A *coord*	set the camera to absolute coordinate *coord*	"a" "g" "e"	command acknowledgment the operation is finished error has occurred
R *coord*	change the camera angle ± *coord* relatively to curr. pos.	"r" "g" "e"	command acknowledgment the operation is finished error has occurred
P	Returns the camera's current absolute ±position	"p" *coord* "g"	command acknowledgment the current position the operation is finished
M	Returns the absolute value of the angle range < 0..*coord* >	"m" *coord* "g"	command acknowledgment the maximal coordinate the operation is finished

mational value is only marginal, because it is not very important to allow a user to scan the room with the camera. On the other hand, this research shows and also solves some of the major problems related to use of input devices based on similar principles.

We expect in the near future, that more systems using a similar structure and input devices will be available. A good example of such an application would be an information system providing data from the environment which is dangerous for human beings or which is rather remote.

The future work on the project will be mainly focused on improving the software part, and mainly the user interface. Also the FIFO management for the camera will be closely examined and tested, which is necessary to propose the best possible strategy for the requirements management. We want to also improve the input device hardware. The micro-controller should gain more independence from the controlling workstation, which will result in a less computationally expensive system for obtaining and supplying data for the information system in real time.

Other extensive research is being conducted in the area of VRML browser design. Extending the capability of the current VRML browsers by adding collision detection and speeding up the visualization during the walk-through should increase the reality of the virtual environment of the three-dimensional database. This could be achieved by applying context sensitive scene subdivision based on global visibility preprocessing.

78

References

1. Herzner W., Kappe F. (Eds.) *Multimedial Hypermedia in Open Distributed Environment.* Springer 94. – Article by Valsky E., Herzog M., Peratello, Slany A., *The Department Information System of the Information System Department at the Technical University of Vienna.* pp. 88 - 102

2. Berners-Lee T., Connolly D., *HyperText Markup Language – 2.0*
   http://www.w3.org/hypertext/WWW/MarkUp/html-spec/

3. Bell G., Parisi A., Pesce M., *The Virtual Reality Modeling Language – Version 1.0 Specification.* http://www.clark.net/theme/vrml/

4. *The Java Language Specification.*
   http://www.javasoft.com/1.0alpha3/doc/javaspec/javaspec_1.html

5. Tanenbaum A. M., Langsam Y., Augenstein M. J., *Data structures using C.* Prentice Hall 1990

A Multimedia Approach of Information Integration

Karin Solka

Fraunhofer Institute for Computer Graphics Rostock
Joachim-Jungius-Straße 9, D-18059 Rostock, Germany
Tel.: +49-381-4024-133, Fax: +49-381-4024-199
Email: karin@egd.igd.fhg.de

Abstract: As quick as computer systems find their way into more and more application fields, on the one hand the variety of information to be computed increases; and on the other hand the requirements on the way of information handling become differently more and more. A practical demonstration of utilizing specific computer technologies for a certain application field may ease the process of system specification and implementation. In a close collaboration with historians a concept of a historical information system has been designed with the objective to demonstrate the utilization of modern computer technology in the rather traditional field of history. It is shown how the variety of historical information and media may be combined and presented with techniques like multimedia, geographical information systems, virtual reality and information networking by means of the World Wide Web.

1 Motivation

A problem for the introduction of modern computer support into a new application field often occur when the professionals of this field are requested to specify their needs and expectations for being supported by a computer system.

Non-computer-scientists usually have difficulties to describe their objectives and to develop scenarios conceptually which are considering the great variety of information and which might be able to be implemented on a computer. They naturally try to map their own knowledge about and experiences with computers on their applicational tasks. Thus, they limit themselves in exhausting the appropriate technological capabilities. A practical demonstration of utilizing specific computer technologies for a certain application field may ease the process of system specification and implementation if it has been created by a close collaboration of professionals of this field and computer scientists.

One of those more traditional application fields which just begins to be open for modern computer technologies is the field of history and historical sciences, respectively. The research work in the field of history usually requires an extensive effort in time and man power for the retrieval and evaluation of information from historical sources which is still done manually in many cases. The intention of following the interests of historians for a modern management of historical information motivated us to design and implement a historical information system exemplarily which integrates various sources of information by utilizing different technologies like multimedia, geographical information systems (GIS), virtual reality (VR) and information networking by means of the World Wide Web (WWW). The first stage of the work resulted in the implementation of the WWW information server KOGGE, the cartography-oriented graphical system for the exploration of the history of Mecklenburg and Vorpommern. Mecklenburg/Vorpommern is one of the 16 federal countries of Germany located in the north-east. The information server has been established as a common initiative of the Department of Historical Sciences at the University of Rostock, Germany, and the Fraunhofer Institute for Computer Graphics Rostock.

2   Concepts of information integration by example of a historical application

2.1 Integration through the multimedia information base

The information obtained from historical sources usually differ in type and amount depending on the variety, quality and completeness of the sources. Every source may be considered as a medium containing information in a certain encoding. Following the description in [1], media are carriers of information which might be understood as multiple layers of encodings whereas we usually refer to the most abstract level (see figure 1).

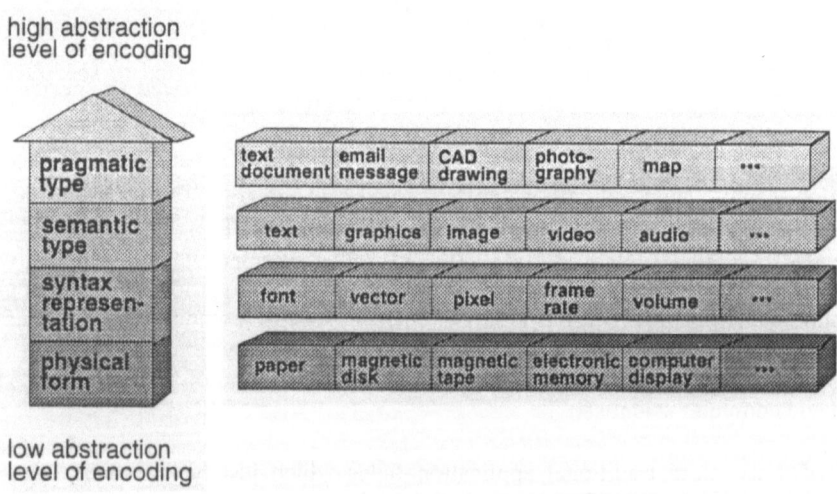

Fig. 1. Encoding layers of a medium

The multimedia historical information base consists of a set of differently encoded information where one pragmatic information type may be composed from multiple encoding types of any layer (see figure 2).

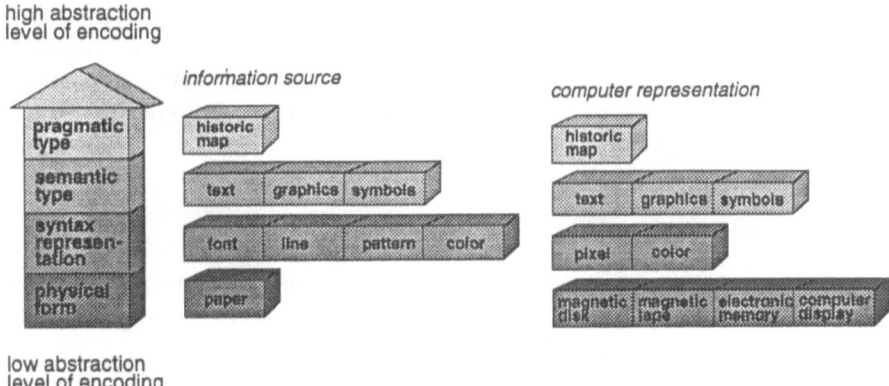

Fig. 2. Example of multiple encoding representations of an information

The way of integrating these multiple media is determined by the covered applicational subjects and has been designed in accordance to the pragmatic encoding level (see figure 3).

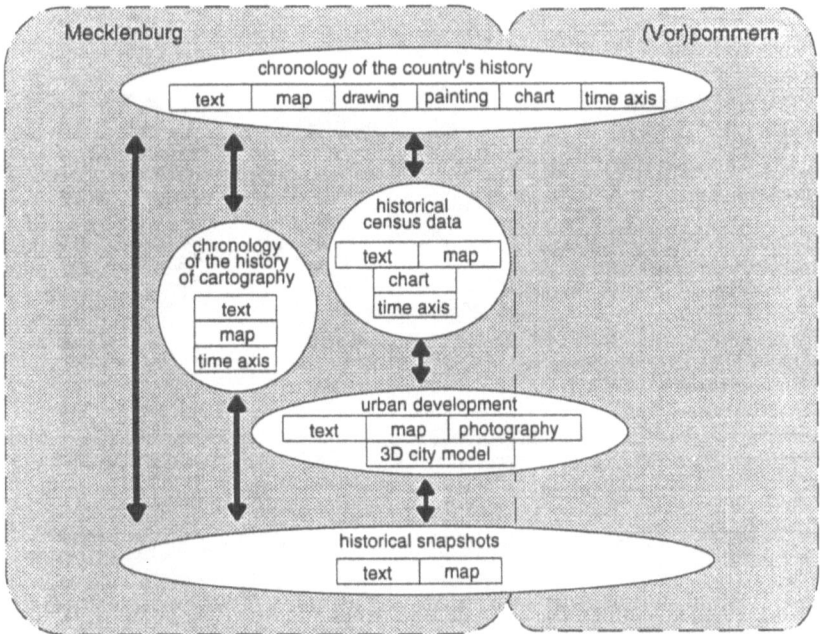

Fig. 3. Pragmatic information types within applicational subjects

In [2] you will find an additional description of the historical information sources used.

Although the requirements for a multimedia system described in [3] have not been fulfilled completely in the current state of the historical information server, the server has been designed as an open system with a multimedia approach allowing the further inclusion of additional static and time-varying information. By now it might be considered as a multimedia system in a wider sense.

2.2 Integration through technologies

According to the applicational objectives, the variety of available information should be represented by appropriate technological concepts. Different objectives and information require different technologies (see figure 4).

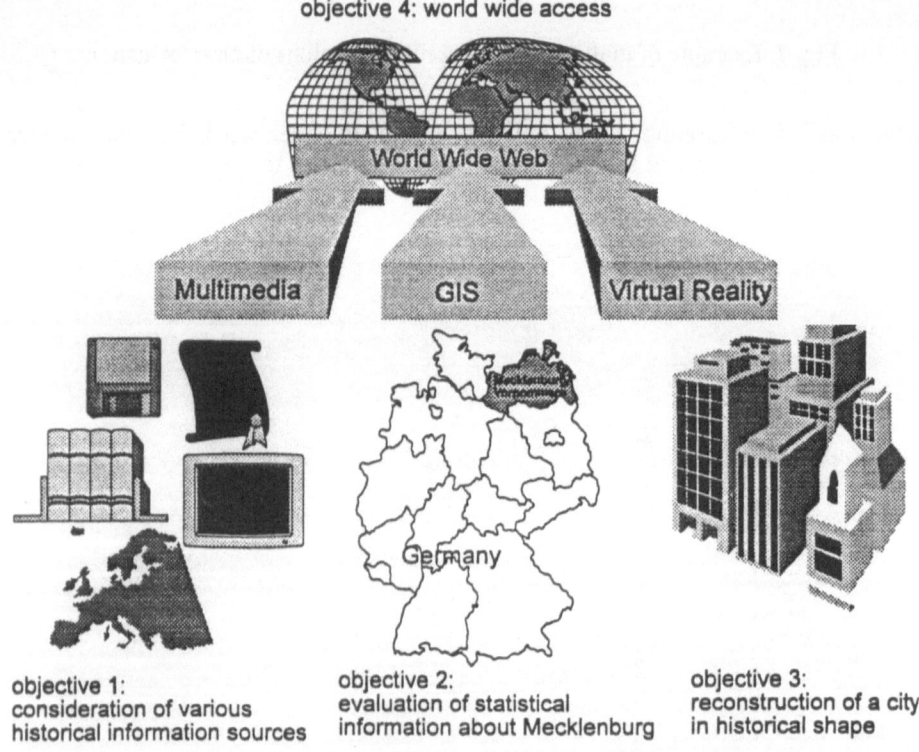

Fig. 4. Applicational objectives mapped on computer technologies

The World Wide Web functions as a final integrator for the multimedia historical information base providing access to the information for the world wide user community. The relationships between the various media of historical information as well as between the different technologies have been established by hyperlinks.

The utilization of the GIS technology was caused by the more detailed objective to provide the capability of an interactive selection of statistical data in conjunction with the graphical representation of the data in its geographical context. The evaluation of historical census data of Mecklenburg and its towns is supported by the graphical presentation of thematic maps which have been produced by means of a geographical information system.

The objective of the reconstruction of a city in its historical shape includes further requirements for the handling and presentation of the results. A reconstructed model of the historical city was requested to be available in a three-dimensional coordinate space. Moreover, the system should facilitate the exploration of this model from different viewpoints. Exemplarily, three-dimensional computer models from a part of the city of Rostock have been provided within a virtual environment using the virtual reality modelling language (VRML) where the user may walk through in real time.

Multimedia usability means giving the user the opportunity for interacting with the system at any time independently of the considered type of information. The user wants to have access to the variety of information without being limited by presentation methods due to the characteristics of an information type; i.e. a user input is allowed at any time. As far as the system contains static information like text, images, photographies etc., this requirement may easily be fulfilled. While presenting time-varying information, specific interaction techniques might be used to provide the opportunity for user inputs.

The exploration of the 3D city model may be executed by two methods alternatively using virtual reality technology. Either pre-defined viewpoints are activated for showing "fly-arounds" by targeting those certain viewpoints like playing a video; or the user controls any step of the navigation through the virtual scene directly.

The pre-defined-viewpoint-method differs from playing a video though, because the sequence of images displayed is not recorded but rather calculated in real time. So the user may select a target viewpoint from any location and viewpoint, respectively, within the virtual environment.

The free-navigation-method allows to determine the direction and orientation of moving through the virtual environment at any time of the interaction.

2.3 Integration through the user interface

As the KOGGE information server was designed as a World Wide Web application, the framework of the user interface is determined by the specific web browser used. The user interface of the application itself integrates the information base and technological approaches described above and offers multiple techniques for the interaction and presentation.

Apart from the usual way of following links through the WWW application, the user may also execute dialogs to determine the next interaction steps and may also navigate through 3D virtual environments in real time. The relationships of information within and between the historical subjects which different technologies are applied to are connected through the representation of the various media.

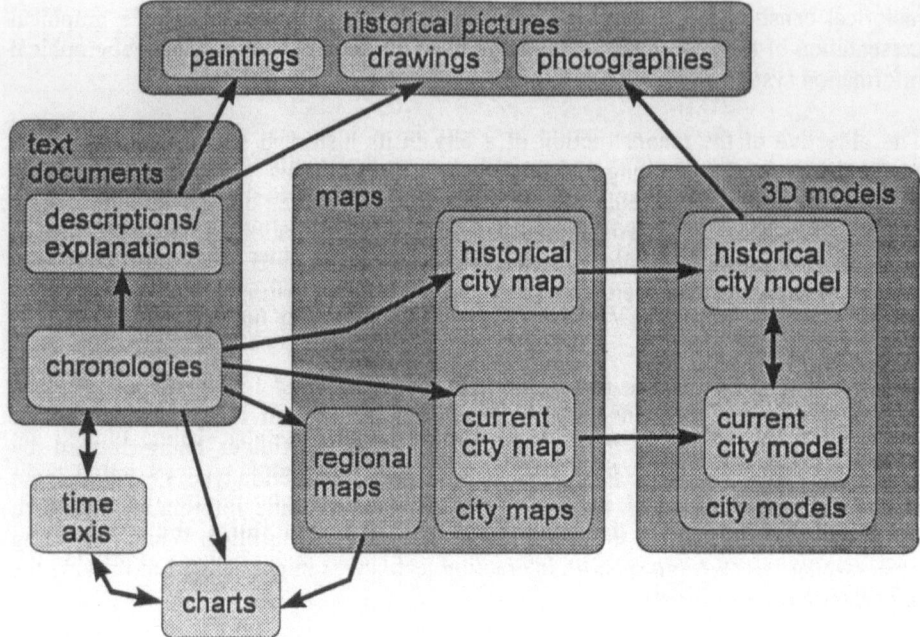

Fig. 5. Relationships between information types

Methods for accessing information through their relationships include:

- direct selection of a geographical feature from a map

- accessing information through a symbolized time axis

- activation of the current and historical 3D model, respectively, by identifying the according part of the city in an appropriate current and historical 2D map

- activation of the historical 3D model from the current 3D model and vice versa through a specific object of the scene

- accessing further information, e.g. texts and photographies, by identifying certain locations or objects, respectively, within the 3D-model (see figure 6)

Figure 5 shows the relationships between the different media which are offered through the graphical user interface and are implemented by now.

Fig. 6. Example of the user interface - virtual environment and further information

3 Evaluation notes

From the applicational point of view of historians the KOGGE server as an implementation of the conceptual idea of an information system about Mecklenburg and Vorpommern provides a new quality of historical information management and usability. Additionally, it is a useful framework for non-specialists of the field of historical sciences who are not only interested in getting information. A system like this also supports the recognition of relationships because information may be accessed and presented in parallel which only would be able to gather otherwise in a time-consuming way with much effort.

Using an interactive 3D representation of the city as a virtual environment, historians get a better understanding of what a city may have looked like in the past and may conclude some additional knowledge, e.g. about structural developments of the population in relation to space and constructional conditions. Moreover, historical models of a city may be a useful decision support for current urban planning and maintenance.

The current implementation of KOGGE has been considered as a proposal rather than a final system. A real-time execution of the VR component requires a high-end workstation with a graphics system supporting graphics calculation and texture mapping. There still might be potentials for the optimization of the performance for interacting with the system generally.

A high level of usefulness of the historical information system will be achieved by defining objectives with some greater detail and including the required information and functionality, therefore. However, the proposed idea has been adopted with great enthusiasm not only by the historians.

4 Further ideas

A further development of the idea of the historical information system will be based on a detailed specification of objectives and requirements in collaboration with the potential users.

Apart from providing completeness of information within the current information server, the following objectives might be taken into account:

- further development of the multimedia approach by integrating audio and video information sources considering approriate user interface metaphors

- extension of the statistical information evaluation by utilizing further GIS methods

- establishing spatial relationships between various historical information, e.g. between maps or between maps and 3D models

- designing the user interface for certain user groups, e.g. scientists (analyzing system), interested people (information system), learning people (tutoring system)

etc.

Furthermore, the VR technology allows the use of alternative interaction techniques, especially gesture control. So it offers a new way of addressing different user groups, e.g. the international user community and disabled people. Gestures are more or less independent of any language, apart from the necessity of a common basis for the semantics of gestures, and might be used more intuitively. In a virtual 3D environment they allow an effective linking of commands with spatial information. Some more detailed descriptions of integrating gestures into user interfaces are given in [4].

5 Summary

A common initiative of the Department of Historical Sciences at the University of Rostock and the Fraunhofer-Institute for Computer Graphics Rostock, Germany, was launched with the objective of the utilization of modern computer technologies including multimeda, GIS and VR, in the traditional field of history. The first stage of the work resulted in the implementation of the WWW information server KOGGE. The interesting aspects of the conceptual idea are to find in a complex approach of integrating multiple information of various characteristics and a variety of historical subjects which the information belong to. Further developments will be motivated by the great interest of historians who have recognized the advantages and potentials of computer assistance in historical research, education and information.

The KOGGE information server is available in the internet through the homepage of the Fraunhofer Institute for Computer Graphics Rostock at the URL http://www.egd.igd.fhg.de/ choosing "information server" or directly through the URL http://www.egd.igd.fhg.de/KOGGE.

References

0. Dannenberg, R.; Blattner, M.: Multimedia Interface Design. ACSM Press, New York 1992. - ISBN 0-201-54981-6

1. Dannenberg, R.; Blattner, M.: The Trend Toward Multimedia Interfaces. In: [0], S. xvii - xxv

2. Solka, K.: KOGGE Kartographie-Orientiertes Graphisches Geschichte-Erkundungssysteme. In: COMPUTER GRAPHIK topics 6/95, Vol.7, S. 14-15

3. Steinmetz, R.: Multimedia-Technologie, Einführung und Grundlagen. 1993

4. Hanne, K.-H.; Bullinger, H.-J.: Multimodal Communication: Integrating Text and Gestures. In: [0], S 127-138

World Wide Conference:
An easy conference connection via a Java application

A. S. Park, J. Meggers, M. Schunck

Department of Computer Science 4
Aachen University of Technology, Germany

Abstract: Multiparty multimedia conferencing has become increasingly interesting for both educational and commercial uses. One major problem lies in the fact that the realisation of multiparty connections is associated with an immense effort, particularly including the selection of the common basis software for the conference and the underlying hardware. One way to cope with these disadvantages and set up group working across the Internet is using the World Wide Web. The Java application, *World Wide Conference* (WWC), will pursue this concept and use World Wide Web as a basis for collaboration and joint editing of documents. This paper describes the design and the initial implementation considerations of the WWC application.

1   Introduction

Multiparty multimedia conferencing has become increasingly interesting for both educational and commercial uses. One major problem lies in the fact that the realisation of multiparty connections is associated with an immense effort, particularly including the selection of the common basis software for the conference and the underlying hardware. In most of the cases there is much work to do installing the essential software - apart from the fact that one common software is not always available for different platforms. For instance, the new T.120 standard of the International Telecommunications Union-Telecommunication (ITU-T) [6] defines management and transmission protocols for multimedia data to realize multiparty multimedia conferencing. The drawbacks of this standard and of several proprietary systems for Audiographic Teleconferencing include price and the difficult installation. On the data communication side the Multicast Backbone (MBone) [1] realizes a virtual network providing a multicasting facility over the Internet. Unfortunately the use of MBone is limited to UNIX based systems. One way to cope with these disadvantages and support collaboration across the Internet is using the World Wide Web. The Java application, *World Wide Conference* (WWC), will pursue this concept and use World Wide Web as a basis for collaboration and joint editing of documents. Multiparty connections will be possible without any additional software and will be independent of specific system architectures. Furthermore, each multiparty session can be set up everywhere totally independent from the location of specific servers. With the unambiguous location of the HTML page providing the WWC application, everyone will easily be able to establish multiparty connections by using a Java Interpreter.

The main goal of this project is the design and implementation of a multiparty conferencing system. The system will enable users to discuss filling in forms or the handling of images on an HTML page. Currently the communication between participants is realized through a whiteboard and a chat box. In later implementations video conferencing will also be realized. The proposed system is very useful for all kind of businesses with a need to fill in forms under expert advice, e.g. tax-forms or diagnostics. Another possible application is education, where students do exercises on an HTML page and can be corrected by their teacher online.

1.1 Scenario

During the redesign of the new Tip-Tronic gearshift for Porsche 911 the engineer Pete has a new idea he wants to discuss with his colleague who is working on a similar job at BMW. He gives Joe a call to set up a conference connection. They have to agree on a password, which is needed to restrict access to the multiparty sessions. Both engineers start the *World Wide Conference* application to begin the communication, during which one of them has the right to lead the session. Pete is the leading person and loads his newly designed Tip-Tronic gearshift into the whiteboard and marks the problem area he has identified. Joe is completely surprised about this brilliant idea, thus he immediately calls the project leader Kevin, who is on the move. Kevin starts his notebook connected to his mobile and accesses the multiparty session (illustrated in figure 1).

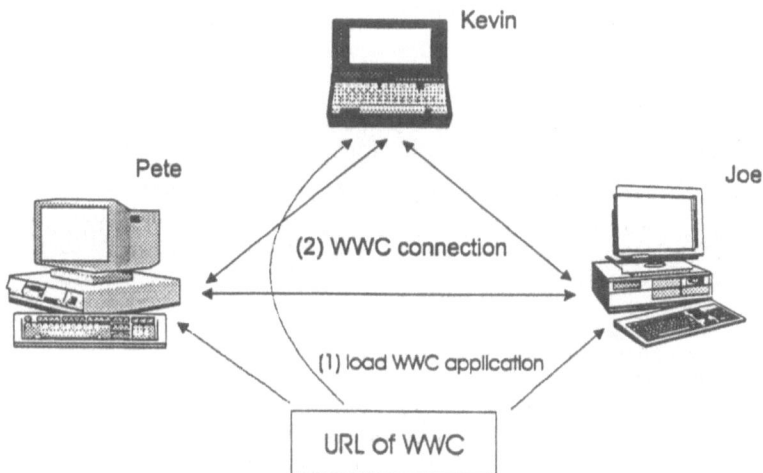

Fig. 1. WWC scenario

When Kevin sees the problem area he remembers an article he saw lately on an HTML page. He directly takes over the leadership and recalls the HTML page on his browser. In the meantime Pete and Joe are looking eager on their screen that also shows the HTML page which Kevin wanted to show them, holding a video sequence. Pete and Joe are amazed about this new information and decide to rearrange a new conference tomorrow with a few more colleagues.

2 Design and implementation

The implementation of this project will be realized using SUN's Java language [2]. Java offers the possibility to embed programs into HTML pages and is independent of any system architectures. HTML pages with embedded Java programs (applets) make browsers start the built-in interpreter, which executes the Java code (bytecode). The Java language is also used to write stand-alone-programs, which are not embedded in an HTML page, but also need a Java interpreter. To distinguish these programs from applets they are called applications. The difference between Java applets and Java applications is essential, because there are many restrictions on applets due to security reasons. In the Netscape browser, for example, an applet is not allowed to read or write to the file system of the local machine. Furthermore, an applet loaded over the net is only allowed to open a socket connection to the location of origin [3]. Applets violating this restriction are stopped by security mechanisms. The security restrictions are controlled by the browser's applet class loader. The loader is established when the browser is started and cannot be changed in any way afterwards. Consideration has also been given to the scripting language called JavaScript [8], which is an extension of HTML. This extension will be supported by various browsers, but is not part of the RFC 1866 [4].

The conference connection will be set up without a central server and therefore should not suffer from delays introduced by a central entity. Furthermore, the installation will be very simple through addressing the Uniform Resource Locator (URL) holding the Java WWC application. Thus only an interpreter for the Java application and a browser with an integrated Java interpreter are needed. The first prototype of WWC will run with a Java interpreter and a Java capable browser. To realize a multiparty session each user needs a *Conference Control Panel* (CCP) and a browser.

2.1 The Conference Control Panel (CCP)

The Conference Control Panel displays different information and manages the communication over the multipoint connection. Each browser in the multiparty session will always show the same HTML page and only the leading participant of this multiparty session is able to manipulate this page (e.g. click on a hyperlink to change the page). This means all changes that are performed by the leader are at the same

time visible on the other browsers of the conference participants. Therefore, the following features will be realized in CCP:

- communication management of all CCPs and the browser,
- shared whiteboards that enable users to exchange any kind of information,
- chat box,
- list of users who join the conference,
- indication of the leading user (who has the right to change the HTML pages),
- connecting and disconnecting to a World Wide Conference.

The CCP is used on the one hand to describe the user interface and on the other hand to communicate with other CCPs and the local browser. It lists each participant of the conference and denotes the leader. The shared whiteboard will be implemented as a pop up window and supports both text and graphics. The CCP also realizes an authentication mechanism to ensure that only users with the appropriate password are able to join the conference. Furthermore, the participants have to define a *start-up* leader and his location address so that each participant is able to enter the announced conference by this address. Hence each user starts a WWC by entering the host address of the start-up leader and the common password.

The communication between the CCPs of the different users will be realized through sockets, which are provided by the Java language. The general functionality of the CCP is depicted in figure 2.

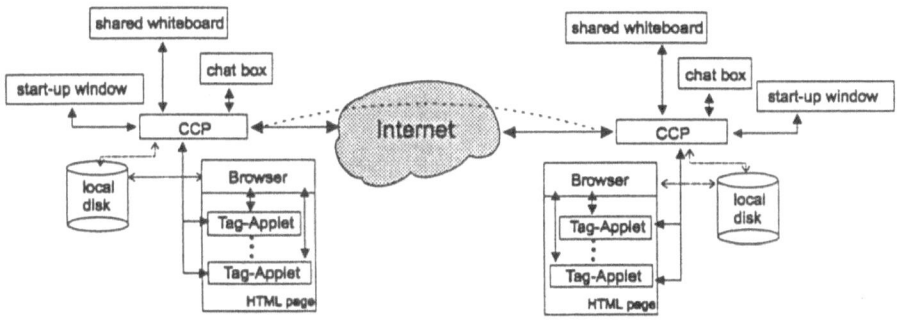

Fig. 2. Diagrammatic composition of WWC

Each CCP will have the possibility to connect to others through sockets to exchange information from one user to the other. This information includes text written in the chat box, the actions on the shared whiteboard and changes that are made to the HTML page of the browser. A first problem that arises is how to multicast the information that the leader has changed the current HTML page. Since at the moment there is no possibility to observe events inside an HTML page (i.e. clicking on a hyperlink or typing in a form), the following idea will be pursued. Whenever the leader changes to a new HTML page the new URL is broadcast to the CCPs of the other users. Each CCP that receives the new URL downloads the requested file and locally scans the HTML page. During this scanning all tags that allow a user activity (i.e. text fields, hyperlinks, etc.) are replaced by Tag-Applets, which are transparent to the user. These Tag-Applets observe any event that can happen on the WWW page (e.g. clicking on a hyperlink applet) and control the information flow to the CCP. The modified pages with embedded Tag-Applets are saved on the local disk of the user's machine. Subsequently, the CCP triggers the browser via the Tag-Applet to load the changed HTML file from the local disk (the browser's disk cache can be used in later versions). The reason for this step is that only applets loaded from the local file system are allowed to establish connections to the server they were loaded from.

2.2   Interaction of the WWC components

The World Wide Conference can be set up when the host address of the start-up leader and the common password have been chosen. The conference begins when the start-up leader starts his CCP. All other users are then able to enter the leader's host address and their CCPs realize the connection to the leader's CCP and transmit all necessary information (host address, password, username, etc.). The leader's CCP again broadcasts this information to all users that are already registered.

Now the leader can work on the HTML page and his changes to the page are recognised by the Tag-Applets, which pass this information to the CCP application. If a hyperlink Tag-Applet is activated by the leader, this Tag-Applet sends the stored hyperlink address to the CCP and then waits for the acknowledgement. In the meantime the CCP broadcasts the new URL to all participating CCPs, so that each CCP downloads the new HTML page and performs the changes. The leader's Tag-Applet receives an acknowledgement as soon as the changes are finished. The last action of the activated Tag-Applet is to force the browser to load the new and modified HTML page from the local disk (see figure 2). For all other participants the same newly selected WWW page is visible. Inputs to forms are realized analogously. Each input will be visible to all participants and thus a common handling of e.g. printed forms is possible.

In figure 3 you can see one possible screen shot with an arrangement of the Conference Control Panel, a shared whiteboard and the Netscape browser in the background. The CCP includes the chat box and the participants' list. The highlighted user (Markus) is the leading person. He is able to hand over this position to some other participant by selecting one in the list. The chat box is independent from the leader and thus everyone can express his wishes. On the one hand each user is able to leave the conference by disconnecting his CCP. On the other hand new participants can join the running session using the connecting button and inserting one of the participants' host addresses and the password. Figure 3 also shows a shared whiteboard that can only be started by the leader. Once the shared whiteboard is in use, each participant can work on it. Only the leader of the session is able to copy images from the actual WWW page to the whiteboard, but then all participants are able to work on this image and discuss it. This use of the WWC is interesting for engineers working on a technical drawing or doctors discussing an X-ray. Additional shared whiteboards can always be opened by the actual leading participant.

Furthermore, each user will get a standard set of drawing functions that he can use; these include lines, circles, rectangles and writing. The leader is able to save the images or load new ones. This enables the user to load images like X-rays, new designs, new architectural studies and so forth.

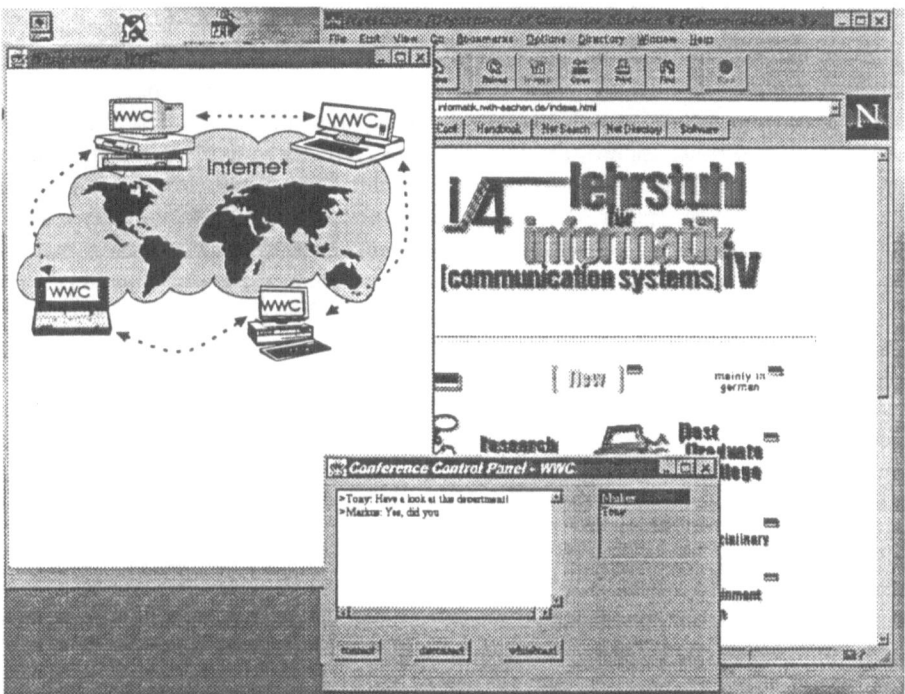

Fig. 3. CCP, shared whiteboard and a Java capable browser

3   Summary and future work

The Java language allows interactions within the widely distributed World Wide Web. The main point at issue of this World Wide Conference project is joint browsing the Internet and handling of forms and images. In this context the Java language supports the realisation of multiparty connections, thus users are able to work with WWC without any specific additional software and independent of any system architecture. Furthermore, each multiparty session can be established totally independent of a central server and therefore the location of the participants is irrelevant. The already well established Netscape browser and the Java interpreter will attract a large number of users to whom such an application is very beneficial. The project of the World Wide Conference is in the initial state. Open problems to cope with include the efficient communication protocol between the Conference Control Panels and the browser. The chat box and the use of the shared whiteboard are already well realized in the Internet; existing ideas will be implemented. The scalability of this WWC application and the performance has to be studied as soon as the first communication between the WWC components is possible. Furthermore, it has to be considered that multimedia applications and multimedia systems become increasingly popular, thus in addition to sound cards also microphones and video cards with little cameras will be standard components shortly. The next development step will be the additional integration of a video conference system with the World Wide Conference application.

References

[1]   Hans Eriksson, "MBONE: The Multicast Backbone", *Communications of the ACM, Vol. 37, No. 8, pp 54-61*, August 1994

[2]   James Gosling, Henry Mc Gilton, "The Java Language Environment: A White Paper" *http://java.sun.com/whitePaper/java-whitepaper-1.html*, November 1995

[3]   Frank Yellin, "Low Level Security in Java", *WWW4 Conference*, December 1995

[4]   RFC 1866: T. Berners-Lee, D. Connolly, "Hypertext Markup Language - 2.0", *MIT/W3C, http://www.cis.ohio-state.edu/htbin/rfc/rfc1866.html*, November 1995

[5]   Reference Material, "On Internet Security", *http://home.netscape.com/info/security-doc.html*, 1995

[6]   ITU Draft Recommendation T.120, "Data Protocols for Multimedia Conferencing", November 1995

[7]   R. Fielding, H. Frystyk, T. Berners-Lee, "Hypertext Transfer Protocol - HTTP/1.1", HTTP Working Group, Internet-Draft, November 1995

[8]   Netscape Communications Corporation, "JavaScript language", *http://www.netscape.com/eng/mozilla/Gold/handbook/javascript/index.html*, January 1996

[9]   Frequently Asked Questions - Applet Security Version 1.0, *http://java.sun.com/sfaq/#summary*, 1995

Collaborative Multimedia Applications and Platforms Integrated with Video-on-Demand

Hideyuki FUKUOKA, Hiromi MIZUNO, Shigehito KAWASAKI

C&C Research Laboratories, NEC Corporation
4-1-1 Miyazaki, Miyamae-ku, Kawasaki, 216, JAPAN

Abstract. Collaborative multimedia applications and platforms integrated with video-on-demand are described. The integration platform is realized by association of a groupware server with a video-on-demand server using a Video Service Bridge. The platform enables application developers to develop collaborative multimedia application systems supporting video-on-demand functions, and provides both realtime and stored video naturally synchronized with audio to group users simultaneously. A collaborative automobile sales support system and a group hypermedia navigational system developed on the integrated platform are interesting examples showing the platform's possibilities. Using these systems, group users can simultaneously share and operate video images retrieved from video servers.

1 Introduction

The remarkable progress of multimedia groupware and multimedia-on-demand, the two major technologies in the multimedia field have brought multimedia distributed applications into practical use in the last few years. Most of the existing multimedia communication services today are realized by either of the technologies. Application systems for multimedia groupware and multimedia-on-demand have been developed, each according to their respective requirements for realtime interactive services and on demand services. Consequently, there is now a serious barrier between the two technologies: the platforms are completely independent.

The multimedia platform proposed in this paper integrates groupware with video-on-demand (VoD) seamlessly. Groupware can be considered as an application technology for VoD, while VoD provides storage services for groupware. The integration objective is to make it possible for a group of users to simultaneously share retrieval and trick play operation as well as view of the stored multimedia information. The integrated platform enables application developers to develop multimedia application systems supporting both groupware and VoD functions.

2 Groupware and multimedia-on-demand

Multimedia groupware services are realtime interactive services which enable users to exchange multimedia information in a bi-directional form. Fig. 1(a) shows a groupware model in which user terminals are interconnected to a centralized multipoint communication server MCU (multipoint control unit), and its data flow direction. User terminals can exchange and share multimedia information sent via the MCU, enabling realtime communication between a number of users. The audio and video information provided in existing groupware services such as video conferencing enables users to see each other's faces and hear each other's voices, and this realtime information must be exchanged within a negligible time delay.

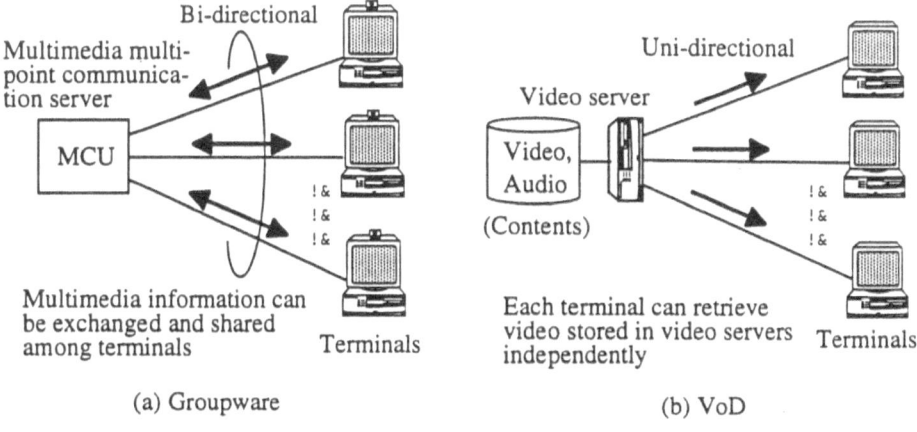

(a) Groupware   (b) VoD

Figure 1: Typical groupware and VoD system models

In contrast, multimedia-on-demand services are information retrieval services, which enable users to access multimedia servers and retrieve multimedia information such as audio, video, images, on their demand. The data flow direction of a typical VoD system is shown in Fig. 1(b). Many user terminals or STB (set top box)s may access the server simultaneously. However, there are no interactions between the users; The stored media is controlled by each terminal individually. The retrieved information arrives at the user terminal within a tolerable delay time depending on the network bandwidth, but users' requirements for the degree of realtime may not be as strict as in groupware services. However, both inter and intra media synchronization are indispensable since the information contents served by VoD services are video programs such as movies or music.

Multimedia groupware and multimedia-on-demand technologies serve as middleware in the multimedia system structure shown in Fig.2. Middleware provides various multimedia services: realtime interactive services such as conferencing, remote education in multimedia groupware middleware, on-demand services such as electronic newspaper, online shopping in multimedia-on-demand middleware.

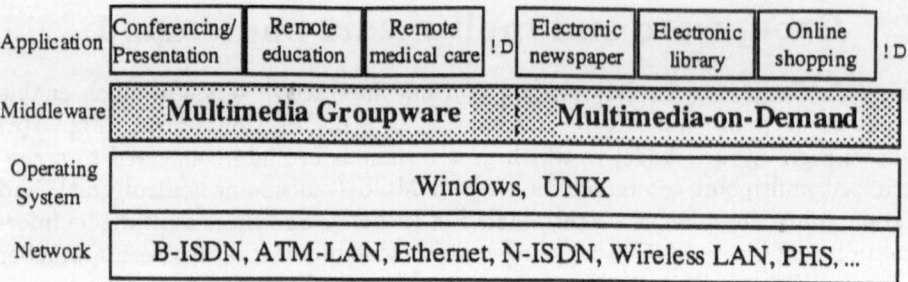

Figure 2: Multimedia system structure

Most of the existing multimedia services are realized either by multimedia groupware or multimedia-on-demand.

A number of studies have been reported on integration of e-mail or workflow based groupware with world wide web, and some of the integrated systems are coming to practical use in recent years. However, integration of multimedia groupware such as conferencing systems and multimedia-on-demand has never been reported. It is considered that multimedia application systems supporting both groupware and VoD functions have never been developed, because multimedia groupware and VoD involve completely separate middleware.

3 Service requirements

Service requirements for groupware and VoD integration have been discussed. The aim is to utilize VoD services for groupware users. The following services are required of the platform integration.

1. A group of users can simultaneously share audio and video retrieved from VoD servers.

2. Users can see each others' faces and hear each others' voices while sharing retrieved audio and video from VoD servers.

3. Users voices should arrive at other users within tolerable delay time.

4. VoD audio should be lip-synchronized with VoD video. (inter media synchronization)

5. VoD audio should be played in uniform speed. (intra media synchronization)

6. Group collaboration in VoD trick play operations such as pause, slow forward, fast forward, jump.

7. Group collaboration in VoD navigation, or video program selection.

The following functions for the integrated platform must be developed, in order to realize the service requirements mentioned above.

- Association between groupware servers and VoD servers

- Group collaborative STB software

4 Server association

A framework for association between groupware servers (MCUs) and VoD servers is necessary to achieve integration of both services. A Video Service Bridge (VSB) is proposed to provide the associative service.

4.1 Integrated system model

Fig. 3 shows a groupware and VoD integrated system model based on system models shown in Fig. 1. The integrated system model is designed to support the service requirements specified in section 3. The integration is realized by a VSB through which stored and retrieval services are provided for groupware systems, and sharing services are provided for VoD systems.

In this model, STBs for group users are realized as application programs on groupware clients. In addition, personal VoD services are also provided for STBs as is in the traditional VoD systems.

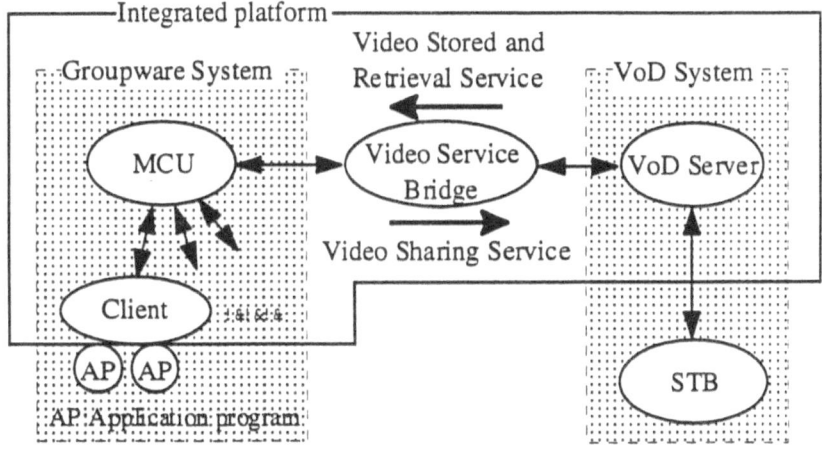

Figure 3: Integrated system model

4.2 Video service bridge

A VSB is a gateway to receive services provided by other systems. A VSB is designed to behave like a client for both MCUs and VoD servers as shown in Fig.4, while groupware systems assume the VSB to be their VoD server. VSB's functional requirements based on the integrated system model is specified:

(1) Pseudo client for VoD:
A VSB behaves like an STB. It makes connection with a VoD server as an STB when groupware users request VoD services. It receives audio and video data sent from the VoD server. VSB also forwards trick play control information from groupware users to the VoD server.

(2) Pseudo client for groupware:
VSB also plays the roll of a groupware client. It joins a conference automatically when groupware users request VoD services, and leaves when they stop using the VoD services. While the VoD services are provided, a VSB forwards audio and video data from the VoD server to the MCU.

(3) Protocol conversion:
Data transmission formats and command formats may be quite different in groupware and VoD systems, and they must be converted. The following functions are required:

 - Data transmission format conversion:
   A VSB converts received data from a VoD server into groupware data transmission format.

 - Command translation:
   A VSB translates received commands from groupware users into VoD commands.

 - Cooperation protocols:
   The connections between VoD servers and MCUs are achieved by the cooperation protocols.

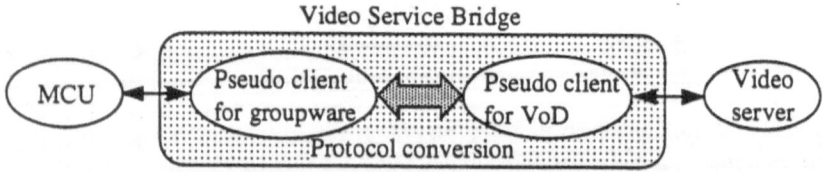

Figure 4: A VSB functional model

4.3   Cooperation protocols

Fig. 5 and Fig. 6 illustrates some examples of cooperation protocols.

Connection setup protocols are shown in Fig. 5. In this example, some clients are already collaboratively working together, connected with an MCU. When a user starts using a VoD service, a connection setup request is sent to the VSB. Whenever the VSB receives connection setup request messages, it establishes connections with a VoD server using VoDStartUpProtocols which are traditional protocols connecting STBs with VoD servers. When the connection between the VSB and the VoD server is established, the VSB requests conference information to the client, and the client sends conferenceID of the attending conference to the VSB. At that time, the VSB sets up connections with the MCU using EnterConferenceProtocols which are traditional groupware protocols. The client requesting the VoD services is informed of the approval of his request by a VoDServerConnectResponse message sent from the VSB.

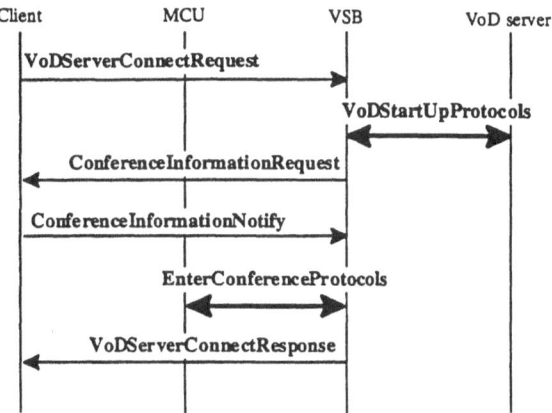

Figure 5: Connection setup protocols

Protocols for VoD trick play are shown in Fig. 6. When a user trick plays the video, control commands such as play, pause, slow-forward, fast-forward are sent to the VoD server via the VSB. The trick played video is sent to the VSB from the VoD server, format translated at the VSB, and broadcast to all the clients by the MCU.

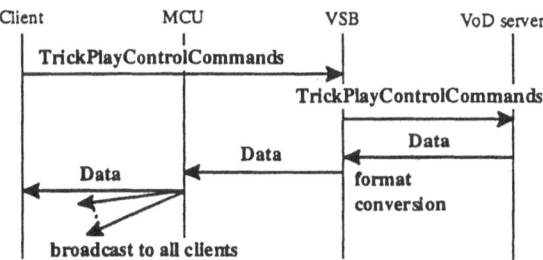

Figure 6: Trick play protocols

5 Media synchronization

In the groupware and VoD integration environment, audio and video data should be managed according to the characteristics of services. As for VoD services, inter/intra media synchronization is indispensable. Audio should be lip-synchronized with video, as well as audio and video recorded in a given amount of time should be played in the same amount of time. However, with regard to realtime communication services, it is required that audio and video are played within as small time delay as possible. Media synchronization is controlled by the following techniques.

5.1 Data transmission rate control

VoD servers respectively control the timing to send audio and video packets according to the required qualities of each medium, so that the transmission rate is maintained as constant as possible and the network is not overloaded. This ensures that audio and video arrives at user terminals constantly in accordance with the qualities. On the other hand, groupware clients send audio and video packets as soon as they are captured at the user terminals.

5.2 Time stamp transfer

A time stamp is attached to each data packet transmitted from VoD servers which is a necessary information for synchronization. Audio and video packets are disassembled, processed, and reassembled at MCUs. When a mixture of user audio and VoD audio is generated at MCUs, VoD audio time stamps are attached to the mixed audio and they are reused as mixed audio time stamps. Similarly, when user video and VoD video are composed into one screen, VoD video time stamps are took over as composed video time stamps. The time stamp transfer scheme is shown in Fig.7. Consequently, time stamps are transferred from VoD servers to user terminals via MCUs.

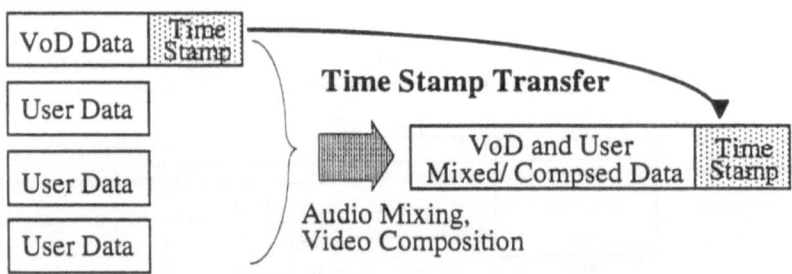

Figure 7: Time Stamp Transfer Scheme

5.3 Media play method

At user terminals, the arriving data are played based on the time stamps. Audio packets are once saved in the queue, and continuously served to each terminal's audio device to assure intra audio synchronization. The audio queue size which determines the time delay of users' voices should be set as small as possible according to the network jitter.

Video packets are also once stored in the queue, and served to each terminal's viewer. Video time stamps are checked against audio time stamps, and video data are played when the video time stamp coincides with the audio time stamp to assure inter media synchronization.

6   Testbed configuration

A groupware platform with a multimedia conferencing system called ATM-Mermaid[1],[2],[3] was developed based on the groupware model shown in Fig.1(a). It supports high quality audio and video communication using high speed networks such as ATM-LAN or B-ISDN. Using the conferencing system, a group of users can share video images up to 30fps, transmitted in motion-JPEG compression format. ATM-Mermaid is utilized in the integration testbed: the media play method described in section 5.3 is implemented in ATM-Mermaid clients, and the time stamp transfer scheme specified in section 5.2 is implemented in the MCU.

A VoD server was also developed for the integration testbed. The VoD server contains motion-JPEG video with PCM audio as well as MPEG. It supports data transmission rate control defined in section 5.1 and provides effective multimedia data transmission using realtime transport protocols RTP[4].

A VSB consists of three modules corresponding to each function defined in section 4.2: a pseudo client module for groupware based on groupware middleware, a pseudo client module for VoD servers based on VoD middleware, and a protocol conversion module, as shown in Fig.4.

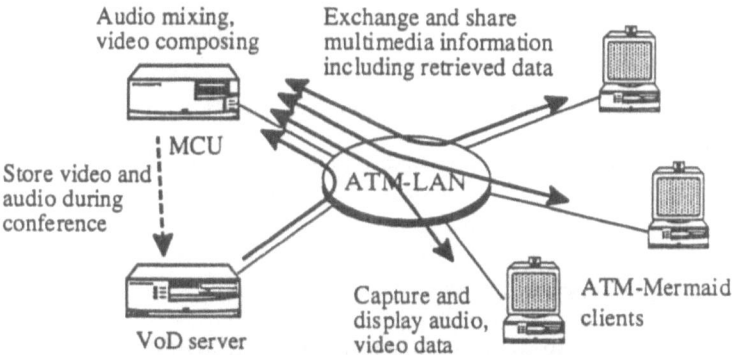

Figure 8: The testbed configuration

The testbed integrating ATM-Mermaid and a VoD server using a VSB is implemented on an ATM-LAN environment. Group collaborative STB software is developed on the ATM-Mermaid platform using the groupware application programming interface (GAPI) [5],[6] provided by ATM-Mermaid. The testbed configuration and its workflow is illustrated in Fig. 8. At least 8Mbps per each client terminal is required to achieve the high quality multimedia communication provided by ATM-Mermaid, however, the testbed system can be utilized in slower communication speed by reducing video frame rate.

A VSB is implemented as a software process which runs either on VoD server or MCU workstations. The VoD server sends retrieved data to the MCU via the VSB. All clients send captured user face data and voice data to the MCU. The MCU mixes audio data, composes video data, and broadcasts mixed audio and composed video to all clients including the VoD server. Consequently, clients can share the retrieved audio and video while seeing each other's faces and hearing each other's voices. The audio and video data sent from the MCU can be also stored at the VoD server, if necessary.

Fig. 9 shows the protocol stack of the integrated platform. The platform enables application developers to develop multimedia application systems supporting both groupware and VoD functions.

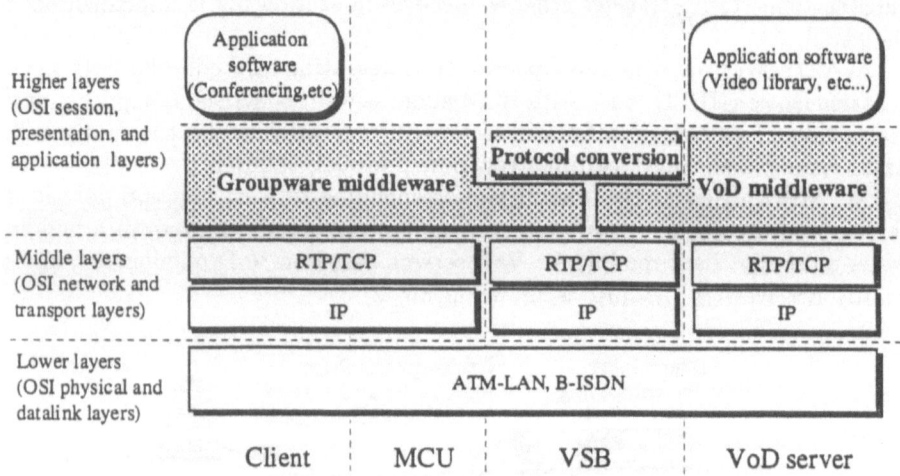

Figure 9: Protocol stack of the integrated platform

7 Applications

The integrated platform makes many different multimedia application systems possible, including conferencing systems and presentation systems supporting a wide range of group users in offices or schools. Other interesting possibilities exist in the field of entertainments, e.g. "karaoke" set-ups and multiple-player game formats for widely distributed users.

7.1 Collaborative Automobile Sales Support System

One particularly interesting example of the platform's possibilities was an automobile sales support system developed on the platform. It enables the customers to share video images of a running car simultaneously with car dealers or, in some cases, engineers, interacting over an ATM network. A screen example of the application system is shown in Fig. 10. The screen is composed of a video window, an image window, and some menu windows. Widely-dispersed car dealers, engineers, and customers are shown in each users' video window by exchanging video data through the network. This enables them to see each other's faces, hear each other's voices, and share the views and operations of all the windows.

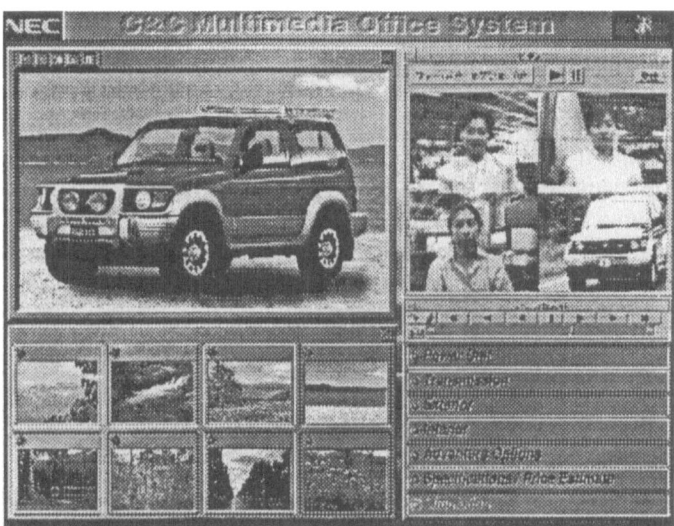

Figure 10: A screen example of the collaborative automobile sales support system

For example, a dealer might display the car he recommends on his menu windows, and its still image will be immediately shown in the image window they are sharing. A customer can select his favorite body color and display it on his menu windows, and the body color of the still image shown in the image windows will change immediately. If they want to simulate running the car, they can see video images of this using VoD services. The video images from the video server are distributed to all terminals through the network, and are displayed with the users faces in the video windows, as shown in Fig. 10.

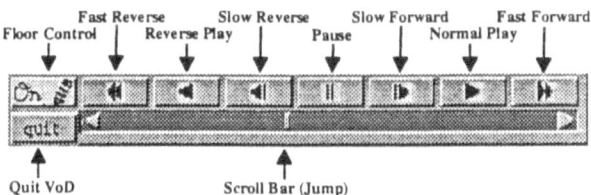

Figure 11: Control-panel

VoD trick play can be operated using a "Control-panel" shown in Fig. 11.

The button functions are described in Fig. 11. Control-panel is a group collaborative STB software, which is shared by the group users. Pressing the floor control button, dealers and customers can get the floor and they can operate trick play of the retrieved video such as play, pause, or fast forward. Consequently, they can use VoD services in collaboration with each other using this system.

7.2 Group hypermedia navigational system

A group hypermedia navigational system is also developed on the platform. The system enables users to simultaneously share hypermedia information including audio and video stored in the hypermedia database. Moving hot-spot navigation can be also shared.

Electronic Aquatic Life[7] is an application implemented on the system which displays fish and other aquatic life in video images while providing interactive exploration through still images, text, and voice, as shown in Fig. 12. Users can listen to and watch explanations of various fish by clicking moving objects in a video scene.

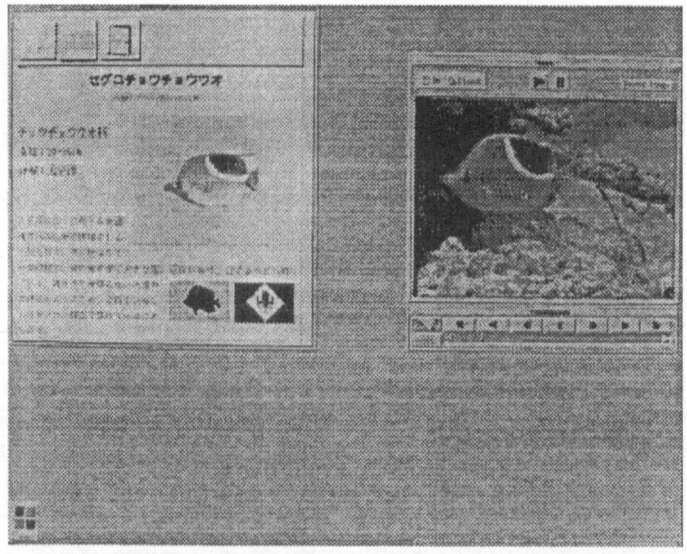

Figure 12: A screen example of the group hypermedia navigational system

This application was build for remote educational use; Widely dispersed students can share virtual aquariums over an ATM network, and learn about marine life together.

8   Conclusions

Collaborative multimedia applications and platforms integrated with video-on-demand are described. A Video Service Bridge is proposed to enable the association between groupware servers and VoD servers, and an integrated platform of groupware and VoD is formed. Multimedia application systems developed based on the integrated platform provides effective and more advanced use of multimedia communication services.

The authors intend to expand the integrated platform functions such as association of MCUs with WWW servers, and develop practical application systems with effective multimedia services on the platform.

Acknowledgments

The authors would like to thank Dr. S. Sakata and Mr. K. Maeno for their valuable advices. They also wish to express words of thanks to Mr. Y. Imahashi and Mr. Y. Kitagawa for their efforts expended throughout the trials developing the platforms and the application systems.

References

1. S. Sakata, K. Maeno, H. Fukuoka, and T. Ohmori, "Distributed multiparty desktop conferencing system: MERMAID," Proc. Conf. on Computer Supported Cooperative Work, pp.27-36 (1990).

2. K. Maeno, S. Sakata, T. Ohmori, K Watabe, and H. Fukuoka, "Distributed desktop conferencing system(MERMAID) based on group communication architecture," Proc. Conf. on ICC'91 (1991).

3. S. Sakata, "Multimedia and multi-party desktop conference system (MERMAID) as a groupware platform," Proc. IFIP Congress, pp.63-68 (1994).

4. H. Schulzrinne, S. Casner, R. Frederick, V.Jacobson, "RTP: A transport protocol for real-time applications," Internet Draft draft-ietf-avt-rtp-0.6.txt.

5. T. Ohmori, K.Maeno, S. Sakata, and H. Fukuoka, "Cooperative control for sharing applications based on multiparty and multimedia desktop conferencing system: MERMAID," Proc. Conf. on ICC'92 (1992).

6. K.Maeno, A.Kurashima "Group cooperative work support system through the mobile and multimedia communications - mobile groupware," Proc. on Telecom95 Technology Summit, Vol.1 (1995).

7. Y.Hara, K.Hirata, H.Takano, and S.Kawasaki, "Hypermedia Navigation and Content-based Retrieval for Distributed Multimedia Databases," The 6th NEC Research Symposium (1995).

Collaboration with
Multimedia Documents

Hans Joseph, Edwin Klement
Fraunhofer CRCG, Inc.
167 Angell Street
Providence, RI, 02906, USA
Tel.: +1 401 453 6363
Fax: +1 401 453 0444
Email: hjoseph@crcg.edu
eklement@crcg.edu

Abstract. Multimedia documents become increasingly important for the success and growth of companies. Communication and collaboration based on documents become critical factors. Documents have to be processed in various ways by various people. Therefore, there is a need for powerful tools, which support the document handling in distributed environments. This paper describes an approach to distributed document handling and discusses the relationship with communication and networking.

1 Introduction

More and more companies are emerging as world-wide operating enterprises, where administration offices and manufacturing plants span different locations and time zones. At the same time individuals as well as groups in those enterprises have to communicate and to cooperate closely; i.e, they have to exchange information. The normal way to do this is by making telephone calls, sending faxes or mails. For example, today people typically fax time-critical documents for review and commenting. But often there is a need to verbally guide a reader or editor through a document (e.g., "change page 6, last paragraph, first line"). Sometimes even time-consuming queries about the meaning of written comments are necessary.

Fax or mail is composed of text, graphics, formulas, spreadsheets, Gantt charts[1], etc. The exchange of this kind of information in digital form is often done by downloading the appropriate files before they are viewed. These documents can be used as a basis for further discussion. Although applicable in some situations, this type of communication is likely inefficient in most cases. People would like to look at and to change simultaneously the same document even in a distributed environment.

---

1. Gantt chart, also referred as a bar chart, is a graphic display of periods of activity; e.g. workpackages of a project. Activities are vertically listed with other tabular information on the left side of the chart. Periods of activity are shown in form of horizontal bars.

Text   Graphics   Image   Audio   Video

Fig. 1. Multimedia Data Types

Within the last few years the traditional field of document editing has met the emerging fields of collaborative work, distributed systems, and multimedia documents. The different fields have grown together to become a single field dealing with collaborative distributed editing of multimedia documents.

2 Collaboration using Multimedia Data

The broad range of information types like text documents, audio and video data, images and sketches, and hyper-linked information structures must be handled uniformly. People who wants to create documents have to deal with five different types of media (Fig. 1).

These media types can be classified into two broader categories using as a criterion the capability of human perception[1]:

- time-independent media (text, images, graphics)

- time-dependent media (audio, video, graphics in animations)

Other criteria to classify multimedia data can be found by looking deeper into distributed environments. Collaboration between partners are done by sending multimedia based information between them. Special tools offer possibilities to support communication and to exchange information more easily. This field has grown rapidly in the last decade to incorporate a wide community of research. Searching the literature for this topic results in a huge list of applications (see [4]). Several categories of collaboration tools are available on the market like conferencing systems (with or without video or audio), shared whiteboards, or application sharing systems (Fig. 2).

Fig. 2. Conferencing Situations

Collaboration means to communicate with partners. In a collaborative environment three types of communication can be identified:

1. *Asynchronous communication*

   means unrestricted transmission delay. It allows collaboration without the simultaneous presence of all users. An example is electronic mail which is already an important tool for the exchange of information between people located around the world. The delivery time is significantly faster than surface mail but the sender does not request immediate response. Therefore, an acceptable latency rate for an email message ranges from seconds to a few hours.

2. *Synchronous communication*

   means bounded transmission delay. It allows collaboration that needs the simultaneous presence of all users. This requires delay restrictions for each message, but the upper delay bound can vary.

3. *Isochronous communication*

   means constant transmission delay under critical time constraints, but only at the final destination of the connection. Examples include conferencing, in which participants can use their computers to see and to talk to each other, and distributed interactive simulations.

The following table tries to assign the five types of media to the three types of communication by using examples from a collaborative environment:

	asynchronous	synchronous	isochronous
Text	Email	Talk	
Graphics	download CAD model	distributed interactive CAD design	distributed interactive simulation
Image	download pictures	shared whiteboard	animation previewing
Audio	download audio clip		audio conference
Video	download video clip		video conference

Table 1: Media types vs. types of communication

Reading text information and the processing by human perception requires time which depends on the context of the information. Therefore, assigning text to isochronous communication makes no sense. Very important in the context of a distributed environment is the isochronous communication. To "see" and, more important here, to "hear" are the communication methods of humans. The human perception is very sensitive to interruptions in the video and, even more, the audio delivery. Therefore, a continuous flow of these data with constant transmission delay is required. Today, in video conference sessions this fact is mostly ignored.

3 Distributed Document Handling

The management of multimedia documents like technical manuals is becoming an increasingly important competitive factor. The problems we face today in document handling are the following:

- to have the documents in the right place at the right time,

- to manage the huge amount of documents that already exists and will be created in future,

- to provide the document in different languages,

- to be able to provide mid- to long-term archiving.

Engineers developing products have to provide documentation concurrently during the whole *product life cycle*. Basically a product life cycle consists of specification, design, test, manufacturing, maintenance, and recycling. In every one of these steps an implementation of a *workflow* has to be met. Workflow are the activities involving the coordinated execution of multiple tasks performed by various groups or persons. By this definition the product life cycle itself is already a workflow. The workflow defines a reporting scheme. This scheme must be supported by the document processing system; especially an annotation mechanism reflecting the workflow has to be in place.

If we look into the document life cycle in more detail we identify the following steps:

- Creation, Integration and Updating
  In this step a document is generated, either originally or by compiling from already existing documents. Links refer to other documents. Once in a while documents have to be corrected or up-dated.
  Nowadays documents consist not only of text. We have to deal with true *multimedia documents*; i.e., documents consist of text, graphics, images, audio, and video. But the most important tool in the creation process is the editor, still.

- Archiving and Dissemination
  Documents are stored in databases, their information is indexed, classified and prepared for efficient retrieval, and further use.

- Use
  Documents have to be presented to a user in an appropriate way. I.e., text docu-

ments have to be presented in an easily readable layout. Hypermedia or on-line systems have to provide a viewer with an easy-to-use user interface and powerful search mechanisms. The same holds true for annotation systems.

The objectives of a flexible and powerful document server, are to develop methods and tools to overcome the problems with today's document handling. Our project focuses on the following goals:

- support of joint editing sessions,

- support of long-term archiving, retrieval and dissemination of documents,

- support of multimedia documents.

These goals will be reached by the following approach:

- Integration
  Existing and well-known software will be used. Missing links will be implemented.

- Use of standards
  The documents to handle have to be described complying with the standards SGML [5], HyTime [3], and others, which are appropriate.

In order to allow the authors access to parts of a document without excluding others totally, the documents stored in the server have to be *well-structured documents*. This is guaranteed by the requirement that the structure of every document stored has to be described in *SGML*.

SGML enables the editing and processing of electronic documents in a vendor- and platform-independent way. The SGML standard provides the approach and means to define the logical structure of a document in a grammar called *DTD (Document Type Description)*. A DTD consists of elements, attributes and entities. Elements are the basis to structure a document hierarchically. For the document server is able to understand DTDs, elements can individually and independently be addressed and retrieved from the document store. This means authors can work independently with elements, which are not sub-elements in use by others.

The architecture of the document server is based on the *client-server model*. Client and server are independent processes running on different hosts. Client and host have to be connected by a local area or wide are network (LAN/WAN) supporting the protocol TCP/IP; e.g., the Internet.

• The Server
  The server has access to the document store. It handles the requests from clients, sends out a directory list of the document store, retrieves DTDs, documents or elements of documents from the documents store, locks elements for write access, and stores documents and elements in the document store again.

- The Client

  The client provides the user interface to the document server and prepares the SGML documents to be processed by a commercial editing tool. In the current implementation the user interface is integrated in the product FrameBuilder of Frame Technology Corp. But our approach is not limited to products of this company. Basically any editing tool for structured documents, providing an Application Programmers Interface (API), can be used.

Another effort is spent in the area of workflow and annotations. The goal of workflow management is to increase the productivity by reducing the time documents need to pass the necessary processing and revision instances. For an efficient workflow management appropriate tools are required. A workflow system has to support all phases of the document life cycle; i.e., creation, dissemination, short-term storage, long-term archiving, retrieval, re-use, printing, and deletion. Workflow management deals with the issues of flow of documents among team members, the ownership of documents, i.e. access rights, and versioning.

The workflow and the revision process can be controlled by making appropriate comments and annotations to a document. For this purpose an annotation management tool is required. It has to maintain the connection between the original document and the annotations in order to guide the user through the revision process.

A document to be annotated has to be a structured, i.e. an SGML or HyTime document. The related document, which holds the annotations and workflow information and which is generated and processed by the annotation manager, is a structured document as well.

The annotation manager supports several types of annotations. There are implemented right now already:

- LongTextAnnotations

  The annotation is displayed in a window of its own. Therefore it can be of unrestricted length.

- ShortTextAnnotations

  This kind of annotation is supposed to look like Post-it' labels. It is displayed on the margin of the original document. Therefore the length of the text should be limited to only a few words like "o.k.", "Change this!", "I don't agree", etc.

- MarkerAnnotations

  This type creates an emphasis of text lines by underlining, double underlining, strike-through and overlining. It is to resume the traditional technique of red-lining a text.

The area of text, an annotation is related to, is marked in the display window of the original text. Clicking on those markers cause the display of the related annotation, if it is not already displayed (e.g. LongTextAnnotations). Annotations can be created, edited, or removed.

The Document Server in the current stage of development is running on SUN and HP workstations.

4 Technical Comments

In a collaborative situation bandwidth and latency time are important factors to implement an useful interactive environment. For example, CCITT has issued a set of recommendations (G.114) for planning networks to achieve quality voice transmission ([2]). A proven solution is to use a connection with guaranteed bandwidth where the line is not shared with other users. Dedicated line and ISDN are examples for this type of connections. The number of lines used between both ends determines the quality of service.

ISDN offers different kind of access to the digital transmission media. The Basic Rate Interface - or BRI - gives a subscriber two Bearer (B) channels occupying a bandwidth of 64 kbps (kilobits per second) each. Additional delta (D) channel[2] handle control messages in order to open, maintain, and close connection across ISDN. Applications using the Internet Protocols TCP/IP, UDP/IP, and Multicast run transparently over ISDN without modification. ISDN gateways can also act as gateways for other non-ISDN equipped systems residing on the same local network. In an ISDN-based connection the bandwidth is guaranteed in both direction because the line is not shared with other users or with the counterpart. To summarize all these facts, applications and scenarios for working collaborative benefits from these advantages.

However, to have a good quality video and audio ISDN connection together with other interactive applications, the numbers of B channels have to be selected carefully to optimize the bandwidth and to reduce the cost. One method to optimize the bandwidth is to take advantage of inverse multiplexing. Inverse multiplexing can be defined as the aggregation of multiple independent information channels across a network to create a single higher rate information channel. For example, if 8 different independent 64 kbps data channels are established between two locations, inverse multiplexing can be used to combine these channels to create a single 512 kbps data stream. This technique is mostly used when only one data stream will be transmitted.

For several independent data streams each with a small bandwidth requirement another approach can be realized. This method takes advantage of UNIX commands *ifconfig* and *route*. *Ifconfig* assigns an address to a network interface and configures network

---

2. Many locations within the U.S. offer B channels with only 56 kbps. This is because much of the older equipment phone companies are using assumes that the D channel is part of the B channel. For this technical reason only n*56 kbps can be used.

interface parameters. *Route* can be used to manually add or delete entries in the routing table to reach remote hosts. Normally, there is no way to specify the data path between workstations at different locations. Only a gateway can be specified to which packets can leave the local network. Between the gateway at sender site and the gateway at receiver site, the flow of the packets can vary. This fact can influence the bandwidth and the latency.

This is not true with an ISDN based connection between LANs. Between two ISDN network routers the bandwidth is fixed and the latency depends on the geographical distance. This configuration looks like the following diagram in an ISDN based connection.

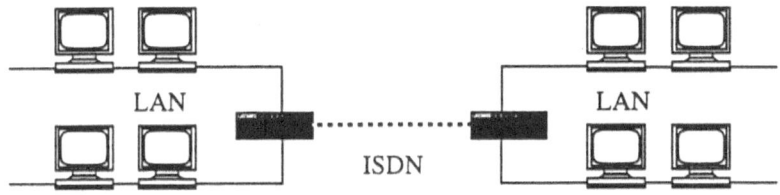

Fig. 3. LAN to LAN connection using ISDN

Normally, routing tables are maintained by the system routing daemon or through default routes and redirect messages from routers. Other remote hosts can be reached through external gateways by adding the routing path.

To increase the bandwidth means to find a way to specify at least two independent routes between two workstations. A solution is to have multiple IP addresses for a single network interface.[3] That allows to specify multiple independent data path between workstations by specifying several gateways. This configuration looks like the following diagram.

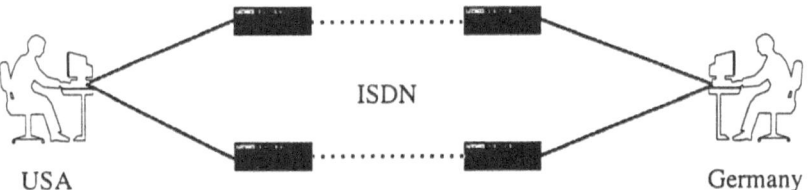

Fig. 4. Using multiple IP addresses for collaboration

The specification of at least two independent data paths increases the bandwidth. This allows to separate the data flow for each application. Lets assume the following situation. A conferencing session is planned with a video and audio connection and two

---

3. This is an undocumented feature of Solaris 2.x. For other operating systems like SunOS, SGI or HP-UX patches are available.

other applications. Usually each application asks for the IP address to establish a point to point connection, or takes advantage of the IP multicast protocol. In this example, a point to point connection is planned in which each workstation is equipped with two IP addresses. Than the video data stream can flow over the first connection, the audio data stream over the second. The data stream for the other applications can be split over both connections.

5 Conclusion

This paper gave a classification of multimedia data with regard to CSCW applications. Furthermore, an approach was presented for the handling of multimedia documents in a distributed environment. Based on the standards of the "SGML family" this joint editing system allows various authors to work with the same document at the same time. In this project we followed the technical approach to use as many commercially available tools as possible. Therefore a text editing tool or a document database was not developed here. But the glue was provided to enhance existing tools with missing CSCW capability. Future work will develop the annotation handling to a workflow management system.

6 Literature

1. K.Aberer, W. Klas, The Impact of Multimedia Data on Database Management Systems, ICSI-TR-92-065, International Computer Science Institute, Berkeley, CA, USA, 1992

2. Comité Consultatif International Telegraphique et Telephonique, Recommendation G.114 - One-way transmission time

3. International Organization for Standardization, Hypermedia/Time-based Structuring Language: HyTime, ISO 10744, 1992

4. Pal S. Malm, The unOfficial Yellow Pages of CSCW - Groupware, Prototypes and Projects, URL ftp://gorgon.tft.tele.no/pub/groupware, 1994

5. International Organization for Standardization, Information Processing - Text and Office Information Systems - *Standard Generalized Markup Language*, ISO 8879, 1986

"Media-On-Demand" Multimedia Electronic Mail: An Approach to Support Online Services

Kei Nam Tsoi and Syed M Rahman

Gippsland School of Computing and Information Technology
Monash University, Churchill, Victoria, Australia 3842.
Email: {Keinamt, Syed.Rahman}@fcit.monash.edu.au

Abstract: The existing design of e-mail systems architecture is effective for exchanging text-only message, but it is not capable of handling the multimedia message which has much larger volume, and requires more bandwidth and storage space than the text-only messages in order to store-and-forward the multimedia message. It is very slow and inefficient if the multimedia message is relaying on a slow network connection with limited bandwidth. Because of limited network bandwidth and disk spaces, some network mail handling system even set quotas for the mail data. In other words, if a mail message exceeds certain size, it will not be delivered to its intended recipients. We propose a "Parcel Collection" approach for exchanging multimedia electronic mail messages. This approach for exchanging multimedia electronic mail messages integrates the current WWW technologies with the existing electronic mail systems.

1 Introduction

Electronic mail system enables the users to send and receive messages electronically and efficiently. Multimedia electronic mail system has extended the power of text-only conventional Internet electronic mail system by enabling the users to exchange electronic messages incorporating multiple media types, such as graphics, still images, motion videos and audio. Some of the prototype systems with diversity of multimedia mail message exchange standards have been studied (Tsoi and Rahman, 1995, 1996). During the recent years, Multipurpose Internet Mail Extension -- MIME (Borenstein and Freed, 1993) has been increasingly adapted by the Internet communities as a standard for exchanging multimedia mail messages. MIME provides a framework for interchange of multimedia mail message contents including multilingual text, images, audio, video and graphs through electronic mail over the Internet. Vast amount of disk storage capacity and substantial network bandwidth are also required to successfully deliver mail messages containing multiple media of data. Most of the existing network environment is not yet favourable to deliver multimedia messages. Delay and failure in delivering multimedia messages are likely to occur due to insufficient network bandwidth and diskspace. Further more, there are too many data types for the mediums and it is difficult to predetermine parameters for the originator to ensure the message can be parsed on the recipient's system. In this paper, we proposed a "media-on-demand" (MOD) approach to ease this situation. The whole idea of this approach is to insert the hypertext reference links in the message and send the message as a MIME body part, instead of sending the actual content of a media data (i.e. Video and Audio) to the intended recipients. Media data are to be delivered only when the recipient is actually reading (has opened) the message. With this method, significant amount of network bandwidth and storage space on the recipient side is saved in contrast to the conventional way of message delivery. Further more, it ensures the mail message to be delivered faster, avoiding many unnecessary delays which is due to limited network bandwidth and storage spaces.

2 The Problem Issues Surrounding the Multimedia Electronic Mail delivery

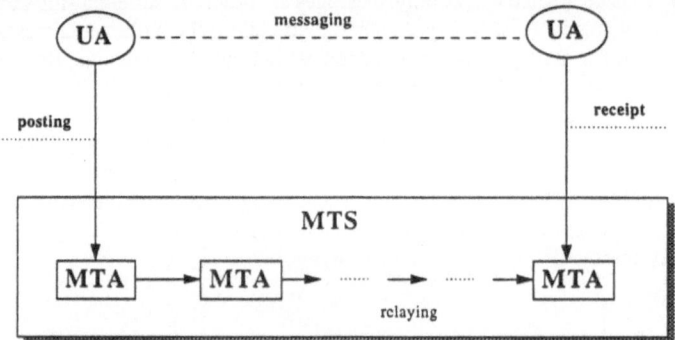

Fig. 1. A Model for Electronic Mail

For some background knowledge on how a mail message is delivered, Figure 1 describes the model for Internet message handling (Rose, 1993), in which, a mail protocol such as the SMTP is the Message Transfer Agent (MTA) providing store-and-forward (relaying) service. A mail message is transferred by a MTA to another MTA until it arrives at the destination. These MTAs are made up of the Message Transfer Services (MTS) on the Internet. This is quite effective in transferring text-only message, but when transferring multimedia message, having much larger volume than the text-only messages, more bandwidth and storage space would be required in order to store-and-forward the multimedia message. It will be slow and inefficient if the multimedia message is relaying on a slow network connection with limited bandwidth.

2.1 Storage Problem

Some mail messages are only sent to one recipient, but some are sent to multiple recipients by its originators. The difference might not be so obvious while these messages are text-only, but what if these messages are conveying multiple media data? It'll make significant differences to the requirement of storage capacities on the recipient's side. Normally the network administrator will set disk quota for the users' mail box. And therefore, if the mail box is full or having insufficient space for additional data, an incoming message is likely to be rejected. Further more, when sending multimedia electronic mail within the same department, it will be very inefficient to make multiple copies of multimedia data to the recipients especially as these messages will be stored on the organization's network server (i.e. POP3 server). Table 1 (Furht, 1994) provides example of storage requirements of some media data. If multiple copies of a single multimedia message are to be sent out, additional storage spaces are required to store the vast amount of media data. As such, it is economically not feasible to store multiple copies of the same message among the local users, because for example a 10 times more storage spaces would be required for storing 10 copies of the same mail message, and if a mail message contains 2 Mbytes of video data, it will require 20 Mbyes or more disk storage.

Table 1 Storage Requirements for Multimedia Data

Multimedia Data	Required Storage
500 pages of Text	1 MB
100 fax line Images (uncompressed)	6.4 MB
100 color Images (compress 15:1)	500 MB
10 min of Animation (compress 15:1)	100 MB
10 min of digitized video (compress 30:1)	550 MB
1 hour of digital video (compress 200:1)	1 GB

2.2 Network Bandwidth

The conventional way of mail delivery for multiple recipients is to make number of copies of a single message according to the number of recipients on the mailing list. More network bandwidth and time are required for the messages to be relayed through the Internet before it reaches all the recipients. Most of the current network capacity are not yet capable enough to cope with such heavy data traffic, specially it is inefficient to transfer a vast amount of multimedia data at the same time. Further more, it is not cost-effective to send redundant data over the network too. If a mail message containing a 320x640x16 pixels/frames (16 color) 16 frames/s animation, it means approx. 2.5 MB/s bandwidth is required for transferring the message. What would be like if there are multiple copies of this message to be sent at the same time? Table 2 (Furht, 1994) shows the network bandwidth requirements for transferring multimedia data. Mail messages with vast amount of data may also failed to be delivered due to the network limitations on the recipient's or the sender's side. In our existing setup, the network mail handling system do not handle messages containing more than 30000 lines or more than 3.6 Mbs.

Table 2 Network Bandwidth Required for Transferring Media Data

Media Data and Size	Bandwidth Required
Voice 8kHZ/8bits (mono)	6-44 KB/s
Audio CD DA 44.1 kHZ/16 bits	176 KB/s
Animation 320x640x16 pixels/frame (16 bit color) 16 frames/s	2.5 Mbytes/s
Video 640x480x24 pixels/frames (24 bit color) 30 frames/s	27.7 Mbytes/s

3 The Proposed Solution

The current network configuration is not desirable for multimedia message interchange because of limited network bandwidth and disk capacities. "Media-On-Demand"-Multimedia Electronic Mail System (MOD-MMEMS) is proposed to overcome the limitations outlined.

3.1 The Conceptual Framework of MOD-MMEMS

This approach is based on the idea of "Parcel delivery" in our physical world. Each mail message containing multiple media data is treated as a "Parcel". Instead of delivering them to the intended recipient's mail-box, the intended recipient will be given a notification indicating the arrival of the "Parcel" and as a reference for a later collection. This notification conveys the description of a "parcel", the date of arrival, recipient's name, where to collect, valid date (until when the "parcel" will still be available) and the methods of collection. When the "Parcel" is due to be retrieved, the collector's ID will be checked for verification.

MOD-MMEMS is basically an adapted system which provides multimedia and HyperMedia capabilities to the existing SMTP/POP electronic mail system. The major characteristics of the proposed system is outlined below:

a) Client-Server Architecture: It is a client-server architecture implementing a "Media-On-Demand" Client-Server framework, optimally utilizing the advantages provided by the WWW technology for message delivery and retrieval.
b) MIME conformance: It is a MIME conformance multimedia electronic mail system featuring that it is platform independent and is exchangeable in a heterogeneous environment.
c) HyperMedia-based message exchange: The mail message is translated into HyperText Markup Language (HTML) (Raggett, 1995) format. The HTML

document is then sent as a sub-type of MIME (i.e. Content-Type: text/html) via the Internet mail system. The actual contents of multimedia data are to be placed onto an OUTBOX multimedia database without inserting into the message body, and only the "reference link" of the media data is conveyed as a HTML document.

d) GUI and Direct Manipulation message composition: A multimedia mail message is authored in a WYSIWYG integrated multimedia environment. A message composer is implemented to serve this purpose.

e) Media Editors of user's choice: The message composer is equipped with various media editors for video, audio, still images, graphics and text, for composing multimedia mail message. Users have choices over which media editor to be used.

f) A multimedia mail message can be viewed on any system platform (either UNIX, PC or Silicon Graphic Workstation) as long as the user agent application supports MIME format and a World Wide Web Browser is available.

3.2 The Design

The system is first implemented on the PC under Windows™ and is scheduled to be ported to the SGI IRIX 5.3™. Design issues of MOD-MMEMS are concentrated on the four major areas; the message composition, translating RTF document to HTML format, delivery/retrieval of MOD-based messages, OUTBOX management and security considerations.

The recipient's mail system can use any type of WWW browser to display the HTML attachment file (i.e. a Web browser such as Netscape). The multimedia data message can be retrieved through hyper-links embedded inside the HTML document. The conceptual model of MOD-MMEMS's "Media-On-Demand" mail message delivery is presented in Figure 2.

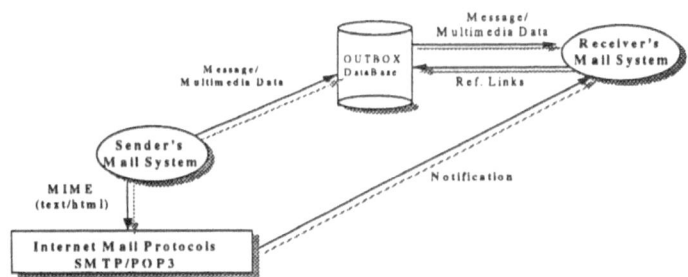

Fig. 2. A Conceptual Model for MOD-MMEMS

This model describes three major components:

• *The Internet Mail protocols:* MOD-MMEMS is designed as an add-on to the existing Internet SMTP/POP3 base MTAs.

• *The OUTBOX DataBase:* It is a MOD database management system located on the existing HTTP-based WWW server. The primary objective of the OUTBOX is to provide services of delivering multimedia data to its intended recipients.

122

Other additional services are such as authentication of the users, providing immediate responses upon the user's input, such as processing customer registration form or marketing questionnaires.

• *The sender's and Receiver's Mail System:* the MOD capable user agents (UA) possess the abilities to compose and deliver MOD multimedia message. A GUI message composer equipped with various media editors, and has routines for writing HTML documents and updating recipient's log for the OUTBOX DataBase. It is not necessary to be MOD capable for every UA on the recipient's side, as long as it supports MIME and has access to a WWW browser.

3.2.1 The Message Composition and Viewing. The sophisticated MOD-MMEMS message composer provides various media editors of user's choice for text (Multiligual), graph, still image, audio and video. The drag and drop, and in-place activation nature of the composer allows the users to copy, paste media data and to activate external programs (i.e. media editor/viewer) seamlessly. Figure 3 refers the procedures for preparing a "Media-On-Demand" multimedia mail message. After the user has composed a mail message, the UA translates the contents of the message into HTML document. The actual contents of the media data together with the HTML document are transferred to the OUTBOX, at the same time updates the recipient's Log.

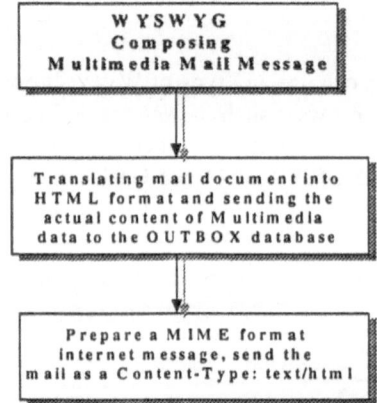

Fig. 3. The Preparation of "Media-On-Demand" Multimedia Mail

A randomly generated message ID, is assigned to the MOD mail notification. The MOD mail notification which contains an explanation of the nature of a message and a HTML document conveying information to request for the actual message contents from the MOD server.

3.2.2 OUTBOX Management and Security Considerations. The OUTBOX multimedia database system is managed by a file loader program. This file loader program is a CGI script which utilizes a server-push and client-pull technique for delivering multimedia data to the client side. A recipient's log is maintained for storing file identifications and the recipient's e-mail address. An entry of the log follows this format:

filename: recipient, recipient

Below is an examples of the log:

1. *For a file with a single recipient*
    Joe12345.html:joe@gcr2.fcit.monash.edu.au

2. *For a file with multiple recipients*
    Joe12345.html: joe@gcr2.monash.edu.au, amy@gcr2.monash.edu.au

The information within the log is added by the UA. When a file has been retrieved by its intended recipient, the loader program will delete the entries from the log (only the recipient's domain name will be deleted in the case of multiple recipients) after the recipient has downloaded the file(s). Figure 4 is the structure of the OUTBOX.

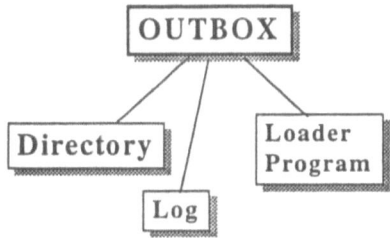

Fig. 4. OUTBOX Structure

Authentication process is carried out by verifying the combination of user's IP address, name and file identification parameter. Thus, the individual file of the OUTBOX is protected in such as way that only the recipient's user ID and password are both matched the entries within the OUTBOX log, in order to gain access to a particular file. When the recipient wants to get access to the files stored in the OUTBOX directory, an authentication process is carried out by the loader program based on matching the accessor's domain name with the records within the log. The loader program will receive the environment variable of accessor's user name and IP address (REMOTE_USER and REMOTE_ADDR, or REMOTE_IDENT, if the HTTP server supports RFC 931 identification) returned by the remote user. When the accessor 's identification is verified, the loader program will then retrieve the message from the directory and send the multimedia data over the network to the intended recipient. Figure 5 demonstrates the process of message delivery. With this message delivery mechanism, the sender is able to send the most updated information to the intended recipients, such information as stock market information. In such case, using a Server-push/Client-pull mechanism, the sender and recipeints may both be able to send and receive the most updated information.

124

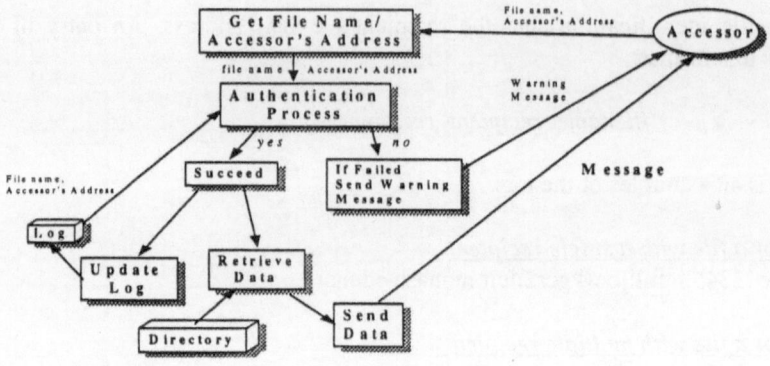

Fig. 5. OUTBOX Functional Model

4 Supporting On-Line Services

The MOD approach for multimedia electronic mail system will be beneficial to the on-line services for many application domains in the commercial area, such as sending marketing advertisement and customer promotion materials containing multimedia information to selected customers. This approach of delivering multimedia messages will not cause conflicts with the limited network resource and storage spaces on the recipient's site. Thus it is also an approach of delivering "customer-friendly" multimedia messages from customer's point of view. It reduces unnecessary consumption of network bandwidth and storage spaces while the customers have choice of what they what to retrieve after inspecting the contents of a multimedia message from the sender's site.

5 Conclusion

The main objective of this paper is to present the architectural design of Media-On-Demand MultiMedia Mail System (MOD-MMEMS). In this paper, we have illustrated an approach to ease the pressure that multimedia electronic message would place on the current network bandwidth and disk storage capacities. Although this approach has solved the problems that we have identified, yet delay in retrieving media data may occur on network which has very limited bandwidth, due to busy line or the file itself being too large. More researches are needed for the security mechanism design of MOD-MMEMS in the near future. And yet, the capabilities and benefits of this prototype can be further enhanced if a MOD server - "Post-Office" for our multimedia electronic mail communication, is exclusively designed.

References

1. Borenstein, N S and Freed, N (1993), *MIME -- Multipurpose Internet Mail Extensions*, RFC 1521 and RFC 1522, Sept. 1993.

2. Crocker, D (1982), *Standard for the Format of ARPA Internet Text Messages*, STD 11, RFC 822, UDEL, August 1982.

3. Furht, B (1994), *Multimedia Systems: An Overview*, IEEE Multimedia, Vol. 1 No. 1, Spring 1994, USA

4. Raggett D. (1995*), HTML 3.0 - Internet Draft*, http://www.acl.lanl.gov/HTML-WG/archives.html.

5. Rose, M T (1993), *The Internet Message - Closing the Book with Electronic Mail*, Prentice Hall, 1993, USA

6. Tsoi, K N and Rahman S M (1995), *Evaluation of Case Studies in Multimedia Mailing Systems*, Research Report - 5/95, Gippsland School of Computing and Information Technology, Australia

7. Tsoi, K N and Rahman S M (1995), *Architecture Evolution of Multimedia Electronic Mail with Conformance to Standards*, ISCA International Conference Proceedings on Computers and Their Applications San Francisco, 1996, USA

Interactive Teletraining Using Real-Time Computer Mediated Communication: Usability Evaluation from Experiences

L. Gradinariu, F. Sandoz,
G. Beuchot, P. Prevot[1]

Abstract The paper presents some original results of experiencing real-time group communication applications in teletraining. We describe the architecture of an open communication environment supporting training strategies specific to engineering domains. In the end we explain the evaluation methodology and the results obtained with some student populations trained in this environment.

1 Introduction

This is a collaborative project involving the Research Group for Multimodal Interfaces and Learning Material for Industrial Training (INSA de Lyon) and ROCAD Network Manager Center (CISM-Univ. Lyon1). It aims to asses usability of multimedia group communication applications for doing interactive teletraining. Our research is actually integrated as a part of TeleRegions Site User Networks (SUN) project from Telematics European Program. The start of our project was motivated (and also facilitated) by two new streams of interest in our university and research community:
- the deployment of video-audio conferencing applications across the campus (ROCAD) and the regional networks (RENATER)
- and the demand of new means for doing continual, distributed, "just in time", "on demand" education and training.
We've guided our research towards specifying a "collaborative environment" built upon a distributed architecture of applications and services able to offer communication functions and training resource access to users. We've looked for merging "classical" distributed computing and real-time communication services to serve user needs related to the collaborative activity they develop. The novelty of our project is that it offers a flexible context for "on field" experiencing of computer mediated real-time communication to achieve training goals. Several training sessions in the domain of mechanical engineering conducted with the first implementation of the environment in-lighted new solutions to accommodate the diversity of group communication during a session. Real needs are largely beyond those of a group conference session. Meanwhile our environment uses a set of

[1]All authors are with GRACIMP Laboratory, Research Group for Multi modalInterfaces and Learning Material for Industrial Training at INSA de Lyon, France. This work was technically supported by the Computing Center for Scientific and Medical Information of La Doua Campus at Lyon (CISM-Lyon1) , France.

conferencing applications made up available by diverse research groups for doing real-time, multimedia communication on the Internet multicast backbone. These applications play the role of communication services that a service integration network might offer to its users. A session specific controller maps user demands on an appropriate communication service application managing this association as required by the context and by the goal of his demand. The idea is to export human comprehensible "functions" to actors involved in training sessions. Using these functions they can set up and maintain an "on demand" communication services with a quality related to each communication role in the training session context.

2 Training Strategies in Computer Mediated Communication Environment

We define learning when students have mastered large, coherent bodies of knowledge and skill. Such coherent patterns of learning usually must accumulate over a series of courses and practical experience.

In the first step of our project, we have took as a model for the experimental environment the context of traditional teaching. The reasons of this choice could be explained by the fact that it was easier to predict their communication needs in a session context and that we can stand on their outcomes. We consider the latter reason very important in assessing usability of virtual environments.

While studying user reaction to limited possibilities to "copy" real-world interactivity in our environment we thought at new solutions to "feed" perception needs with other representations for the information they expect in order to obtain the same result and without affecting the quality of training. This is the most evolutionary part of our project.

Therefore we have paid a special attention to educational strategies, and then, we have studied which technologies are best for supporting those strategies. In this effect, we have identified strategies that students need to study and respects end-user communication needs. Strategies are defined in three different activities during a training session :

2.1 Perception

Perception is the first stage of learning. It consists of the "assimilation" or "memorization" of fundamental concepts during a course session. The teacher presents the knowledge and more specifically concepts with some slides and illustrates them by some examples and eventually technical demonstrations.

In this stage, students learn by heart : there is no integration of knowledge.

Students have the video of their professors on their monitor and have the possibility to ask to him some questions about specific points.

2.2 Understanding

This stage is assured with some cases of studies ; there are direct applications of the concepts previously presented. Students access to practical tools during a surveyed training session. To solve these exercises, they dispose of a hyper-media contextual help and courses slides from their "copybook". They navigate through them in a different way and at a different rate.

The teacher supervises, in real time, the work of the students and explains their eventual errors. So, students rectify mistakes and try the exercise again. They learn by doing it again or by solving an analogous problem.

2.3 Mastery

This stage is the higher level of learning. It integrates cooperative and collaborative strategies through any project.. Students work in group : they subdivided the project into tasks and into sub-group. They can collaborate by using a cooperative editor of text or drawing and more generally groupware to provoke active learning through work on complex projects, rethinking of assumptions and discussion.

In perspectives, we allow for extension of training strategies by using multimedia communication facilities :for example; in some specific domain, common video training support are very adapted to knowledge transfer. The professor has difficulty in teaching in computer mediated context because he has no visual perception of the comprehension feeling of students. So, we look for the future to introduce some indirect information representation (a visual indicator like colored flag) to replace visual perception needs.

3 CETTE: A Communication Environment for TeleTraining in Engineering

3.1 General Background

Since open distributed systems and multimedia applications have been involved in information technology projects, many research programs were carried on to improve learning systems and lately distant learning systems on these basis. We may cite some large programs like DELTA with CTA - Common Training Architecture[1] group of projects oriented towards defining standards for a distributed learning and training system, Telematics with MICE/MERCI [http://www.cs.ucl.ac.uk/mice] projects for improving research Collaboration through multimedia conferencing or Annenberg/CPB [http://www.learner.org] program an innovative movement in higher education to apply new developments in information and telecommunications technologies to teaching and learning (cost-accessibility-quality). We have retained from their experience some important aspects in designing an open learning environment:

- *generality* in order to accommodate different user profiles and pedagogical technics while standing on common, well-known technologies;
- *seamless communication* support as one of the most motivating factor in acquiring efficient learning;

- *accessibility* both for users and administrators and reported to costs and goals of the learning system.

We may also remind here some major issues which are not yet solved by actual implementation of open learning systems [6]:

- support for large scale use and experience with real users;
- accessibility from different locations;
- hardware support heterogeneity;
- architecture flexibility to tailor various organizational and functional models.

One may notice that the first three issues (so that the great majority) mainly address the communication subsystem of a learning environment. The ReLaTe project [21], a working demonstrator of multicast-based conferencing system for remote language tuition, proves that video, audio and shared whiteboard communication applications actually running across the Internet are potential solutions.

Our project uses communication tools of the same family but the approach we've taken towards designing the communication subsystem is different as discussed below. The goal is to develop a flexible environment which can accommodate styles, methods, behaviors specific to learning activity in respect of learning actors profiles and of learning objectives. Therefore we situate our research in the realm of the last major issue cited before.

In order to meet both the principles derived from other research experiences and our own constraints we have done the development and carried experiences within an intranetwork environment philosophy.

3.2 Approaches to a Flexible Communication Subsystem Architecture

There are few researches oriented to deepen the impact of real-time multimedia communication applications in open distance learning. We went further than other projects oriented towards using conference paradigm for doing teletraining. In our approach, video and audio channels are opened in response to user needs, they represent fonctionalities that the training environment offers to its actors to let them pursuit and accomplish each training step: talking to one's mate, finding trainer and asking him a question , see what others are doing on their screens or talking and designing in a group. Furthermore training activity itself seems to change to become more efficient by emphasizing the constructive aspect of learning through interactivity, collaboration and knowledge integration. Teaching migrates towards collaborative learning and transfer of knowledge and skills towards the development of competencies.

Designing a communication support for an open training system becomes a complex task as it is very difficult to find a model that can incorporate concrete representation of all these knowledge and ideas about the training system usage. The global behavior of the communication system is to network training agents and to link training resources to provide continuity, integrity and coherence to the training process. Diversity of communications and communication roles and representations in training activities complicates the communication system specification. Therefore starting from a toolkit framework like those proposed in [4], [18] was not a satisfactory design solution. Toolkits assume that communication is application independent [15] so that they can not accommodate diversity neither tailor communication quality to application context.

130

The scope of our project is within the synchronous systems for training in engineering. Consequently, the design of the communication subsystem is oriented towards supporting actors collaboration and training process on session basis. Sessions are computer mediated that is actors and resources access and interaction during a training session are completely integrated in a computer network environment.

The general quality requirement for information systems designers is to orient system conception towards satisfying user-needs and behavior minimizing technical influences and constraints. Within this aim we chose from the beginning to provide an environment that can support a large number of synchronous (hard and relax real-time) training activities. We also decided to consider that the high-level behavior of the communication system is to enable occurrence of each real-time training strategy specific to engineering domain (presented earlier in this paper) at distance and in single or multiples groups. This decision is motivated by the great need of training systems that support people in the execution of real job task (thus promoting the development of competence in an in-the-job learning)[10] as it is the case for engineering (chiefly design engineering). On one hand, in-the-job training is more motivating for learners and, on the other hand, it demands "just in time" access to the right "knowledge source" in an interactive and dynamic manner (enter and leave an ongoing session, alternate individual practice and work with real-time group training).

Taking as abstraction the training scenario, our communication environment has the following generic architecture offering a unifying interface to its actors:

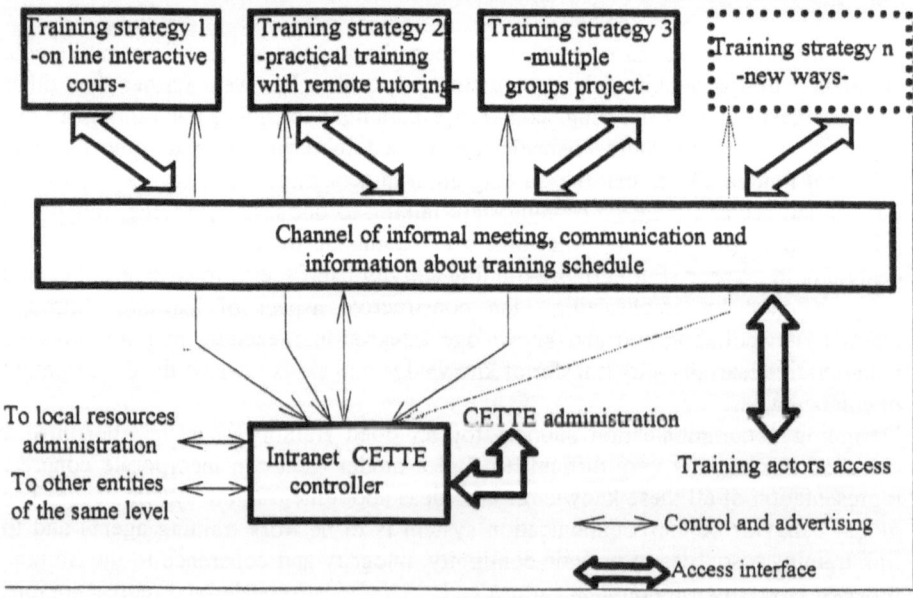

Fig. 1. CETTE, a flexible Communication Environment for TeleTraining in Engineering: generic architecture

The flexibility of this architecture is reflected by the fact that it is composed of slightly independent modules and each module might be instanciated. That means that in an intranetwork environment (the geographical scope is related to network administration and resources issues) we may have:
-concurrent environments;
- concurrent different modules within the same environment;
- concurrent instanciations of the same module within the same environment.
One of the most important tasks of the local controller is to solve this concurrence in respect of training actors (through the training scheduler), of the availability of local resources and of coherence with cross-environments sessions. As there is a single "informal" communication channel per environment (as well as local controller) we think that in an intranet context (or a well defined administrative domain) an environment may be associated we a certain category of users and/or training discipline within engineering domain. This makes easier training resource management and more coherent the contents of sessions schedule.

3.3 A Training Module Architecture

The usefulness of CETTE stands on its ability to interact with and to concretize a large variety of application programs in order to instanciate all functional aspects concerning a training session just in time and with an appropriate quality. Each session means instanciation of one or more training modules, at user demand and in respect of the session schedule. One may notice that there is not necessary that all training actors get into the session at the same time or for the same duration. They may have different access terminals [9] and different communication applications treating the same media. Therefore a centralized session control may be hard to implement to meet real-time session requirements. The light-session model was preferred [13]. Figure 2 presents the generic architecture of a training module with the classes of applications that might be involved in a training by its actors or by CETTE local control process. An alternative to the controller architecture would be the control channel. We did not explore this approach and in its actual version, CETTE starts a local control process whenever an actor connects to a session. This process takes into account what resources are needed by the training activity, identifies actor's profile and exports a functional user interface. While most of the audio-video and shared whiteboard communication control is dispensed to each communication application "called-up" by the controller at user demand, all aspects related to media presentation quality, communication channels priorities, failure on communication, dynamic groups communication, etc. are relevant to CETTE local control process. For many reasons [15] [20] it is implemented in Tcl/Tk language [16].

3.4 About CETTE Functional Specification Towards Supporting Teletraining

While the complexity of system architecture was generically solved by a "constructive" approach (specific to engineering domains), the functional specification is more complicated and relieves rather to phsyco-pedagogical knowledge and pedagogical experience. We pursued and discover rather by experience then by prediction how people organize their work and interact within each type of training strategy. We tried to respect natural feeling of group awareness (therefore we modeled multivue communication channels following the role of the actor involved in communication), or to substitute functions too hard to

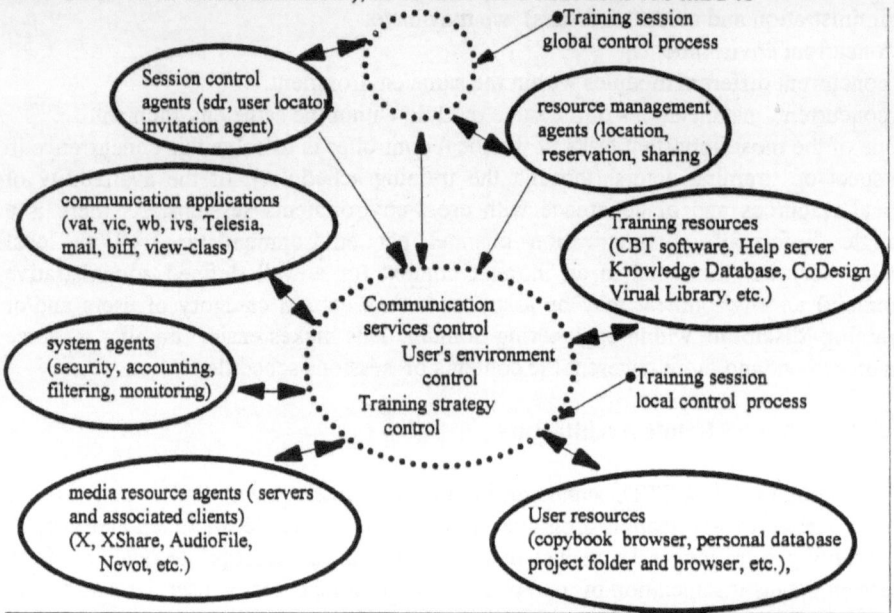

Fig. 2. Architecture of a local CETTE controller

implement in our development platform bounds with simples representations of the result of human perception (like feeding back to the trainer some information on students understanding of his talk by a system of color flags).

Following is a list of high-level communication functions and their scope in CETTE context.

Course:
- Class audio channel (floor controlled by trainer) (multicast to all)
- Trainer's video presence channel (multicast to all)
- Awareness on talk contents channel (multicast to trainer)
- On demand video channel for video clips included in course support (multicast to all)
- Shared whiteboard with attached telepointer (floor controlled by trainer) (multicast to all)
- Synchronous up-to-date of the knowledge database with the course contents (unicast to servers)
- Synchronous "personal copybook" associated with the shared whiteboard (local)
- Copy-book browser (unicast to server)

Remotely tutored practice:
- Class audio channel (multicast to students, on demand to trainer)
- Group audio channel (multicast to group)
-Trainer's audio channel (multicast to nobody, on demand to interested students)
- Student's screen feed-back to trainer (multicast to trainer)

- Help Desk access (unicast to server)

Collaborativ Project:
- Group audio channels (multicast to each group)
- Ringing video-phone (unicast)
- Group video-phone (multicast to group)
- Collaborative writing tool (multicast to group)
- Co-design tool (multicast to group, unicast to server)
- Group project viewer (multicast to group, unicast to server)

A snapshot on each actor's interface during a practical training session with remotely tutored (surveyed works) is presented below.

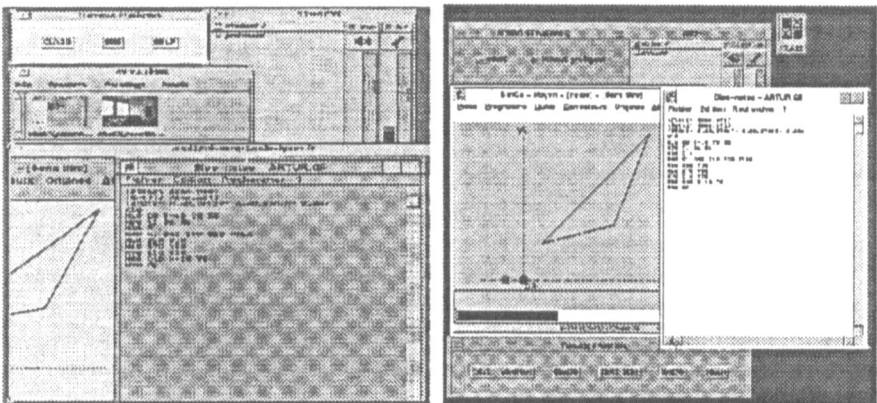

Fig. 3. Trainer surveying some students (left); Student discussing with the trainer about a command line (right);

The most important aspect here was to "qualify" different conferencing applications to answer these functional needs (which is to evaluate their usability in our environment). Actually, CETTE offers a static mapping between perceived quality (evaluated from subjective test results) and communication applications parameters. We envisage a dynamic mapping (managed by the session controller) using methods of assessing subjective (perceptual) quality based on evaluation of each media objective parameters.

4 Usability Evaluation and Assessment

4.1 Technology Usage Assessment

Developing good training evaluation procedures is difficult and expensive. Evaluation must take into account both training strategies and training environment. Their diversity is opposed to the generality aim of an evaluation method. Meanwhile there are two major issues to evaluate with a learning systems [Car94]:
- short term and long term training outcomes;
- user satisfaction.

We remind here that the goal of our project is not to evaluate training strategies (which we have considered good strategies!) but how computer mediated

134

technology is used to make effective these strategies. Therefore we consider that technology usability might be assessed starting from training evaluation results within CETTE.

4.2 An Evaluation Methodology for Computer Mediated Training Systems

Our evaluation method consists of sets of measurements on:
- training outcomes (knowledge transfer, concepts understanding and mastery of learned material);
- user behavior in the training environment (user satisfaction with the perceptual/usage quality of communication applications and access interface to CETTE);
- ongoing session parameters (timings of communication channels usage, latency, software fault rate, etc.).

A first series of experiments were conducted on two student populations with a course and a surveyed practice on numerical command language for mechanical tools:
- 19 students with a bachelor in manufacturing engineering (GPR) all knowing the trainer from their scholarship time and have a good background for attending the training subject;
- 6 undergraduate students (EURINSA) prepared for engineering domains therefore having general background for attending the training subject but never having encounter this discipline during their scholarship (they didn't know the trainer at all).
Sessions were carried with two or three students during one hour. The same kind of session with the same contents of the training material (course support, CAM software tool) was carried in a classical environment (class for course and practical laboratory) with two series of 4 students preparing their master in mechanical engineering. Definitely neither participant had knowledge of the training subject before the session.

4.3 Results of Tests on Training Outcomes

The aim of comparing training outcomes evaluation from tests done on people doing training in a traditional environment and those using CETTE is not to see which is the best way of doing training. This could not be done at our scale and with our means.
All participants followed the course (with one exception, a student looking rather for fun) and only one failed to finish the training exercise after the last delay (40 minutes). Undergraduate students were particularly serious and this is reflected in the results of their understanding and mastery tests. Bachelor students were rather enthusiast ones. Objective tests results (written answers at questions on trainer talk contents, a practical application of the talk and a technical problem to solve) showed clearly the limited role of multimedia as communication technology. Even though the sound was good people have selective memory on talk topics (gaps may be filled by background knowledge on domain as test "audio 2" shows it).
People working seriously can be trained to mastery even though they do not have a priori knowledge on concepts treated during the session. Consequently computer

mediated communication is not the barrier when integrating training at work place and using such technologies to develop collaborative learning.

Table 1 Short term memory and training outcomes tests results

population /environment		GPR/classic		GPR/CETTE		EURINSA/CETTE	
test	Max.	Mean	Std. Dev.	Mean	Std. Dev.	Mean	Std. Dev.
visual-graphics	1	1	0	0.84	0.37	0.83	0.4
visual-text	1	0.11	0.33	0.3	0.48	0.16	0.4
audio 1	2	1.44	0.72	1.23	0.72	1.16	0.98
audio 2	2	1.22	0.97	1	0.81	0	0
visual-audio 1	2	1.66	0.70	1.23	1.01	1.5	0.83
visual-audio 2	2	0.88	1.05	0.15	0.37	0.33	0.51
contents understanding	5	4.1	1.69	2.07	1.93	3.8	1.47
mastery	5	3.5	1.33	2.46	1.61	3	1.41

4.4 Results of Tests on User Satisfaction

In order to appreciate the satisfaction with a teletraining session, we proposed to each student trained on CETTE platform a subjective test. Because all students (and the trainer) were new to such an environment, questions are often addressed comparatively to a traditional environment to offer them a value reference. Answers are codified by affecting a value on a 1 to 7 scale were small values express better satisfaction. The choice of questions was very difficult. Questions role is to reveal not only satisfaction with technology, with communication using this technology but also personal opinion on training fulfillment and personal investment to achieve training goals. [11] and [17] were good starts for building our questionnaire.

Table 2 Satisfaction with a teletraining session: test summary

Topic of questions	Possible answers (and their codification)
Perception of teletraining environment	A1. frustrating (7), disturbing (5), without importance(2) A2. favorable to your training (1), unimportant (4), unfavorable(7)
Quality of access interface	A3. good(2), acceptable(4), inadequate(7)
Use of computer tools during the mediated session	A4. good (6), acceptable (4), inadequate (1) A5. very disturbing (7), moderately disturbing (4), not very disturbing (2)
Effectiveness of new technology	A6. sufficient (1), acceptable (3), insufficient (6)
Concentration	A7. more important (7), similar (4), less important (1)
Participation	A8. more important (1), similar (4), less important (6)
Interaction with the trainer (communication set in)	A9. easier (1), identical (4), more difficult (6)
Need to solicit the trainer	A10. amplified (2), similar (4), less (6)
Training without colleagues by your side is:	A11. a penalty (7), unimportant (4), a benefice (6)

Need to solicit colleagues	A12. more (7), the same (4), less (1)
Quality of feedback (conversation quality)	A13. good (1), similar (3), insufficient (6)
Existence of an on-line help desk is:	A14. necessary (1), normal (3), superfluous (7)
Accessibility of information from the on-line help desk	A15 difficult (7) normal (3) easy (1)
Motivation of students	A16. their reasons of motivation : novelty of technology (), direct relation with the teacher (), better knowledge acquisition (), their reasons of non-motivation : atmosphere (), difficulties to use tools (), not any faith in the environment ()
Part of video	A17. insuring (3), a help for better understanding (3), useless (7)

The same questionnaire was proposed to the trainer (questions that fit his role in the mediated environment). We present below the table of simple statistics on actors answers orderd by the result of an analysis of possible pricipal factors in their appreciations.

Table 3 Simple statistics of subjective tests

Answer	Mean	Std. Dev.	Trainer's answer
A4	2.14	1.93	4
A9	3.33	1.87	6
A10	3.52	1.53	2
A6	3.57	1.53	6
A8	3.00	1.70	4
A13	2.42	1.74	
A14	2.8	1.99	
A2	2.76	2.27	4
A11	4.95	2.5	5
A15	1.76	0.99	
A1	3.85	2.03	5
A12	4.85	1.19	
A17	2.95	1.62	3
A16	3.19	1.83	3
A3	3.76	1.84	4
A5	3.23	1.3	4
A7	4.04	2.26	7

In our codification we have considered that people's (trainers or students) need to interact more in this environment is good for achieving training goals. Meanwhile all subjects explained this need as being the compensation of their isolation (therefore telepresence implementation was not very effective).

We performed a factor analysis to identify if answer variables form clusters. As it is stated in [17] the clustering that results from factor analysis could be motivated either by wording patterns in a question or by the existence of a common construct.

Table 5 Oblique Principal Component Cluster Analysis
Total variation explained = 11.01372 Proportion = 0.6479

	variable	own cluster	next cluster	1-R**2 Ratio
		R-squared with		
cluster 1	A4	0.7396	0.3757	0.4171
	A9	0.7905	0.2385	0.2751
	A10	0.7665	0.2155	0.2155
cluster 2	A6	0.3125	0.0362	0.7133
	A8	0.5460	0.0363	0.4711
	A13	0.7483	0.1811	0.3074
	A14	0.6496	0.0534	0.0534
cluster 3	A2	0.6884	0.1750	0.3777
	A11	0.7317	0.0307	0.2768
	A15	0.6451	0.0901	0.3901
cluster 4	A1	0.5270	0.0180	0.4817
	A12	0.5098	0.0491	0.5155
	A17	0.5389	0.1663	0.5531
cluster 5	A16	1.0000	0.0829	0.0829
cluster 6	A3	0.4654	0.2141	0.6802
	A5	0.6588	0.2830	0.4759
	A7	0.6957	0.1651	0.3645

Table 6 Cluster Structure

Cluster	1	2	3	4	5	6
Eigenvalue	3.01	1.72	1.52	1.09	1.01	0.83
A1	0.134	-0.078	0.044	0.725	0.088	-0.062
A2	0.181	0.182	0.829	0.392	0.418	0.190
A3	-0.462	0.141	0.231	0.063	0.354	0.682
A4	-0.860	0.013	-0.040	-0.120	-0.121	0.612
A5	-0.532	0.236	-0.023	0.088	-0.145	0.811
A6	-0.097	0.559	-0.007	-0.132	0.190	0.177
A7	-0.314	0.129	0.072	0.249	0.406	0.834
A8	-0.064	0.738	0.095	-0.174	-0.032	0.190
A9	0.889	0.119	0.130	0.210	0.488	-0.383
A10	0.875	-0.048	-0.081	-0.035	0.140	-0.464
A11	-0.049	0.158	0.855	0.147	0.175	0.170
A12	-0.221	0.034	-0.192	-0.714	0.104	-0.036
A13	0.104	0.865	0.197	0.070	0.425	0.236
A14	0.078	0.805	-0.231	0.064	0.120	0.059
A15	-0.046	-0.300	0.803	-0.050	-0.083	-0.095

| A16 | 0.287 | 0.242 | 0.208 | 0.088 | 1.000 | 0.254 |
| A17 | -0.105 | 0.025 | 0.196 | 0.734 | 0.204 | 0.407 |

These results are provided by an Oblique Principal Component Analysis (VARCLUS procedure from SAS[SAS]) which identify 6 clusters based on variables correlation matrix. Clustering reflects that somehow items addressed by the questionnaire reflects some subjective factors characterizing user activity and satisfaction with the environment. The Eigen values of all 6 factors are high enough (the last is almost 1) and not very different so all factors are important.

We interpret the *first factor* as reflecting student position vis-à-vis of communication tools, training tools and trainer accessibility (*accessibility* to training elements). These are the two most important poles of the training environment (as knowledge and communication).

The *second factor* regroup items related to user *interactivity* with the elements of the environment (a measure of how active users are and if their perception of interaction is "synchronized" with what the environment offers to support interactivity).

The third and the fourth factors reflects user's satisfaction with the environment conditions of *awareness* (of training actors or of information sources). The *third factor* express this satisfaction from training goals point of view whilst the *forth* reflects the subjective, perceptual aspect of this satisfaction.

The *fifth factor* is *motivation* to be trained in a mediated environment which in turn reflects both actors satisfaction with the usage and their personal reasons.

The *sixth factor* reflects personal effort or investment cooperate with the environment which we call *tolerance* to implementation and tools imperfection.

This is a first, rough qualification of factors that influence .

Table 4 quantify these factors in the experimental version of CETTE. We may observe the difference between trainer's appreciations of these factors and students appreciations. This observation might be related to the difference between speaker role and listner role in a conferencing session remarked in [17]. Further experiences with more "collaborative" strategies (which attenuate role differences as users change oftenly the role in communication) shall elucidate this aaspect.

We may notice the correlation between tolerance and accessibility in Table 6.

Table 6 Intercluster correlation

Cluster	1	2	3	4	5	6
1	1.00	0.02	0.03	0.11	0.28	-0.55
2	0.02	1.00	0.02	-0.04	0.24	0.21
3	0.03	0.02	1.00	0.19	0.20	0.10
4	0.11	-0.04	0.19	1.00	0.08	0.17
5	0.28	0.24	0.20	0.08	1.00	0.25
6	-0.55	0.21	0.10	0.17	0.25	1.00

4.5 Measurements on ongoing session parameters

Within this class we include measurements (actually took "by hand") on:

- each training strategy session duration both in traditional and computer mediated environments. Each first usage of CETTE by an actor is preceded by an introduction to environment. Hereby are some results of these measurements (we recall that training support and subject are the same for each session of new users and in both environments):

    - course duration: 15 - 20 minutes (traditional)
    　　　　　　　　　　15 - 20 minutes (mediated)
    - practical training:　　20 - 30 minutes (traditional)
    　　　　　　　　　　20 - 40 minutes (mediated)
    - learn about the
    mediated environment:　15 - 30 minutes;

- latency of interaction
    - time to get effectively the floor:　0 - 135 seconds (mediated), mean=12s
    　　　　　　　　　　　　　　　　0 - 30 seconds (traditional), mean=5s;
    - time to get the image of what
    the student is doing on his screen:　3 - 10 seconds (mediated)
    　　　　　　　　　　　　　　　　3 - 10 seconds (traditional)
- communication tools failures　　2 X-server errors when loading new slide in
    　　　　　　　　　　　　　　whiteboard (students lost their "copybook");
- level of activity of training actors in mediated environment:
    - average number of questions per course:　2 (mediated)
    - time to answer a question:　　20 - 50 seconds (course), mean=25s
    　　　　　　　　　　　　　　5 - 100 seconds (practical training),
    　　　　　　　　　　　　　　　　　mean=40s;

These are rather maintenance and monitoring measurements. Their role of evaluating communication channels usage and tools latency will be undertaken by the accounting, filtering and monitoring module of user environment controller/

5 Conclusion and Further Work

The most important outcomes of our project are:
- an evaluation of feasibility of real-time, interactive teletraining across local/metropolitan area networks, argued by training outcomes and end-user satisfaction evaluations;
- a specification of communication application roles in teletraining environments and related assessment of quality requirements based on" in field" observations;
Our further research is oriented towards three important aspects of the environment:
- better interface between users and communication functions (new GUIs for communication service applications) and exploration of multimodal interfaces benefit;
- assessment of the relationship between perceptual quality and communication service parameters specific to teletraining activities in order to dynamically control the quality of services from information exported by communication applications;
- improving efficiency of training by using multimedia representation of knowledge and information and by exploring them in collaboration

- integration of new training strategies experienced by teachers and students and validated by evaluation tests results.

Acknowledgments: We want to express our gratitude to all researchers of the Internet community for making available their applications which are fundamental bricks of our environment. We think that discovering new ways of using, mastering or adapting such applications to real work environment get them more reliable and contribute to their promotion as new services across computer networks.

References

1. Alins, W.A. Verreck and P.I. Zorkoczy (eds.) Using Technology in Education and Training: Recommendations for a Common Training Architecture, Inderscience Enterprises Ltd, 1995

2. Caristan, P. Leonard, Usage and Quality Enhancement in Videoconferencing systems: The Telesia Approach, Technical Report, INRIA-Rocquencourt, FRANCE, 1995.

3. Carroll, M. B. Rosson, Managing Evaluation Goals for Training, Communications of the ACM, Vol. 38, No. 7, July 1995, pp. 40-60.

4. Craighill, M. Fong, K. Skinner, R. Lang and K. Guenefeldt SCOOT: An object-oriented toolkit for multimedia Alaboration, Proceedings of ACM Multimedia'94, October 1994, ACM, pp. 41-49

5. Deering, Host Extensions for IP multicasting, RFC 1112, August 1989

6. Derycke, C. Smith, L. Hemery Metaphors and Interactions in Virtual Environments for Open and Distance Education, Proceedings of ED-MEDIA95, Ed. Hermann Maurer, Graz, Austria, June 1995

7. Ehrmann What Does Research Tell Us About Technology and Higher Learning, Change magazine of Higher Learning, XXVII:2, March/April 1995, pp. 20-27.

8. Frederick, "nv" Unix Manual Page, Xerox PARC, CA, 1992.

9. Gradinariu, P. Prevot Local and Distant Aspects of Exchanging Multimedia Information in Distributed Class-room, in Multimedia and Video Coding, Plenum Eds, NY, 1995, pp 39-46.

10. Gredtschenko, M. Nysen, W. Stevens Education on the move. Alcatel Telecommunications Review, Special Issue for Telecom95, October 1995.

11. Hecht, Measures of Communication Satisfaction, Human Communication Research, Vol 4, No 4, Summer 1978, pp 253-264.

12. McCanne, V. Jacobson, Using the LBL Network "Whiteboard", Lawrence Berkeley Laboratory, Berkeley, CA, 1993.

13. Jacobson Multimedia Conferencing on the Internet, SIGCOMM94 Tutorial, London, UK, August 1994.

14. Jacobson, "vat" Unix Manual Page, Lawrence Berkeley Laboratory, Berkeley, CA, 1992.

15. McCanne, V. Jacobson vic: A Flexible Framework for Packet Video, Proceedings of ACM Multimedia'95, November 1995, San Francisco, CA.

16. Ousterhout, Tcl and the Tk Toolkit, Reading, Massachusetts, Addison-Wesley,1994.

17. Rao Dimensions of Satisfaction in Teleconferencing: An Explanatory Analysis Proceedings of the Twenty-Seventh Annual Hawaii International Conference of System Science, 1994, pp 124-133.

18. Roseman and S. Greenberg GroupKit: A groupware toolkit for building real-time conferencing applications. Proceedings of CSCW92, october 1992.

19. *** SAS User Guide, Version 6, First Edition, SAS Institute Inc., Cary, NC, USA, 1990.

20. Schulzrinne Dynamic Configuration of Conferencing Applications using Pattern-Matching Multicast, NOSSDAV95, Durham, New Hampshire, April 1995.

21. Watson, M. A. Sasse, J. Hugues Evaluating the Potential of Multicast Conferencing for Distance Education: A Case Study of Remote Language Tutoring, submitted to CSCW96, Boston, MA, november 1996.

A Content Based Retrieval Video System for Educational Environments

Antoni Bibiloni, Ricardo Galli
Depart. Matemàtiques i Informàtica
Universitat de les Illes Balears
Ctra. de Valldemossa Km 7,5
E-07071 Palma (Baleares)

Tel: 971 173204
Fax: 971 173003
e-mail: dmiabc0@ps.uib.es

Abstract. The interest in indexing and querying video data is growing rapidly. Desktop video is a new and attractive medium for communication between people using computers and networks. The main focus in any video information system is to develop a database management system with a friendly content-based retrieval of the digital video information.

In this paper, we present an on-line video system for educational purposes. The interface consist of two modules. An *annotation-video-interface* which can be used to put keywords, comments, proposal exercises, recommended lectures and so on in video segments. The annotations specify video sequences information for the automatic generation of a video library indexed by content. And a *query-video-interface* which can be used to extract the relevant segments of video that satisfy the specific query condition.

Also we will show how a standard relational database management system can be extended in order to handle queries by content. Based on these ideas, we have built a prototype video content-based retrieval system called *Educational Video On Line*.

1 Introduction

If we take a look to multimedia applications, their composition is defined by a *multimedia knowledge* (made up of text, images, video, audio, databases, etc.), a *user interface* (which shows multimedia knowledge to the user in an attractive way), a group of *interactive functions* (allowing the user to manage the multimedia information through the interface) and *network functions* (that connect clients with servers in a distributed environment).

We propose a way to structure video and two user interfaces that make video easier for annotation, browsing, searching and content retrieval [1][8][9][10]. Each video sequence should be indexed using the extracted content of their images and audio sequences. When we save this resultant information (start-finish, key words, date, etc.) we have the objects, backgrounds and actions descriptions of a structured video. We used this technique to develop an educational video information system able to run in different environments, platforms and networks.

Our system is highly dependent of the source nature (educational video) and it is oriented to solve the necessities at level of queries by content desired by students. Few years ago, the main problems were the storing of huge amount of information and the hardware limitations for real-time visualisation. Nowadays, these limitations are being overcome by new video compression/decompression techniques and network technologies. At present, the mainly problem resides on the difficulty to classify, store and retrieve video sequences based on content criteria when they deal with large video databases. Our aim is to provide a new digital video data model with content-based access to alleviate these problems and to motivate an extensive use of video resources for distant education.

2 Data Model

The methodology of educational video information system consists in using a defined model where the human intermediary (teacher) interprets and transcribes the semantics of the video sequences over this model. The computer-based transcriptions using automatic techniques from computer vision are not satisfactory enough yet. The use of the system consists in that only the indexes or combination of them can be used for building queries.

The data model that we propose for indexing educational video data is structured as trees [2] and follows the segmentation of shots, scene and segment presented in [1].

Our definition of the previous terms are:

Shot: *a minimum unit of continuous video frames, defined by its beginning and ending temporal points over the digital video source.*
Scene: *a set of sorted linked shots creating a compact content.*
Segment: *the presentation to the user of linked scenes under a criteria.*

Combining concepts of video indexing and characterising the queries, we noticed that three classes of entities should be interpreted and indexed to offer a good content-based retrieval:

Objects: They appear in the sequences and they can be lecturers, graphics projections, diagrams, etc.

Activities: They describe the subject of a given sequence.

Context Classes: They represent the general structure of the contents that reside in the video library.

For a better understanding of these structures we show some queries examples. The normal queries have the form : "Find all video sequences in which one context appears, where this context belongs to a specific activity and particular objects are involved in this activity". That means compound queries, comprising complex relationships among different objects and activities in a given context.

Examples:

a) Find all the video classrooms (activity) of mathematics (context class) where the teacher is Prof. Braun (object).

b) Find all the video conferences (activity) of computer science (context class) where the speaker is German (object) an the subject is Databases (object).

c) Find only the questions of the audience of the previous query example.

3 Architecture

The system architecture we propose is composed of:

1. DBMS.
2. Archive servers.
3. Annotation-interface.
4. Query-interface.

The DBMS stores the metadata files that contain attributes and relations among objects and activities. They also contain concise information about the location of the video data. The advantage of the metadata approach is that allows the user to examine the contents of a database without having to retrieval large video data [3][4]. The metadata concept is adequate for interactive multimedia applications, where a single presentation might involve different media sources (video, text, audio, etc.).

The archive servers store the digital video sources, which can be stored in different servers and are pointed by the metadata files. The servers run independent user processes that allow clients to retrieve the video segments. The processes are in charge of the implementation of different communication and retrieval protocols. By this approach we make the storing and retrieving tasks independent of the storage devices and network technologies. Indeed, changes on the archive servers and communication technologies do not affect the structure nor the indexes of the DBMS.

The annotation-interface is a client program that indexes objects, activities and context classes of the video source and then automatically updates the tables in the DBMS.

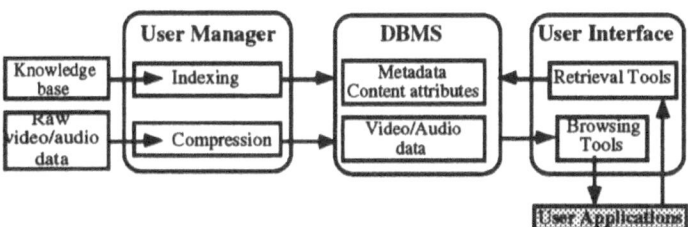

Fig. 1. Diagram of video management architecture

The query-interface is another client program. It connects to the DBMS to retrieve the metainformation and thus can get the corresponding video segments from the archive servers. The retrieval criteria is defined interactively by the user using the existing keywords and relations in the DBMS.

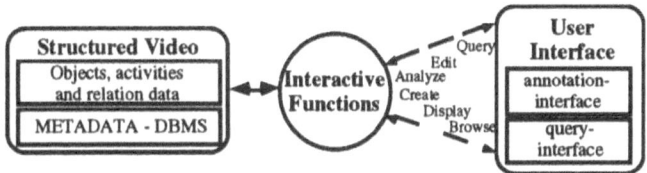

Fig. 2. Interactive user functions

4 Implementation Details

The goal of the project was to define and to implement a digital video database based on the object oriented approach proposed by S. Gibbs [11]. The video sequences come from the university lectures, conferences, workshops and seminars. Thus, the knowledge base covers a specific domain and it is enough to use keywords to provide consistent descriptions of the content. This set of keywords do fit in with the index of the courses' curriculum.

4.1 DBMS

The DBMS is the relational database Oracle, which is used to create and update the metadata files needed for video information management [5]. The metadata files store the attributes, the structures mentioned before and the pointers to the raw video files.

1. Course (*Carrera*)
2. Subject (*Asignatura*)
3. Lecturer (*Profesor*)
4. Lecture (*Clase*)
5. Topic (*Tema*)

CARRERA		
Codigo	N	4
Nombre	C	20
Descripción	C	Memo

PROFESOR		
Codigo_Prof	N	4
Nombre	C	40
......		

ASIGNATURA

Codigo_A	N	4
Codigo_C	N	4
Nombre	C	20
Curso	C	5
......		

TEMA

Codigo_T	N	4
Codigo_CL	N	4
Inicio	SMPTE	11
Fin	SMPTE	11
Descripción	C	20
Dependencia	N	4
......		

CLASE

Codigo_CL	N	4
Codigo_A	N	4
Codigo_Prof	N	4
Apunt_Vídeo	C	30
Fecha_grab	D	8
......		

Fig. 3. Index Tables

To describe the entities mentioned in section 2 (Data Model), we have implemented five tables (figure 3). Another table represents the relationships and hierarchy between keywords of the tables just described. Actually, this table implement a tree where the leaves are the logical video segments and the intermediate nodes represent video attributes.

4.2 Archive Servers

Although the video objects can be stored in different servers in the University's network, they are currently stored in an Alpha DEC server and it runs user processes that allow MacOS to mount its directories as remote file systems. The video source are stored as standard MacOS files in the server and they are accessed and read by the clients.

We film, digitalize, compress and save the video data of each lecture as a QuickTime file with sound track. To test the implementation we built a video database that contain approximately 10 hours of video material from course lectures given in our University.

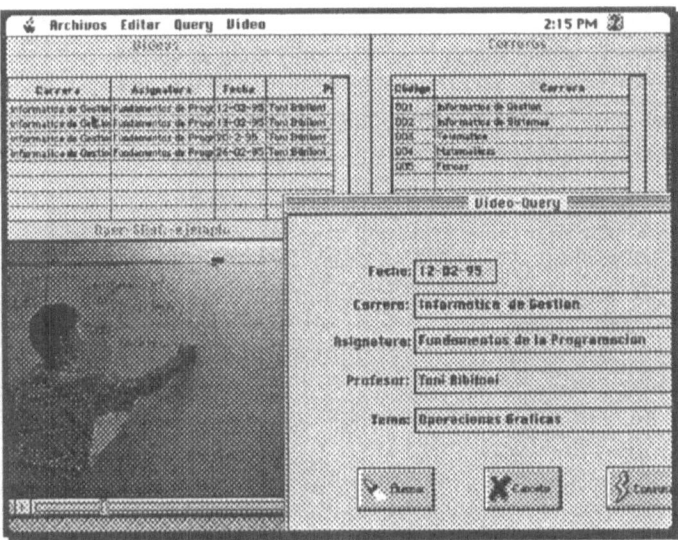

Fig. 4. Query Interface

4.3 Query Interface

We developed a graphical menu-driven user interface (query interface) which can interact with the DBMS and archive servers through the network. The query interface shows all keywords existing in the index of the DB to the user and allows her/him to compose a complex query by a combination of them. The user can consistently retrieve related portions of video by content using the keywords (see figure 4). This way of constructing the queries assures that no empty answers can be generated. The query can be constructed by a combination of logical operation on attributes such as courses, lectures, subjects and topics [6][7]. The query interface is also able to create new "virtual" video presentation from existing sequences.

The interface was designed in such a way that an user can use it without knowing neither the database's details nor any query language. The interface runs on Macintosh computers and it was implemented using the C++ language and the Oracle toolkit for Macintosh.

4.4 Annotation Interface

Another interactive program (annotation interface, figure 5) helps teachers to add annotations and to update the related metadata. The annotation process is a computer-assisted environment, where teachers can index their own lectures previously digitalized and saved in the archive servers. Users watch to the video sources and add keywords by selecting an initial frame by clicking on the window when the frame is displayed. The program asks for the keyword and then waits for the user to select the

148

final frame. During an indexing session, users can look up and select previously recorded keywords. The metadata is automatically updated on-line.

The program runs on Macintosh computers and it modifies the metadata tables through network connections to the Oracle DBMS.

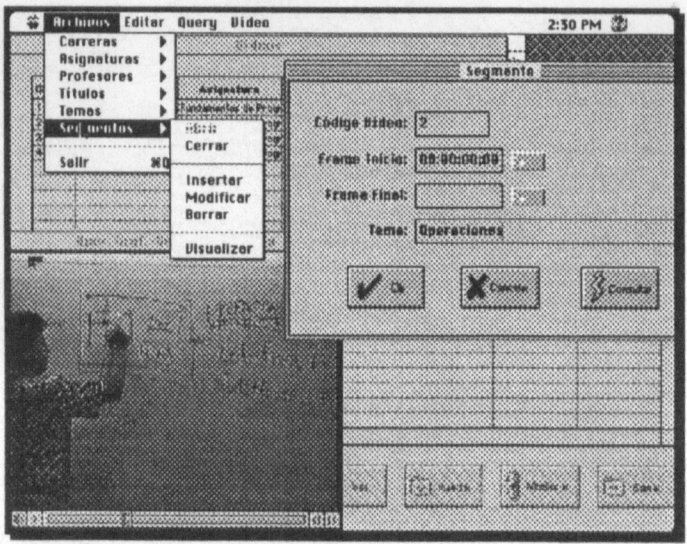

Fig. 5. Annotation Interface

5 Conclusions

With the spectacular growing of information networks (Internet) and with new tertiary storage systems like juke-boxes and compression techniques, a huge amount of video data is available. As such video data becomes more and more widely accessible, the necessity of indexing this data becomes more and more significant. Furthermore, translating the user interface to WWW can exploit the benefits of using Web technology.

As result of our experiments with the system we realised that the teacher's extra work for indexing and metadata updating is relatively small compared to the time we took just to compress the sequences in a Quicktime file. This demonstrates that for educational purposes, where the contents of the topics are well defined previously, our indexing techniques have shown to be adequate.

On the other hand, when testing the system with the students, they understood very rapidly how to use the program to construct complicated queries in order to retrieve desired lectures' segments. Indeed, they were motivated and satisfied with the possibility of attending the desired lectures as many times as they wanted.

Although we accomplished our major goals, we faced several problems due basically to the local network technology. The UIB LAN is divided in Ethernet (10 Base-T) segments connected to a FDDI ring. Our Macs were attached to a different segment that the DEC server was, so the bridges increased round-trip times and lowered speed transmissions, so no real-time could be achieved. The latter forced the query interface program to read all the video segments from the server, save them in a local hard disk and just at that time display them in order to get a reasonable visualisation quality.

6 Future Work

The next step is to add new features to the system, mainly those aimed to offer automatic concatenation of sequences given the specific (an combined) content. The last may turn out in a system able to provide a full-course video presentation from isolated indexed sequences.

To improve video quality for real time transmission, we are setting up a 16 Base-T segment which will provide us with a reasonable quality of service. For long distance transmission, we are developing network modules for ISDN boards for both sides, the server archives and the user interface programs.

On the other hand, we are investigating the complexity of to adapt the system to CATV technology. Getting a circuit oriented communication in these systems is very complicated due mainly to the topology of the network, which is composed of one-way repeaters and coaxial cables. Exploiting the high bandwidth of the cable channels, we can broadcast the video segments and metadata at higher velocities. To allow the home computers (query interface) to select those parts that the user is interested in, we send an extra "directory-metadata" information which gives the indexes and time-codes of segments.

References

1. Yoshinobu Tonomura, Akihito Akutsu, Yukinobu Taniguchi, and Gen Suzuki. "Structured Video Computing," IEEE Multimedia Magazine, Fall 1994.

2. Stephen W. Smoliar, HongJiang Zhang. "Content-Based Video Indexing and Retrieval," IEEE Multimedia Magazine, Summer 1994.

3. Little, et al. "A Digital On-Demand Video Service Supporting Content-Based Queries," Proc. ACM Multimedia 93, Anaheim, CA Aug 1993.

4. Little, Dinesh Venkatesh. "Prospects for Interactive Video-on-Demand," IEEE Multimedia Magazine, Fall 1994.

5. Samuel DeFazio, Bruce Croft, et al. "Integrating IR and RDBMS Using Cooperative Indexing," SIGIR´95, Seattle, Washington, USA, July 1995.

6. Louis Weitzman, Kent Wittenburg. "Automatic Presentation of Multimedia Documents Using Relational Grammars," *ACM Multimedia 94*, San Francisco, California, 1994.

7. Sibel Adali *et al*. "Advanced Video Information System: Data Structures and Query Processing," http://www.cs.umd.edu//projects/hermes/publications.

8. Antoni Bibiloni, Ricardo Galli, Bartomeu Estrany. "Content Based Retrieval in an Education Video System," to be published in *ED-Media 96*, AACE, Boston, June 1996.

9. Antoni Bibiloni. "Representación, Indexación y Recuperación del Contenido Vídeo", *CEIG 95*, Palma de Mallorca, Spain. 1995.

10. Subrahmanian. *Multimedia Databases Systems*, Sushil Jajodia (Eds.) Springer-Verlag 1996.

11. Gibbs, D. Tsichritzis. *Multimedia programming: Objects, Environments and Frameworks*, ACM Press/Addison Wesley. 1995.

Evaluation and communication techniques in multimedia product design for "on the net university education"

Francisco V. Cipolla Ficarra

Universitary Audiovisual Institute
Pompeu Fabra University
La Rambla 31, E08002 Barcelona, Spain

and

Department of L.i.S.I. — FIB
Polytechnical University of Catalonia
c/ Pau Gargallo 5, E08028 Barcelona, Spain
E-mail: ficarra@goliat.upc.es

Abstract. We consider how the quality of software — in this case multimedia "on the net" — is influenced by several factors that are exogenous to a programming code. The analysis of a layout, a dynamics, a content, a structure, facilitates the acceptance of multimedia products. In other words, the objective here is to present the advantages of having a method for the evaluation of multimedia usability, the results of which can be used to improve the design of interactive applications with a certain level of complexity, such as distance university education. This paper presents the communication recourses and the methodology employed in the design of educational multimedia packages for the first virtual campus of an open university based in Barcelona. It also explains circumstances that affected directly or indirectly its creation.

1 Introduction

Electronic networks will create a supple environment for corporate and university training and management programmes. An on-line, networked conferencing and instructional facility can provide a real-time "ecology" of extensible and interactive systems. Such a facility integrates various pedagogical and communications media such as the computer, telephone, modem, handbook, and video film, for example. There has been a steady growth in open and distance learning as an alternative and a complement to face-to-face teaching in education by mail or correspondence courses. The advantages of distance education include economies of scale, the possibility of students combining study with full-time paid work or domestic duties and versatility in patterns of study [14].

There is a consensus that future generations of computer system for open and distance learning must incorporate various tools and activities in order to provide the flexibility required by new learning situations and different learner needs [7]. Multimedia technologies inspire active learning by letting students participate in the instructional process, and advancements in these technologies may significantly improve education. The use of multimedia technologies is known to be extremely effective for many diverse educational scenarios. Visual technologies, i.e., static graphics and animations, are beneficial to learners in many ways. Also, it is widely recognised that multimedia offers means of improving education and learning environments: it provides more objective and expressive presentation of knowledge. Furthermore, it makes simulation-based learning possible [12] [20] [22].

The main aim of the project was to enable people with no previous experience of working with a computer to:

- Become acquainted with the basic functioning for the input and output of data.
- Handle the main options in an operating system, a word processor, a spreadsheet, a database, a electronic mail, etc.
- Communicate with the university by E-mail, sending or receiving information in order to participate in classes, conferences, etc.

2 Techniques for design oriented multimedia evaluation

The first question to ask when embarking on an evaluation is: what makes for educationally effective multimedia?. This is very important question, because the effects of multimedia may be subtle. Therefore, evaluations of multimedia must be carefully performed in order to prevent a piece of software from being prematurely accepted or rejected [13] [15]. The usability concept is of great help here. But usability is frequently associated whit five parameters: easy to learn, efficient to use, easy to remember, few errors, and pleasant to use [19].

The minimal criteria when designing an interactive product for student could be summarized thus:

- Ease of use (can a student use it with minimal help?).
- Educational rating (what can a student learn from this program?).
- Entertainment rating (is this program fun to use?).

Evidently, an interactive program should be interesting for both partial and complete navigation. Besides giving the information, a multimedia system should offer entertainment and maintain the attention of the user. That is to say, the contents could permit a diversity of focuses, and should have audio-visual abundance and attractive resources. But it is necessary to measure the components. We need evaluation methods and quality criteria for this goal.

The HDM model facilitates the task of evaluating of interactive systems [8] [9] [5], because it permits the detailed analysis both of elements of content and of structure in interactive multimedia products. The outputs in the HDM model are very important, because their concepts can be extrapolated to various areas of the social sciences, for example semiotics [3].

From the point of view the content it is interesting to analyze the homogeneity of the multimedia product, i.e., what elements are necessary in order to achieve the unity. This problem finds a solution with the notion of isotopy [3]. The notions of entity, collection, index links, etc. (in order to extend these concepts, consult [10] [11]) are employed in the function of evaluation. The following diagram is based on a heuristic analysis process:

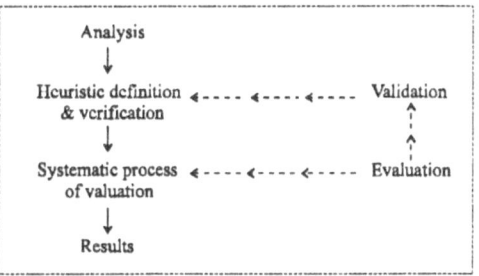

Fig. 1.

We have elaborated an index similar to a chart (see Appendix 1) with all elements and criterium that we considered necessary into a first stage in order to evaluate the quality of an application of multimedia —this chart is constantly updated. This chart has been tested with a set of 60 commercial CD-ROMs. They are commercial products from North America and Europe, widely distributioned and internationally commercialised. Here the principal criteria adopted are: richness, ease, consistency, self-evidence, predictability, readability and reuse [8]. Also, we introduce other criteria of analysis in order to increase the quality: isomorphism, transparency, motivation, autonomy and control, naturalness [5]. In brief, decrease the noises into the process of communication between the multimedia applications and the user.

For example, in this project when two users or more have been observed having problems with a specific aspect of the interface, then that aspect is refitted. Designs are modified, extended and refined according to findings suggested by the testing stage. The main obstacles proved to be handling the operating system — Windows or System 7 — and sending E-mail, and in an attempt to overcome this the signs used for navigation were changed, mainly to red circles, with some arrows. The latter were originally thin, but were later made thicker, and an eye was introduced to denote the emulation of real processes. A series of orange ellipses for use within the text was also incorporated.

It is the first attempt to assemble several criteria in function of four dimensions through the analysis of commercial CD-ROMs: content, layout, structure and dynamics. Thus, a primary one-to-one relationship exists between content and structure. However, between the four basic components there is a bi-directional relationship and each of their constituent parts often function as small units or subclasses which are themselves interrelated. Multimedia could be described as a joining together of media, on different levels and with more or less recognisable forms, towards an intersection of media with "a language of its own". Graphically, this could be represented as:

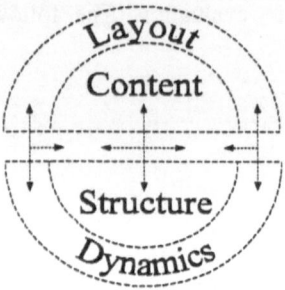

Fig. 2.

After the analysis of the group of CD-ROMs, we are currently working on four new sub-categories inter-related with the previous ones. These are: resources of acceleration in the interaction, and principal elements for basic and efficient navigation (inter-related with the dynamics aspect). Isotopy lines, and a tendency toward the simulation of the reality (inter-related with the layout aspect).

3 Planing the work

The short time of production (the production period was barely one month) made it necessary the application of several methods of elaboration to the environment of the social sciences as to the computer sciences. We are at a stage in that the software requires social sciences [2]. For example, a multimedia product must not ignore the cultural differences that exist between different geographical points of same country.

If the degree of success of a multimedia application is directly related to making a complex subject matter clear and accessible to a wide audience, then in designing interfaces for learning we need to take into consideration the same principles that good teachers use when they prepare a lesson for a new group of students. In order to do this, it is necessary:

• to highlight the main centre of interest;
• to reduce the presence of secondary elements;
• to eliminate superfluous details.

The design stage is the key *par excellence* to the success of a product, since its consequences may be economically negative if there is no type of evaluation that can be encountered by users.

4 Resources of communication

4.1 Comic and characters

As well as the obvious geographical drawbacks, one of the obstacles to overcome within distance education is that of the different levels of education and/or knowledge among prospective students that must be taken into account when designing a software package. As a result, it was decided to use the animated character or comic as a medium, since it has yielded highly positive experiences in education. The comic is an important recourse of communication and of teaching.

In these educational multimedia packages there are two characters, one a young man casually dressed so as to be readily identifiable as a student, whose main role is to be a friendly, ever-present guide through each sections. The other character is a young woman teacher with a more formal look, whose function is to evaluate the knowledge acquired.

Care was taken in the portrayal of facial features (the area of strongest expression in comics), arms and so on, in order to communicate as directly and colloquially as possible, because the human face plays the most important role for identification and communication [17].

4.2 Animation and graphic features

How can we use animation to create more attractive, useful, and efficient interfaces?. Animation can help cut through the complexity of an interface. For example, it can show what can or cannot be done, guide a user as to what to do or not do, or review what has been done. In other words, animation can help us review the past, understand the present, and describe the future. It can help us answer the questions: Where am I?, What else is there to do?, Where should I go next?, and How can I get there? [1]. That is to say, it helps navigate around the multimedia. Furthermore, animation in the multimedia can:

- Represent complicated sequences of steps and bettering situations more realistically and convincingly than textual explanations.
- Maintain the user's interest in the navigation and promote their progress in the topics.
- Increase the sensation that the user is making considerable progress (gaining time).

The graphic appearance is a principal factor in the acceptance or in the rejection of multimedia. We have basically employed two-dimensional graphics. However, there are a numbers of items into the menus. The numbers are on spheres. This is a small simulation of 3D. The graphic features can be divided into three groups:

- Those used for the characters (movement of arms, legs, hair, etc.).
- Those simulating the real effect of options of the programmes, such as the opening of certain windows. After the trials an eye was inserted (which closes when the option is chosen) to offer the student the option of seeing the simulated version of what is being explained.
- Graphic tools (arrows and circles for highlighting words or options). This method avoids the need for extensive simulation and leaves space free for data storage.

Also, there is just one fade-in screen, featuring a photograph of the university building and one fade-out screen (see fig. 6).

4.3 Colours

Colours are for the most part warm, to catch the eye: red for arrows and circles highlighting buttons and bars, green for the eye, and yellow for the character's hair. The text is black on a white background. Users of an interactive system should feel as if they are reading a newspaper [4].

Most people, in a communication process, absorb the message in the following way: 10% of what is read, 20% of what is heard, 40% of what is seen, 80% of what is both heard and seen [6]. The coherence of graphic aspects is therefore important, 40% is what is seen being absorbed, yet, to give an example, certain norms regarding colour are violated a priori, due, for example to anthropological or psychological factors. Colour is not an absolute. It is a perception [21].

Adults have a preference for cold colours (blue, grey, etc.), children the warm colours. Claims that blue is the preferred colour in Western countries are confirmed for 50% of persons questioned. Green follows with 20% and white and red with 8%. This occurs throughout western Europe, North America and Australia. Spain is the exception, where red in first place [16]. In Argentina and Brazil the favourite colour is blue, before red and white. In Japan the favourite colour is white (40% of those polled) then black and yellow [16]. One must think about these axes, because they have influence regarding the acceptance or rejection of an multimedia product.

4.4 Text and style

The text attributed to each of the characters is presented in speech balloons telling the user what to do –continue, repeat, consult the manual, etc. Users disliked pages with one or more screens of unstructured text. They do not want to read much [18].

The information in each section is stored as an inverted pyramid, that is, a topic is first approached in terms of its basic, general concepts, the details being followed up subsequently. Graphically, one begins at the base of the pyramid and progresses towards the top. This is a way of focusing the attention of the user at the beginning of the text, since it decreases as the reading advances.

The language used is colloquial, with short sentences (not more than 15 words). Understanding is difficult when there is more than 20 words and few verbs — a good proportion is 7 words approximately for each verb. Vocabulary is thoroughly comprehensible, avoiding abstract words. Verbs are in the present tense and active voice, which makes it more expressive and is easier to understand. Style should be simple, clear, and exact. Phrases have been included to evaluate and encourage the learning process, such as "very good", "carry on", "excellent", etc. (see fig. 6).

4.5 Structure and arrangement of information

Everything that is on the computer screen has a communicative value. The aim is to structure these elements so that the attention of the user is drawn towards the areas that the designer considers most important rather than randomly. Consequently, one of the priorities is to establish a centre of interest in which the most important element is highlighted and made evident to the user.

This centre of interest is not a simple geometric centre such as those found in the works of Escher. It is also an expressive centre, linked to the elements of the layout and accentuated by the contrast factor, for example. The types of contrast include lines, forms, dimensions, tones, colours (cold and warm, leaving the warm ones closer to the eye of the user and the cold ones further away), light, etc.

Leonardo da Vinci spoke of "La divina proporzione", that is to say, dividing the space in which to paint the proportional form. By drawing a cross on a sheet of paper there are four areas: upper right, upper left, lower right and lower left. The upper right zone has a greater intensity for Latin people.

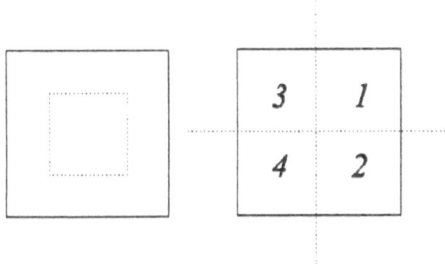

Fig. 3. Number 1 indicates the area of the most important visual centre of interest and number 4 that of the least important one. The navigation keys are located in area 2. The characters will change position to leave the central area free for choosing options or reading an explanation.

The arrangement of elements on the screen of these educational multimedia packages is similar to the design of the first page of a newspaper [4], and this is a diagram of the structure (E-mail multimedia product):

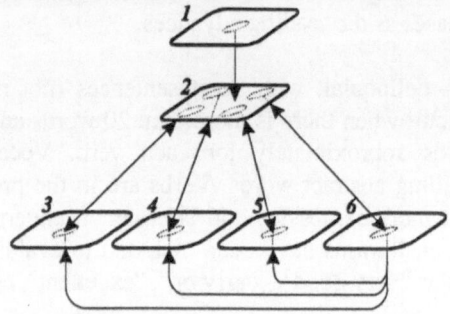

Fig. 4.

Sequential explanation of the basic concepts and the navigation keys (screen 1). List of subjects with 3 options plus self-assessment and indication of the path followed (screen 2). Between screen 2 and each of its derivatives there is a two-directional relations (options of forward, back and go to main menu). Self-assessment (screen 6). The exit option is always present in all screens.

Now we consider other characteristics of the arrangement of information on the screen in these educational multimedia packages:

Fig. 5. The young boy, ever-present guide through each of the sections.

a) The central part of the screen displays everything concerning the topic being explained. Here we find the characters, their speech balloons, windows for programmes (if applicable) and other signs (circles, ellipses, arrows, etc.). The windows for the applications presented in the contents area were obtained from the real programmes.

b) There is a main menu for each of the main topics, and submenus for the secondary ones. The options are numbered, the number turning grey when selected. Users who are acquainted with the contents can do only the exercises.

c) The buttons for navigation, with simple options ("continue", "return", "go to main menu" and "exit") are along the bottom of the screen.

d) There are two types of flat screens, superimposed on a background which serves for identification and navigation, arranged according to the vertices.

e) In the top left corner there is an icon which represents the topic currently being explained, for example the operating system Windows. Next to this is the title and below the sub-title selected in the secondary menu. On the opposite edge is an icon with the name of the university. On the bottom left there is the exit option next to the principal topic. On the right, there are buttons for continuing, returning and going to the main menu or list of contents.

f) In the event of having to consult the manual, an additional icon appears, in the form of an open book.

These features remain constant throughout. The main reason for this is that through their semiotic function they provide an anchor for the contents, and mark isotopes (lines of meaning) between the various parts of the interactive system [3]. In this way, homogeneity is guaranteed throughout the communication process.

4.6 Exercises

Here the exercises perform the function of consolidating the knowledge that has been acquired, and force the user to pay more attention.

Once a topic has been presented there are several evaluations of the learning process, in which the teacher appears and presents the user with a blackboard showing questions on the topic concerned, along with several possible answers from which the user must choose the correct one.

If the answer is correct (see fig. 6), the teacher shows her satisfaction by animation techniques (raising her arms and smiling); conversely, in the event of a wrong answer, the teacher's hair stands on end. However, the user will always be presented with the right answer, and advised to repeat the topic if mistakes have been made.

160

Fig. 6. The young woman teacher evaluates the knowledge acquired.

4.7 Manuals and video film

Within distance education there are two fundamental variables: place and time (i.e., same time: conference, different time: mailing). Educational multimedia can provide the basis for an exploratory learning system but that by itself it is incomplete, needing to be supplemented by more directed guidance and access mechanisms. There is a need to reinforce the multimedia message in a virtual campus or in networked university education through the use of manuals and videos.

In our project the multimedia system is on diskettes rather than CD-ROMs, since many home users in Spain still lack facilities for CD-ROMs. This makes it necessary to reduce the interactive message and use other means of communication:

1) Manuals: a number of manuals have been published to explain in greater detail some concepts displayed on the screen. These manuals reproduce the original software on the screens. However, the handbooks have an important function in the process of distance education.

2) Video film: there is also a video film on hardware aspects.

5 Conclusion

The results obtained in an analysis of usability improve the design of multimedia products, even when the public is heterogeneous and from different parts of the world. The key word for these cases is "simplicity". The traditional strategies of communication used in the different media still help — to a certain extent — to eliminate the problems raised by new technologies that can be encountered by users.

Of course, there are a number of guides available for designing multimedia products, but none of them include precise keys for a perfect. It is necessary continuously to measure each aspect of usability, and the iterate in a hill-climbing manner toward a better system.

To conclude, we believe that the presentation of educational topics through animated character or comics can be highly positive, and this medium has already proved its worth as an educational tool. Given the characteristics of the students (different ages, different locations, lack of previous experience with computers), navigation through the text has been kept as simple as possible. The colloquial language also helps to make the topics more readily understandable. The text is presented in short sentences, in black on a white background, in the style of a newspaper. In brief, the package combines communication strategies used in mass media, human-computer interaction, computer animation, education, and has shown highly satisfactory results to date.

Acknowledgments

Open University of Catalonia.

References

1. Baecker, R., Small, I.: The Art of Human Computer Interface Design. Addison-Wesley, pp. 251-267 (1992).

2. Basili, V., Musa, J.: The Future Engineering of Software —A Management Perspective. IEEE Software, Vol. 24 N° 9, pp. 90-96 (1991).

3. Cipolla-Ficarra, F.: A Method that Improves the Design of Hypermedia: Semiotics. In: International Workshop on Hypermedia Design, Montpellier. Springer-Verlag, pp. 249-250 (1995).

4. Cipolla-Ficarra, F.: The Importance of Visual Components in the Creation of Educational Hypermedia Packages for a Virtual Campus. In: Evaluation panel at the Hypertext '96. Seventh Hypertext Conference ACM, Washington (1996).

5. Cipolla-Ficarra, F., Berenguer, X.: Towards a Set of Rules for Evaluating Interactive Multimedia Products from the Viewpoint of their Content, Structure, Dynamic, and Layout. In: First International Workshop on Evaluation Methods and Quality Criteria for Multimedia Applications: Garzotto, F., Thuring, M. (eds.): ACM Multimedia, San Francisco (1995).

6. Fidalgo-Blanco, A.: Multimedia for education and productivity. Objectives vs. objects. In: Proceedings of World Congress Multimedia, Sitges (1993).

7. Derycke, et al.: Metaphors and interactions in virtual environments for open and distance education. In: Proceedings of ED-MEDIA 95, Graz, pp. 181-6 (1995).

8. Garzotto, F., Mainetti, L., Paolini, P.: Multimedia Design, Analysis, and Evaluation Issues. Communications of the ACM, Vol. 38, N° 8, pp. 74-86 (1995).

9. Garzotto, F., Mainetti, L., Paolini, P.: Multimedia Application Design —A Structured Approach, Designing Multimedia User Interfaces. W. Shuler, J. Hanneman (eds.): Springer-Verlag (1995).

10. Garzotto, F., Paolini, P.: Design and Usability Criteria for Multimedia Application Evaluation. In: First International Workshop on Evaluation Methods and Quality Criteria for Multimedia Applications: Garzotto, F. and Thuring, M. (eds.): ACM Multimedia, San Francisco (1995).

11. Garzotto, F., Paolini, P., Schwabe, D.: HDM: A Model-Based Approach to Hypertext Application Design. ACM Transactions on Information Systems, Vol. 11, N° 1, pp. 1-26 (1993).

12. Hawkins, J.: Technology and the Organization of Schooling. Communications of the ACM, Vol. 36, N° 5, pp. 30-34 (1993).

13. Hutchings, G., et al.: Authoring and Evaluation of Multimedia for Education. Computers & Education, Vol. 18, N° 1-3, pp. 171-177 (1992).

14. Jones, A., et al.: Providing Computing for Distance Learners: A Strategy for Home Use. Computers & Education, Pergamon Press, Vol. 18, N° 1-3, pp. 183-193 (1992).

15. Lee, A. et al.: Is multimedia-based training effective? Yes and no. Human Factors in Computing Systems (CHI'95). ACM Press, pp. 111-112 (1995).

16. Maffei, L.: In International Conference: Colours of Life, Torino. Hubel, D., Hillman, J. et al. (eds.): La Stampa, pp. 60-67 (1995).

17. Magnenat Thalmann, N., Thalmann, D.: The World of Virtual Actors. Virtual Worlds and Multimedia, Wiley, pp. 113-126 (1993).

18. Nielsen, J.: A home-page overhaul using other Web sites. IEEE Software, Vol. 12, N° 3, pp. 75-78 (1995).

19. Nielsen, J.: Hypertext and Multimedia, Academic Press, pp. 143-162 (1990).

20. Owen, S., Morris, M., Fraser, M.: The Development of a Multimedia Training System for a Water Treatment Plant. Computer & Graphics, Vol. 17, N° 3, pp. 243-249 (1993).

21. Vetter, R. et al.: Using Color and Text in Multimedia Projections. IEEE Multimedia, Vol. 2, N° 4, pp. 46-54 (1995).

22. Woolf, B., Hall, W.: Multimedia Pedagogues —Interactive Systems for Teaching and Learning. IEEE Computer, Vol. 37, pp. 74-80 (1995).

Appendix 1 — Set of rules for evaluating interactive multimedia products

[C] = Content [L] = Layout [S] = Structure [D] = Dynamics	
• Static (passive) media:	[C]
a) Formatted date. b) Text strings. c) Images. d) Graphics. e) Maps.	
• Active (dynamic) media:	[C]
a) Video. b) Sound. c) Animation.	
• There is a predominance of:	[C]
a) Animation. b) Sound. c) Video.	
• Synchronisation between: audio, text and images.	[D]
a) 0/1 sec. b) 2/5 sec. c) 5/10 sec. d) More.	
• Different languages:	[C]
a) English. b) French. c) German. d) Italian. e) Japanese. f) Portuguese. g) Spanish.	
• Interaction direction: a) By queries. b) Explorative.	[D]
• Input and output interaction time:	[D]
a) 0/1 sec. b) 2/5 sec. c) 5/10 sec. d) More.	
• Input recognition (cursor and symbolic for recognising the input)	[D]
a) Sandglass icons Windows: Static. Dynamic. b) Special: Static. Dynamic. c) None.	
• The user and navigation:	
1. Feed-back levels: a) Only visual. b) Visual and sound. c) Nothing.	[D]
2. Constant possibilities for:	[D]
a) Escape. b) Option changes. c) Content printing. d) Message writing.	
3. Content levels: a) Only one. b) Several.	[C]
4. Advance motivational effects through the multimedia environment:	[C]
a) Phrases. b) Sound. c) Images: Static. d) Animation.	
• Error treatment: a) Feed-backs in order to avoid them. b) Various levels of helps.	[D]
• Explanation of the functions of the navigation icons:	[L]
a) In the presentation. b) In the help. c) When the arrow is placed over them. d) None.	
• Organisation of textual: a) Normal pyramid. b) Inverted pyramid.	[C]
• Focal point of the narration (the narrator):	[C]
a) The narrator says more than the characters know.	
b) The narrator says the same as a particular character knows or sees.	
c) The narrator says less the main character knows.	
• Semiotics:	
1. Isotopy:	[C]
a) Homogeneity between the main topic and secondary topics.	
b) Correlation between images and texts.	
2. Topology:	[L]
a) The same position for the navigation keys. b) Shared text and image screen position.	
3. Coherence of graphic aspects:	[L]
a) Base colour: Primary. Secondary. Primary & Secondary combination.	
b) Base texture: Text, colours and images. Only text and images. Only images.	
c) Transparencies: All screen. Frame.	
d) Illumination effects: Ambient. Omni-directional.	

e) Effects of 3D: Borders with shades. Reflection of light. Diffuse of the image.	
f) Video: Colour. Black & white.	
g) Camera effects: Zoom in. Zoom out. Horizontal movement. Vertical movement. Angular movement.	
h) Plane: General. Medium. First.	
i) Emission movement: Constant. Stop or break.	
j) Animation classes: Morphing. Only 2D. Only 3D. 2D and 3D.	
k) Typographies: Classical. Special.	
l) Object or image presentation: With rendering (a perfect finish). Without rendering. Wire.	
m) Photographies: White & Black. Colours. Wire.	
n) Drawings: White & Black. Colours. Wire.	
o) Key of navigation: 2D. 3D. Static. Animation. Arrows. Special Icons. Draws.	
• Effects of images motions: Zoom in. Zoom out.	[D]
• Printer: All screen. Part of screen.	[D]
• Plays:	[C]
a) Classical: Chess. Checkers. Puzzle. Reversi. Others. b) Special development.	
• Sounds:	[D]
a) Possibility of changing the volume. b) Possibility of eliminating the volume only.	
• Screen aspects:	[L]
1. Transition types:	
Cut. Dissolve. Random Bars Horizontal. Split Vertical Out. Split Vertical In. Wipe Up.	
Vanish. Blinds vertical. Blinds horizontal. Blinds central. Checkerboard. Diagonal.	
Spiral. Uncover. Strips. Cover. Box in. Box out. Fade Through Black.	
2. Screen content attention elements:	
a) Special symbols: Circle or ellipse. Squared or rectangle. Arrows. Icons.	
b) Sounds. c) Words.	
3) Space occupied by animations and videos on the screen:	
a) Full screen. b) A frame on the screen.	
• There are a map of the structure (tree and roots).	[C]
• The content of the text is on lines.	[L]
• Available browsing methods:	[S]
a) Single word or phrase search. b) Alphabetical index of node names.	
• Number of quantity nodes displayed at one time: a) Only one. b) 2/3. c) More.	[S]
• One node and one frame.	[S]
• Do similar nodes have similar frames?	[S]
• Nodes: a) Go home. b) Go back one node. c) Go back several nodes.	[D]
• Structural links: a) Unidirectional. b) Bi-directional. c) Grouping.	[S]
• Entities: a) Sequences of components. b) Trees of components.	[S]
• Entity types: a) Physical objects. b) Abstract objects.	[S]
• Collection of entities: a) 1/5. b) 6/10. c) More.	[S]
• Web index.	[S]
• Components have two or more perspectives.	[S]
• Basic types of access structures:	[S]
a) Graphic: Circle. Arbitrary. b) Linear. c) Circular. d) Indexed. e) Tree.	
f) Free-form network.	

adVISer –Application of a Visualization Paradigm to Multimedia Design

Ulrike Spierling, Tanja Koop
Computer Graphics Center, DECADE
64283 Darmstadt, Germany, email: [ulisp,koop]@igd.fhg.de

Wolfgang Müller
Fraunhofer IGD, Dept. Animation & HD Image Communication
64283 Darmstadt, Germany, email: mueller@igd.fhg.de

Abstract. The problem of how to find an appropriate design for a user interface for hypermedia applications has certain similarities with the problem of finding a suitable visualization for data and information, which is a central topic in the area of Scientific Visualization. In this area a paradigm based on the determination of user, data, domain, and resource model has been proven to be a suitable approach for the selection of an appropriate visualization method. In this paper we will introduce this paradigm in more detail and propose how it can be transferred for the design of hypermedia user interfaces. We explain how this paradigm was applied for the design of a specific hypermedia application, the visualization assistant adVISer. Finally, we discuss the additional constraints to the paradigm imposed for applications in the WorldWideWeb.

1 Introduction

With the strong growth of the WorldWideWeb, hypermedia applications are finding increasing resonance in very different domains such as electronic banking and on-line magazines. This involves an increasing need for multimedia interfaces which are specifically designed for the various application domains. A central problem in hypermedia and multimedia design lies in finding appropriate media and representation forms for the information to be presented. Even today, the successful design of a multimedia user interface is still considered an art. Interestingly enough, the similar question of how to find an appropriate visual representation of certain data has been a topic in the field of Scientific Visualization for a long time. In this paper, we want to discuss the relationship between these two areas. This relationship will be illustrated in conjunction with a specific application, a multimedia visualization assistance tool. First, we will briefly discuss the problems in the field of Scientific Visualization and justify the requirements for a user support tool for the visualization process. We will present the solution strategies applied to the development of this tool, and will give a short overview of the underlying visualization paradigm it is based on. Then, we will show how this paradigm and similar approaches could be applied for the design of a multimedia interface. As a concrete example for the application of this paradigm, we present the hypermedia visualization assistant adVISer. Finally, we will discuss the presented multimedia design principles in the context of the WorldWideWeb.

2 Scientific Visualization and User Assistance

Scientific Visualization exploits human visual capabilities for the detection of correlations and structures and has been proven to be a good (and sometimes the only) way to gain information concerning unknown data. However, deciding on the most appropriate visualization method is a very difficult problem. Often, it is not obvious which technique should be applied, and on which kind of graphical primitive the data should be mapped. This problem is of great importance, since an unsuitable visualization may lead to wrong conclusions.

Certain rules and rule systems exist for the support of a user during the visualization process [1, 18, 2, 15, 5], but not only is their scope generally very limited, they are also not available as an on-line help system and are consequently not appropriate as a support for daily work. Moreover, they are not appropriate for modern, time-dependent visualization techniques such as animation. On the other hand, a couple of different automatic visualization systems exist [9, 14, 12, 8]. Most of them, however, are also practically limited to a specific application domain and do not provide an introduction or any additional information concerning the suggested visualization techniques, which might be needed for a successful interpretation of the visualization results. Furthermore, these systems do not provide any means to identify related techniques which might be more appropriate. This is a problem if, for instance, the user could not give a detailed specification of his visualization goal.

As a consequence, a different approach to support the user during the visualization process is necessary, which
- provides an on-line tutorial on different aspects of visualization,
- can be used as an on-line glossary to look up specific visualization methods and techniques,
- can be used as a workspace for an intelligent search of appropriate visualization techniques for a given problem, and
- allows the direct application of the selected technique to the given visualization problem

all at the same time. Information about the different visualization techniques has to be available in a complete and comprehensive form. Thus, presentation and interaction means, such as text, still images, video, animation, interactive animation, sound, and hyper-navigation need to be applied to introduce the various topics. As a result, an intelligent visualization assistant based on hypermedia technology is required. In the following paragraphs, we discuss the theoretical framework such a tool has to be based on.

3 Underlying Visualization Paradigm

The central part of every visualization process is the classification and selection of the visualization techniques according to their appropriateness for specific application problems. A general solution for this problem does not exist; however, we can present a paradigm which may direct the user to the selection of a suitable visualization method. This paradigm we are relying on is based on the complete definition of the following components for every visualization problem [11, 3]:

- a *data model*, which describes the content data as well as the structure and source of this data,
- a *user model*, which describes the user's visual skills, his experiences, his preferences, and his specific aims and expectations of the visualization,
- a *domain model*, which consists of information about usual presentation types and metaphors of the application area, and the application-specific tasks to be performed, and
- a *resource model*, which contains a description of the available resources, such as the display and hardware system used, and the available visualization and interaction techniques.

Once these components are fully defined for a specific visualization problem, it is possible to classify the available visualization methods and techniques according to their expressiveness and effectiveness in this context [9]. In general, this results in the selection of appropriate visualization methods and corresponding mappings of the data and information onto the visual attributes of a presentation. Similar strategies for manual and automatic selection of visualization methods and mappings have been successfully applied in the field of Scientific Visualization in the past [1, 9, 8].

It is worthwhile to discuss these different models in more detail. The *resource model* defines the starting list of visualization techniques and mappings. In addition, qualitative descriptions of the available hardware and software packets [4] may define further constraints on the usability and effectiveness of visualization techniques in certain cases.

The basis of the *data model* is a classification of scientific data. Here, two aspects are most important: the type data values and the dimensionality of the data. Regarding the first aspect, scientific data can usually be divided into qualitative and quantitative data. For qualitative data, one can further distinguish between nominal data and ordinal data, thereby defining an additional order relation of the data. Quantitative data is usually divided in data based on an interval scale and data based on a rational scale [17, 13]. While data of the first type enhances ordinal data with the possibility of measuring distances between data values, data of the second type also allows for the calculation of ratios. Moreover, data sets are usually classified with respect to the dimensionality of the independent and dependent variables. Since it is possible to classify visualization techniques in a similar way, a list of techniques an be generated, whose, so-called meta information, could potentially express and visualize the information in the data set. Additional meta information may provide additional clues for an appropriate mapping of the data. Knowledge about a potential spatial and temporal relation of the data, for instance, can be exploited to map these dimensions onto the corresponding dimensions in the visualization, thus optimizing the effectiveness of the visualization.

Similarly, the *domain model* describes factors which mainly impact the effectiveness of a visualization. Domain-specific tasks, and, thus, domain-specific visualization aims, knowledge about valid metaphors and standard visualization methods in the specific application domain can be exploited for an appropriate ranking of visualization techniques.

Finally, additional constraints on the selection of visualization methods are imposed by the *user model*. Aside from providing a description of the visual abilities of the user, the goal of the visualization represents an important element of the user model. This element has a certain impact on the expressiveness and effectiveness of a visualization, since not all techniques and mappings are appropriate for the different aims the user wants to achieve. While such aims can be very complex in general, the following basic goals can be identified when analyzing unknown data, which are: summary reading, elementary reading, and comparative reading [2]. During elementary reading, the user performs a directed search and tries to identify certain elements and their attributes. Comparative reading is characterized by performing comparisons between different elements and their attributes. Summary reading describes the general process of exploration, when the goal is the detection of structures, correlations and trends. Here, preserving the global structure of the data during the visualization mapping is more important than a direct mapping of each data element attribute.

In a standard application environment, resources and domain model do not change very often and, thus, can be well defined. Consequently, a pre-selection of visualization techniques fulfilling the expressiveness criteria can be performed in advance. The data model and parts of the user model, however, have to be determined for each visualization problem anew.

4 Application of the Visualization Paradigm to Multimedia Design

In the design of multimedia and hypermedia applications, different kinds of information have to be mapped on media elements, which again have to be arranged on the computer screen in spatial, temporal and conditional layouts. Screen Design Techniques, which represent a very important part of multimedia design, are problem-solving models for visualizing information in a way that reduces complexity and transmits correlations directly to the user in concise ways. Similar to the field of Scientific Visualization, the most appropriate representation for the different kinds of information has yet to be found.

The visualization of information for communication purposes is the traditional domain of artists and designers. In general, design strategies are learned through practice. Therefore, typical designer know-how is based on experience and the ability to anticipate the effect of a visualization intuitively. The idea of having set rules for design is largely unacceptable to professional designers, although guidelines on design fundamentals relying on perception theory and Gestalt principles exist [10, 16]. Consequently, in most cases, today^s multimedia interfaces rely on the intuition of the responsible designer. Since the complexity of hypermedia and multimedia systems is steadily increasing and development times are decreasing, this situation is no longer acceptable. Models and approaches for a more systematic analysis of design problems for hypermedia interfaces are necessary to help us find appropriate structures and basic presentation concepts for the design process to start with.

The approach presented here results from the observation that the specific problem of presenting visualization rules using hypermedia concepts is recursive in nature. On the one hand, visualization methods and corresponding rules have to be classified in such a way that it is possible to identify an appropriate visualization method for a specific visualization problem. On the other hand, this classification and the complex information about the various visualization methods has to be visualized and communicated itself, thus defining a new visualization problem. Consequently, applying the paradigm used for the classification of the visualization techniques and mappings to the design of the hypermedia user interface is a natural approach.

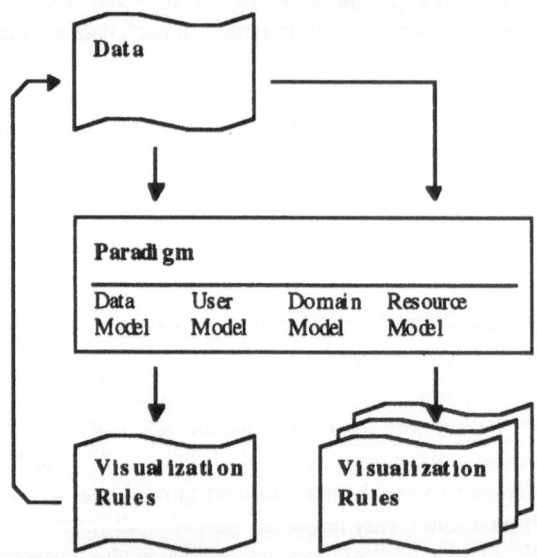

Fig. 1. Recursive Application of the Visualization Paradigm

Similar to the field of Scientific Visualization, data model, user model, domain model, and resource model can be defined. However, aspects of human computer interaction have to be considered in a much greater extent, thereby lending these models a somewhat different character. Data model, user model, domain model, and resource model may provide a basis for a classification scheme of multimedia presentation techniques and multimedia data mappings. This classification makes it possible to group information in order to make basic decisions on how to map information on media. However, the final design decisions can only be made by a human operator [6].

Although these models can easily be defined for hypermedia applications, there are certain differences to the corresponding models in the field of Scientific Visualization. The most obvious difference can be seen in the data model. For hypermedia applications, the most important distinction is between content information and meta information. Content data is information that is already available as a media element, such as text, images, visualizations, or sound. The information as a whole might have an implicit structure which is part of the content. Meta information, on the other hand, concerns the dialog with the user. System messages and status display are to be distinguished from navigation and interaction guides that support the access of the document content structure. The visualization of these interaction means concerns navigation structure as well as system behavior. A consistent visualization of these elements supports an intuitive and easy to understand navigation and the generation of a mental model of the content structure.

Visualization goals also depend on the user model, which slightly differs from above. Here, the user from the above paradigm can be classified first of all regarding the role he has in the visualization process. As an end-user of the hypermedia application, he has to be modeled according to his requests and goals as pertains to receiving the visualized information; he also can be considered as the visualizing designer of the application, who probably has goals in the area of communication or teaching and needs to apply the visualization rules. In the case of scientific visualization for data analysis, these two roles merge into one person, since communication is not involved.

The *resource model* determines the availability of features that can be used for mapping and, therefore, may act as a filter for the sum of possible presentation types.

5 The Hypermedia Visualization Assistant adVISer

adVISer is a prototype of a hypermedia visualization assistant for various problem areas in the field of visualization and supports the user during the generation of a visualization. adVISer provides an overview of the most important visualization methods in different areas of Scientific Visualization and explains the advantages and disadvantages to be considered in a specific application context.

During the development of the hypermedia application, the visualization paradigm based on *user model*, *data model*, *domain model*, and *resource model* was applied in

172

order to design a structured document with an adequate visual representation of the information about Scientific Visualization. In the following, the main design decisions will be derived from the specified models.

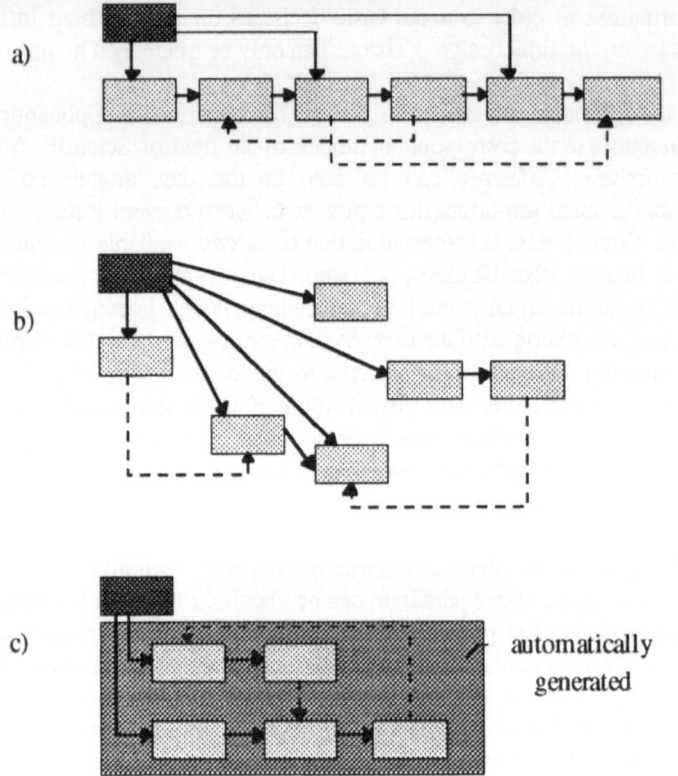

Fig. 2. Task-Specific Structures of the Hypermedia Document
a) Sequential Tutorial b) Glossary c) Workshop.
Solid lines mark main connections. Dashed lines mark additional hyperlinks.

Domain Model and Task Model. The domain is defined as on-line teaching and assistance software. Consequently, the resulting hypermedia application has to be provided with several access methods that meet the didactic requirements of educational software. In respect to a flexible user model, three different access modes have been specified:

- The *tutorial mode* provides newcomers with a comprehensive introduction to the visualization process including detailed information on different data types, appropriate visualization techniques with general descriptions, illustrations and visualization rules.
- The *glossary mode* supports experts with detailed information on searched topics.
- The *workshop mode* offers problem solutions to specific situations that the user can define interactively.

In all these different modes, the user is given a different view into the underlying information network.

Data Model. The underlying content database contains general information, occasional definitions and explanations, a table presentation of a general data classification scheme, and illustrative examples. Different media such as images, graphs (e.g. AVS pipelines [19]), animation, sound, and written text are provided. The real structure of the information net offers high complexity, since correlations are hyperlinked, not linear. The mental model of the hyperstructure noticed by the user is supported by the three different modes which are provided in parallel according to the above *domain model* (see Fig. 2). However, the *tutorial mode* delivers the most complete view of the database.

Access to the content information is arranged by meta information, which can also be classified according to its function, appearance, and type. Navigation and status elements help define a mental model of the content structure (building the interaction structure) and sometimes come along only with specific information to work as an access tool for higher dimensional content such as animation, 3D objects, and sound. As these elements are to be operated by the user, they have to be visualized in a way that makes their function obvious and does not interfere with the representation of the content data. A detailed listing of all information types used in adVISer and their (visual) representation is given in Table 1 and Table 2.

Table 1: Types of Content Information

Information	Type	Behavior	Applied Visualization Method
Main text, general information	Written text	Static, with hyperlinks	Consistent spatial layout
Accompanying information to main text, examples, illustration, animation, video	Images, graphs, frame series	Static or loop through frames series	Consistent spatial layout, framed by an outline, accessed by navigation devices
Occasional additional explanations and definitions for main text parts	Written text, graphs	Temporal appearance	Apparent only during user interaction (mouse down on keyword), fixed space in spatial layout
Additional explanation of illustrations or examples	Spoken Text, Sound	Temporal appearance	None (hearing)
Overview of classification	Table with text	Function as distribution table	Whole extra screen
Titles, headlines	Short written text	Static	Placement, boldness, size

174

According to [1], there is a hierarchical order in which various mappings on visual variables are perceived, being size and position at the top of the line, since they support the perception of shapes according to Gestalt principles. Consequently, the best way to distinguish between content and meta information was to separate them spatially. Another basic decision was not to use color excessively as a coding variable. The media part of the content data model offers nearly the whole color spectrum, so that most of the color-coded meta information would compete with the content. An exception was made for to hyperlinks, emphasizing just one color.

Table 2. Types of Meta Information

Information	Type	Behavior	Applied Visualization Method
Main navigation devices: next, previous, trace back, home, literature, help, quit	Button series	Static, shows pressed state while mouse down	Consistent static spatial layout, grouping by placement and labeling by set of icons
Occasional media control devices, example access aids: play/stop sound/animation, toggle AVS graph, adjust values	Button series	Temporal, status display	Set of icons with consistent spatial layout, placement close to the controlled media within frame, blue color -coding
Hyperlinked keywords in main text to switch to another part of the document	Part of main text, hyperlink	Static	Words color-coded blue and underlined
Keywords in main text which provide optional short definitions	Part of main text, link	Static	Underlined word
Distribution table within the overview of classifications	Table with text including hyperlinks	Static	Whole extra screen, hyperlinks color-coded blue and underlined
State indicator: tutorial chapter numbers	Bitmap	Static, not sensitive	Placement, color-grouped to the background

Resource Model. The hypermedia application adVISer was developed with the multimedia authoring system Director 4.0 from Macromedia. Director allows the combination and integration of a number of different media types (text, still images, animation/video, sound, and complex behavior) within a single application. Using the Director projector, resulting applications such as adVISer can be played cross-platform on Macintosh and PC. In order to support a large number of users, the resolution of the adVISer pages was restricted VGA (640 x 480) and can be played with 256 colors.

Since the WorldWideWeb meanwhile provides more possibilities for designing integrated hypermedia documents, we will discuss a transfer of adVISer to the

WorldWideWeb – keeping the layout and interaction possibilities – using different techniques in more detail in the next part of the paper.

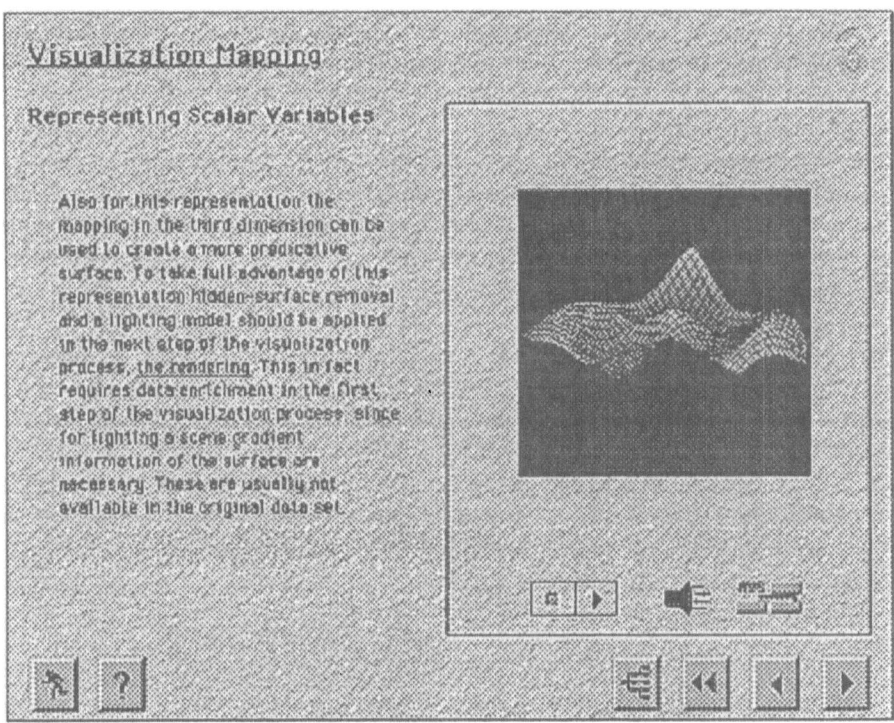

Fig. 3. Example of an adVISer Page

6 Multimedia Presentation in the WorldWideWeb

In the last chapters, we presented a paradigm for the design of a hypermedia user interface and discussed its application for a specific stand-alone application, the visualization assistant adVISer. The question arises in how far the results of the discussion above are also valid for an application in the WorldWideWeb. Apparently, there are two central problems:

- Although neither the data model nor the domain model are affected by a transfer of a multimedia application to the WorldWideWeb, the user model and the resource model may be the subject of change.
- Until now, it was assumed that all phases of the visualization process could be controlled by the visualization designer. This, however, is only true if the data is transferred in its final form and no different mapping or distortion is applied to the hypermedia document thereafter. For certain content description formats such as HTML and VRML, this is not the case and an interpretation and final rendering is

performed on the client-side, introducing the risk of manipulation of the overall design as well as content mapping.

The first problem mainly illustrates the higher complexity WorldWideWeb applications have to deal with. Through the distribution on the WorldWideWeb, any application can be accessed by an enormous number of users with very different backgrounds and different aims. Any part of a complex document may be accessed from another application and with a very different context. Similarly, the application may be started on very different hardware configurations with varying display systems. Applications can react to the latter either increased flexibility or with a restriction to the smallest common display. Loading times are in most cases a factor applications needs to be adapted to.

The second problem is based on the drawback that for certain encodings, the resources and mappings can not be sufficiently restricted. Fonts, and to some extent also color, may be exchanged under HTML on the client side. Even more importantly, spatial distances and relations cannot be guaranteed in HTML. Only through the use of frames can at least spatial relations be preserved to a certain degree and, thus, ordinal information can be maintained in those cases (see Figure 4). Again, the solution to this problem is either an increased flexibility of design, or the complete avoidance of content data with these drawbacks.

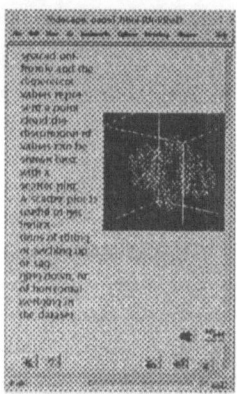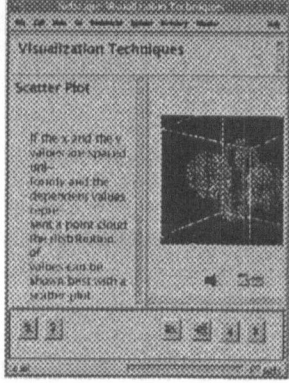

Fig. 4. adVISer Page in HTML – without and with Frames

7 Conclusion

In this paper, we showed how a paradigm from the field of Scientific Visualization can be applied to information visualization for the purpose of structuring the first stages in the process of designing a hypermedia interface. We used this paradigm to analyze the application requirements for the visualization assistant adVISer, to classify its information elements, and to decide on the appropriate presentation techniques for this information. Moreover, we showed the fundamental differences in designing such an application for the WorldWideWeb, and that the flexible resource management of certain content types has to be seen as a general problem of screen design and information visualization in the Web.

References

1. Bertin, J.: Semiology of Graphics. The University of Wisconsin Press, 1983.

2. Cleveland, William S.: The Elements of Graphing Data. Wadsworth Advanced Book Program, Pacific Grove, 1985.

3. Domik, G.O., and Gutkauf, B.: User Modeling for Adaptive Visualization Systems. Proc. IEEE Visualization '94, IEEE Computer Society, 1994, pp. 217-223.

4. Gerfelder, Norbert, and Müller, Wolfgang: Quality Aspects of Computer-Based Video Services, In: Heitmann, Jürgen (ed.): Proc. 1994 European SMPTE Conference - Convergence of Imaging Media, SMPTE, September 1994, pp. 44-67.

5. Keller, Peter R., and Keller, Mary M.: Visual Cues - Practical Data Visualization. IEEE Computer Society Press, Los Alamitos, 1993.

6. Laurel, Brenda (ed.): The Art of Human-Computer-Interface Design. Addison-Wesley, Reading, 1990.

7. Levine, Michael W., and Shefner, Jeremy M.: Fundamentals of Sensation and Perception. 2nd Edition, Brooks/Cole Publishing Company, Pacific Grove, California, 1990.

8. Lange, Susanne, Schumann, Heidrun, Müller, Wolfgang, and Krömker, Detlef: Problem-Oriented Visualization of Multi-Dimensional Data Sets. Scateni, Riccardo (ed.): Proceedings of the International Symposium on Scientific Visualization '95, Chia, Italy, World Scientific Pub., Singapore New Jersey London Hong Kong, 1995, pp. 1-15.

9. Mackinlay, J.: Automating the Design of Graphical Presentations of Relational Information. ACM Transactions on Graphics, vol. 5, no. 2, April 1986, pp. 110-141.

10. Marcus, Aaron: Graphic Design for Electronic Documents and User Interfaces. ACM Press, New York, 1992.

11. Müller, Wolfgang: Visualisierungshilfe zur Visualisierung von Multiparameterdatensätzen. Technical Report GRIS-92-5, Darmstadt Technical Unversity, Dept. of Computer Science, Interactive Graphics Systems Group, December 1992.

12. Rogowitz, Bernice E., and Treinish, Lloyd A.: Using Perceptual Rules in Interactive Visualization. SPIE Proc. vol. 2179 on Human Vision, Visual processing, and Digital Display V, SPIE, 1994, pp. 287-295.

13. Schmidt, Robert F., and Thews, Gerhard: Physiologie des Menschen. Springer-Verlag, Berlin/Heidelberg/New York, 1987.

14. Seligmann, Dorée Duncan, and Feiner, Steven: Automated Generation of Intent-Based 3D Illustrations. Computer Graphics, vol. 25, no. 4, July, 1991, pp. 123-141.

15. Senay, Hikmet, and Ignatius, Eve: Rules and Principles of Scientific Data Visualization. SIGGRAPH '90 Course Notes #27 State of the Art in Data Visualization, 1990.

16. Spierling, Ulrike, and Koop, Tanja: Screen Design. ZGDV Course Notes, Computer Graphics Center, Darmstadt, 1995.

17. Stevens, S.S.: Psychophysics. John Wiley & Sons, New York/London, 1975.

18. Tufte, E. R.: The Visual Display of Quantitative Information. Graphics Press, Cheshire, Connecticut, 1983.

19. Upson, Craig, Faulhaber, Thomas Jr., Kamins, David, Laidlaw, David, Schlegel, David, Vroom, Jeffrey, Gurwitz, Robert, and van Dam, Andries: The Application Visualization System: A Computational Environment for Scientific Visualization. IEEE Computer Graphics & Applications, July 1990, pp. 30-42

SpringerEurographics

Remco C. Veltkamp, Edwin H. Blake (eds.)

Programming Paradigms in Graphics '95

Proceedings of the Eurographics Workshop
in Maastricht, The Netherlands, September 2–3, 1995

1995. 41 partly coloured figures. VIII, 172 pages.
Soft cover DM 85,–, öS 595,–
ISBN 3-211-82788-9
Eurographics. Edited by W. Hansmann, W.T. Hewitt, W. Purgathofer

The papers in this volume are a good sampling and overview of current solutions to the problems of creating graphically based systems. The presentations investigate the applicability, merits and problems of various programming paradigms in computer graphics for design, modelling and implementation.

The papers are grouped into four parts: Object-Oriented, Constraints, Functional, and Multi-Paradigm. This essentially takes the reader on a tour of the issues. Firstly there are the impressive benefits and power of object-oriented approaches, both as conceptually tools for design and as programming frameworks. In constraints, though, the limitations are exposed, and addressed. Functional programming provides a clear alternative approach with some impressive recent breakthroughs conceptually (e.g., the use of monads to express state) and in practice. Finally some approaches to resolving (or at least enumerating) the multiplicity of approaches encountered are presented.

SpringerWienNewYork

P.O.Box 89, A-1201 Wien • New York, NY 10010, 175 Fifth Avenue
Heidelberger Platz 3, D-14197 Berlin • Tokyo 113, 3-13, Hongo 3-chome, Bunkyo-ku

SpringerEurographics

Patrick M. Hanrahan, Werner Purgathofer (eds.)

Rendering Techniques '95

Proceedings of the Eurographics Workshop
in Dublin, Ireland, June 12–14, 1995

1995. 198 partly coloured figures. XI, 372 pages.
Soft cover DM 118,–, öS 826,–
ISBN 3-211-82733-1

Martin Göbel, Heinrich Müller, Bodo Urban (eds.)

Visualization in Scientific Computing

1995. 150 figures. VIII, 238 pages.
Soft cover DM 118,–, öS 826,–
ISBN 3-211-82633-5

Wolfgang Herzner, Frank Kappe (eds.)

Multimedia/Hypermedia

in Open Distributed Environments

Proceedings of the Eurographics Symposium
in Graz, Austria, June 6–9, 1994

1994. 105 figures. VIII, 330 pages.
Soft cover DM 118,–, öS 826,–
ISBN 3-211-82587-8

 SpringerWienNewYork

P.O.Box 89, A-1201 Wien • New York, NY 10010, 175 Fifth Avenue
Heidelberger Platz 3, D-14197 Berlin • Tokyo 113, 3-13, Hongo 3-chome, Bunkyo-ku

SpringerEurographics

Demetri Terzopoulos, Daniel Thalmann (eds.)

Computer Animation and Simulation '95

Proceedings of the Eurographics Workshop
in Maastricht, The Netherlands, September 2–3, 1995

1995. 156 partly coloured figures. VIII, 235 pages.
Soft cover DM 89,–, öS 625,–
ISBN 3-211-82738-2

The sixteen papers in this volume present novel animation techniques and
animation systems that simulate the dynamics and interactions of physical
objects (solid, fluid, and gaseous) as well as the behaviors of living systems
such as plants, lower animals, and humans (growth and metamorphosis,
motion control, locomotion, etc.). The book vividly demonstrates the con-
fluence of animation and simulation, a leading edge of computer graphics
research that is providing animators with sophisticated new algorithms for synthesizing dynamic scenes.

Riccardo Scateni, Jarke J. van Wijk, Pietro Zanarini (eds.)

Visualization in Scientific Computing '95

Proceedings of the Eurographics Workshop
in Chia, Italy, May 3–5, 1995

1995. 110 partly coloured figures. VII, 161 pages.
Soft cover DM 85,–, öS 595,–
ISBN 3-211-82729-3

13 contributions cover a wide range of topics, ranging from detailed algo-
rithmic studies to searches for new metaphors. The reader will find state-
of-the-art results and techniques in this discipline, which he can use to
find solutions for his visualization problems.

 SpringerWienNewYork

P.O.Box 89, A-1201 Wien • New York, NY 10010, 175 Fifth Avenue
Heidelberger Platz 3, D-14197 Berlin • Tokyo 113, 3-13, Hongo 3-chome, Bunkyo-ku

SpringerEurographics

Philippe Palanque, Rémi Bastide (eds.)

Design, Specification and Verification

of Interactive Systems '95

Proceedings of the Eurographics Workshop
in Toulouse, France, June 7–9, 1995

1995. 153 figures. X, 370 pages.
Soft cover DM 118,–, öS 826,–
ISBN 3-211-82739-0

Twenty-one contributions cover the different aspects of interactive systems, from formal user modelling to formal techniques for prototyping, and describe the state-of-the-art on these topics, also giving new directions for future research.
The book is an obligatory piece of literature for all scientists working in the formal aspects of the interactive systems field, but it is also valuable for the practitioner involved in the design of reliable interactive systems.

Martin Göbel (ed.)

Virtual Environments '95

Selected papers of the Eurographics Workshops
in Barcelona, Spain, 1993, and Monte Carlo, Monaco, 1995

1995. 134 partly coloured figures. VII, 307 pages.
Soft cover DM 108,–, öS 756,–
ISBN 3-211-82737-4

The book contains 22 selected and revised papers that have been presented in EG workshops in Barcelona and Monte Carlo. The areas covered are visual presentation aspects, gesture and speech interaction issues, applications and VE system, demonstrating very clearly the emphasis and the results of various research activities in the field.

 SpringerWienNewYork

P.O.Box 89, A-1201 Wien • New York, NY 10010, 175 Fifth Avenue
Heidelberger Platz 3, D-14197 Berlin • Tokyo 113, 3-13, Hongo 3-chome, Bunkyo-ku

Springer-Verlag
and the Environment